50 Shared texts

NON-FICTION

Year 4
Scottish Primary 5

C000217292

INCLUDES CD-ROM

Chris Lutrario and Andrew Taylor

Credits

Authors
Chris Lutrario
Andrew Taylor

Series Consultants
Huw Thomas
Melissa Mackinlay

Project Manager
Elizabeth Dalby

Editor
Roanne Charles

Assistant Editor
Catherine Gilhooly

Series Designer
Anna Oliwa

Designers
Lynne Joesbury
Helen Taylor
Micky Pledge

Text © 2007 Chris Lutrario and Andrew Taylor
© 2007 Scholastic Ltd

Designed using Adobe InDesign

Published by Scholastic Ltd
Villiers House
Clarendon Avenue
Leamington Spa
Warwickshire CV32 5PR

www.scholastic.co.uk

Printed by Bell and Bain Ltd, Glasgow

123456789   7890123456

British Library Cataloguing-in-Publication Data
A catalogue record for this book is available from the British Library.

ISBN 0-439-96567-5
ISBN 978-0439-96567-5

The right of Chris Lutrario and Andrew Taylor to be identified as the authors of this work has been asserted by them in accordance with the Copyright, Designs and Patents Act 1988.

Extracts from the National Literacy Strategy © Crown copyright. Reproduced under the terms of HMSO Guidance Note 8.

System requirements
- Supported PC operating systems: Windows 98 SE, Windows ME, Windows 2000, Windows NT, Windows XP
- Supported Mac operating systems: Mac OS9 with CarbonLib 1.6[1], Mac OSX
- Recommended minimum processor speed: 1GHz
- Recommended minimum RAM: 512MB

Mac OSX version 10.1 and Intel-based Macs
If you are experiencing problems, please double click the icon named "os9 autorun" on the CD-ROM. This will run the Mac OS9 version of the program.

[1]Some versions of Mac OS9 do not have CarbonLib 1.6 installed. Please visit the Apple website (www.apple.com) to download and install CarbonLib 1.6.

Contents

N Teachers' notes   P Photocopiable

 *Teacher's notes*    *Photocopiable*

Introduction

The new *50 Shared Texts Non-fiction* series follows Scholastic's previously published series, *50 Shared Texts*. It picks up on two comments received from a number of teachers in response to the initial series. Firstly they welcomed the notes that accompanied each text, providing various avenues for discussion with a class as part of the shared or guided reading of the text. Secondly, they wanted more non-fiction. By 'more' they meant both 'more texts' in general, and texts from a wider range of backgrounds.

This new series aims to meet those needs, by building on the most valuable aspects of the original series. The provision of a range of high-quality extracts gives you the time to focus on teaching rather than sourcing material; relevant links with other areas of the curriculum are highlighted; and the book can be easily used in a flexible way and dipped into as required.

Shared reading

Shared reading has been around as a specific term since the work of Don Holdaway in New Zealand. The idea gained momentum during the 1980s but the main push for both 'shared' and 'guided' approaches to reading took off with the arrival of the National Literacy Strategy, introduced by the Government to schools in England and Wales in 1997. The approaches have also found a home in classrooms in Scotland and further afield.

Shared reading is the strategy in which the teacher reads a text with the whole class. This can be everyone reading along together or the teacher giving instructions such as 'read the first paragraph in your head'. It can include the teacher reading and pointing to the words while the children observe, or the teacher asking a child to read a portion of the text aloud. The key ingredient is everyone having sight of the same text and taking their eyes along the same lines at the same time.

This series incorporates a range of approaches to shared reading, dependent on the age of the children, the best approach to the specific text and the method that best suits the learning activities accompanying it.

While the series is entitled 50 Shared Texts it also allows for the fact that some teachers may want to use certain texts in the context of guided reading. Guided reading involves a teacher or teaching assistant working with a small group of children to guide them through a text, setting them off on their reading to a particular point, stopping them along the way and asking questions or discussing observations. The texts and notes in this resource can be used in this context.

What's in the book

The texts in this book are organised term by term, and cover a range of examples of non-fiction tailored to each year group. Each text appears in two forms. The small, annotated version and accompanying page of teachers' notes guide you through features in the text that lend themselves to learning objectives. The larger, un-annotated version is to use with your class and can be copied or enlarged.

What's on the CD-ROM

All 50 texts from the book also feature on the CD-ROM, in a variety of full-colour formats designed to maximise their potential for sharing with a group.

The CD-ROM contains:
- Colour versions of all 50 core texts.
- Fully annotated versions of the 50 core texts.
- Half-annotated versions of the 50 core texts, designed for use with interactive whiteboard tools – providing you with the opportunity to highlight, circle and underline key words and phrases.
- The 50 core texts in an editable format, allowing you or the children to make changes to the document and print out the results.
- Differentiated full-colour versions of all 50 texts. These are designed to support less able learners, though most can also be used with the whole class: to teach the structure of the various non-fiction genres, to scaffold writing tasks, or alongside the core text as a comparison between written and visual methods of presenting information.
- Print options for all the text versions.

The texts

The 50 core texts featured in the book and on the CD-ROM have been either gathered from a range of diverse backgrounds or specially written for this resource to fit with the objectives for each term. The crucial aim of this gathering is that it should save you time, providing you with a ready-to-use range of stimulating and appropriate magazine articles, website extracts, newspaper cuttings, reference material, advertisements, posters and leaflets to explore, rather than expecting you to spend time hunting them down yourself. For most text types, there is more than one example, allowing you to select the one that best supports your planning requirements.

The purpose-written texts have been devised to provide texts that dovetail with the objectives being explored in a particular unit of learning. The authors have aimed to cover a range of learning objectives, making full use of the texts to support text level objectives while also ensuring there is coverage at sentence and word level.

Background

Notes are provided about the text that may include details about its origin or author, the story behind it or the context in which it was printed. This section can also include notes from the author about the rationale for using a particular text in the way it is dealt with in this resource.

Discussing the text

Guidance is provided as to how each text can be explored in the classroom setting. The aim is to avoid bland questions and answers and to provide ways of engaging children in reading and interpreting the text. This can include discussion points, activities they may undertake that weave their way through a reading of the text, points of contention where they may disagree with it and language features that will lead them to further explore their own grasp of words.

Some of these sections contain a lot of material and it is up to you to be selective. The aim in each section is to provide more material than needed.

The texts

The choice of texts has been driven by the need to ensure that these are quality texts both in content and language. It is hoped that among the selection you will find a mixture of authors and texts, both familiar and new. Whole texts have been provided as far as possible so that children have the satisfaction of reading and appreciating a coherent and complete piece of writing.

Talk, read and write

This section leads on from the reading to provide activities stemming from the text. Following a discussion of the text, this section provides activities that link with the reading. These may lend themselves to independent or group work within literacy lessons or they could be activities that will fit in with other areas of the curriculum.

Extension

This section provides ideas for further exploration of themes covered in the text, and relevant homework activities suitable for the year group.

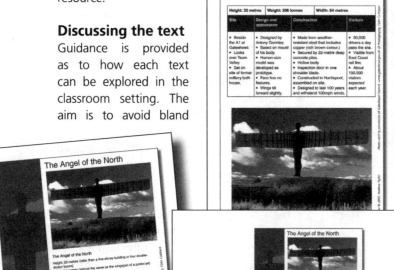

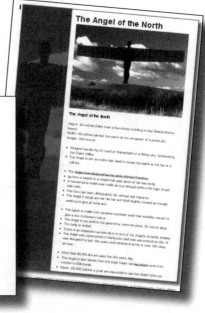

Range and objectives

Year 4 Term 1

Range	Text	NLS references
Newspaper article	**'Treats with a bit of Wonka magic'** from the *Sussex Express*	T20, T21, T24, S5
Newspaper editorial	**'Serve the kids better'** from 'Voice of the Mirror' (the *Daily Mirror* website)	T16, T19, T20, S3
Newspaper article	**'Why is Ellen such a star?'** from *The Newspaper*	T16, T18, T19, T21, T24, S3
Newspaper review	**'Charlie and the Chocolate Factory'** from 'Voice of the Mirror' (the *Daily Mirror* website)	T16, T19, T20, T24, W11
Advertisement	**'Free book'** from *Nursery Education*	T16, T17, T20, W9
Newspaper letter	**'Write here right now!'** by 'Brenda Harley'	T16, T19, S2
Magazine article	**'Animal magic'** by Tina Baker	T19, T21, T24, S4, S5
Newspaper article	**'School thinner'** from the *Daily Mirror*	T18, T20, T21, T24, W5
Instructions text	**'Brush and ink paintings'** by Fiona Watt	T16, T25, S2, S4
	'Down the slippery slope' by Chris Lutrario	T17, T22, T25, T26, S2
	'Pancakes' by Sam Stern	T22, T25, T26, S2, S3, S4
	'Lewes town walk' by Chris Lutrario	T16, T22, T25, T26, S2
	'Albert Park' by Chris Lutrario	T16, T17, T22, T25, S2
	'Race to 100' by Chris Lutrario	T17, T22, T25, T26, S2, S5
Magazine article	**'Feng-shui for your bedroom'** from *Poppi Extra!*	T16, T22, T25, S2
Non-chronological report	**'Daily life'** by Andrew Solway	T16, T17, T19, T27, S5

Year 4 Term 2

Range	Text	NLS references
Explanation text	**'Rivers'** by Andrew Taylor	T16, T19, T20, S4
	'Tornadoes' by Andrew Taylor	T16, T19, T20, T25, W13
	'Mummies' by Andrew Taylor	T16, T19, T24, W3, S3
	'RSPCA' by Frazer Swift	T16, T17, T18, T19, T20
	'Detectives of the past' by Andrew Taylor	S4, T19, T20, T24, T25
	'What is a Tudor theatre?' by Gillian Clements	T24, W11, W13, S4
Persuasive text	**'Polka Theatre'** from www.polkatheatre.com	T17, T19, T21
Information text	**'The Angel of the North'** by Andrew Taylor	T16, T17, T19, T21
	'Animals of the rainforest' by Suzanne Kirk	T17, T21
	'Glossary' by Laura Howell	W3, T17, T18, T21, T23
Persuasive text	**'National Coal Mining Museum'** from The National Coal Mining Museum for England	S2, T17, T18
Biography	**'The early life of James Cook'** by Andrew Taylor	T15, T16, T17
Information text	**'Physical activity'** by Nuala Mullan	T17, T18, T23
	'Vikings' from Scholastic Ltd	T16, T17, T23, S1, S4, W6
	'Operation Pied Piper' from http://clutch.open.ac.uk	T16, T17, T23, S4, W1
Website news report	**'A new resolution'** from www.whitbytoday.co.uk	T16, T18, T21, S2
Website review	**'Wallace and Gromit'** from the *Radio Times*	S1, T14, T21, T22

Year 4 Term 3

Range	Text	NLS references
Persuasive text	**'A magical day in history!'** from the Malcolm Group Events Medieval Festival	T18, T19, T25, S2
	'The great escape!' from www.acornadventure.co.uk	T18, T19, T25, S2
	'Staying fit & active' from Tesco Ltd	T18, T25, S4, W3, W8
Letter – advice	**'Dear Holly'** by Chris Lutrario	T16, T18, T23, S3, S4
Persuasive text	**'Vote for me'** by Chris Lutrario	T18, T21, T23, S3, S4
	'Welcome to North Devon & Exmoor…' from North Devon Marketing Bureau	T18, T19, T25, W11
	'What Champs will do for you' by Colin Rose	T17, T19, T20, T25, S4
	'Book Power' by Chirs Powling	T18, S2, S3
Discussion text	**'Evacuation'** by Vince Cross	T16, T20, T21, T23, W9
	'Should children follow fashion?' by Adam Hibbert	T16, T17, T18, T21, W8
	'Zoos – good or bad?' by Jane Bingham	T17, T21, T23, S4, W6
	'The death of the dinosaurs' by Fiona Chaplin, Sam Taplin and Jane Bingham	T16, T17, T21, S4, W7, W8
	'Owning a car' by Chris Lutrario	T16, T17, T21, T23, S2
	'Animal rights and human wrongs' by David Bellamy	T16, T23, S2, S4, W6
	'Telling about bullying' by Rosemary Stones	T16, T21, S2, S4
Newspaper editorial	**'Slam brake on carnage'** from 'Voice of the Mirror' (*Daily Mirror* website)	T16, T17, T23, S2, S4, W8
	'Clean up this mess' from 'Voice of the Mirror' (*Daily Mirror* website)	T17, T18, T23, S4, W9

Treats with a bit of Wonka magic

from the *Sussex Express*

Background

This story appeared in the *Sussex Express* in August 2005. It describes how a local student set up a sweet shop. The journalist has added interest and appeal by linking the story with the film of Roald Dahl's *Charlie and the Chocolate Factory*, which was released that summer and much in the news. The text illustrates many characteristic features of a news story: an attention-grabbing headline and opening sentence, a non-linear structure and direct quotations from those involved.

What's on the CD-ROM

This is a straightforward list of the story facts. It offers a supportive way into the more complex news story. Comparison of the two texts highlights the way in which journalists work with the facts to make an appealing story and how information in news stories is organised.

Discussing the text

● Read the headline. Ask: *What do you think this news story is going to be about?* (If necessary, explain the Roald Dahl reference.)

● Next, study the first three paragraphs and confirm the gist of the story.

● Continue reading to the end of the article, then ask the children to recount the facts. Highlight where these come in the text, noting that they are not in chronological order. For example, information about opening the shop comes before information about sourcing the sweets. Explain that this is typical of news stories, where information is usually organised in order of importance rather than time.

● Ask the children what is significant about the text in speech marks in the fourth paragraph. (These words were actually spoken by Iris Elliott.) Discuss the use of direct quotes in news stories and their importance in establishing the truth of what happened. Ask children to find other examples. They might also be interested to consider why Mrs Elliott rather than Chantel is quoted.

● Switch the focus to style and presentation by asking: *How does the journalist try to make the story interesting?* Look in particular at the headline and the opening sentence. They are intended to catch a reader's eye and play on his or her curiosity. Draw attention also to the links between this story and the film *Charlie and the Chocolate Factory*, making the story have additional relevance. Challenge the children to find the play on words in the final paragraph (*sweet rewards*) and explain that journalists often enliven stories in this way.

● At sentence level, focus on the complex sentence beginning *The shop…*, which makes up the third paragraph. Ask the children to identify all the facts conveyed in this sentence. Distinguish between the central idea (*The shop is owned by 17-year-old Chantel Elliott*) and additional information in the two sub-clauses. Note how commas help the reader to pause and to understand how the sentence works. Explain that news stories often include sentences like this to pack in lots of information. Develop this by asking the children to write a simple sentence about a person (*Tom is my best friend*) and then incorporate other information, using commas where appropriate (*Tom, the best singer in our class, is…*).

Talk, read and write

● Consider the effectiveness of the story. Do the headline and opening sentence make the children want to read on? Does the writer succeed in holding their interest? If so, how? If not, why not?

● Ask the children to imagine themselves in the place of the journalist, and ask: *Who do you think they spoke to? What questions did they ask?* Explain that interviews are one of the ways in which journalists gather information. Then ask who else might have been interviewed and what questions might have been asked. This is a good way to discuss how the story could have been developed in other ways.

● Use shared writing strategies to experiment with alternative headlines and opening sentences. Evaluate their impact.

● Challenge the children to write just a headline and first two sentences for a news story about an event of current interest.

Extension

● Ask children to write and design a poster for the Sugar Mouse sweet shop, drawing on information in the news story.

● Children could search for interesting headlines for discussion and display.

4: 1: T21: to predict newspaper stories from the evidence of headlines, making notes and then checking against the original

4: 1: S5: to practise using commas to mark grammatical boundaries within sentences

wordplay to enliven the story and amuse the reader

conclusion anticipates future developments

Treats with a bit of Wonka magic

Willy Wonka would be right at home in Uckfield's newest sweet shop.

The Sugar Mouse at Bridge Cottage sells the kind of handmade confectionery that would not look out of place at his sweet factory: from humbugs to old-fashioned lemonade sherbet.

The shop, opened only three weeks ago, is owned by 17-year-old Chantel Elliott, who is in her second year of Business Studies at Sussex Downs College.

Chantel's mother, Iris Elliott, said, 'Chantel has been so focused on this venture. She has personally picked every sweet, sweet jar and wrapper. Her father and I have helped out but this shop is testament to her hard work and dedication.'

After dreaming up the idea Chantel spent a considerable amount of time sourcing the best confectioners in the country and eventually discovered 72-year-old sweet maker Dave Keyanne.

Mr Keyanne, who owns Keyanne

Confectioners, served as a consultant to the sweet manufacturers on Tim Burton's new film *Charlie and the Chocolate Factory* starring Johnny Depp. He not only makes the vast majority of the products sold in the shop but has also given Chantel invaluable advice and expertise.

Iris said: 'The list of sweets we stock is never-ending, everything from broken rock, original cough candy, bullseyes and carbolic drops to liquorice and sour plums.'

'We get so many different types of people in here. Some of our older customers say they haven't seen some of these sweets since their childhood. Sometimes people ask for specific sweets that we don't stock, so Chantel phones Dave and he either makes them for her or finds out where to get them.'

Not one to sit back and enjoy the sweet rewards of all her hard work, Chantel is looking to expand her empire and is considering the possibility of opening another shop in the foreseeable future.

Text from "Sussex Express" Friday 5th August 2005 © 2005, Sussex Express; photo posed by model © 2006, Jupiter Images Corporation/John Pilge

eye-catching headline mentions popular character

opening statement intrigues reader

sentence gives the gist of the story

complex sentence, packed with information; commas mark grammatical boundaries

direct quote from someone involved in the story

information not in chronological order; events referred to in this paragraph precede the opening of the shop

4: 1: T20: to identify the main features of newspapers

4: 1: T24: to write newspaper style reports

Serve the kids better

from 'Voice of the Mirror' (the *Daily Mirror* website)

Background

This is an editorial from the *Daily Mirror* website of 12 May 2005. It expresses the newspaper's view on an issue being much debated at the time – school meals. This topic had been propelled into the headlines by a series of television programmes in which the chef Jamie Oliver exposed the current state of affairs and set out to improve school meals in the borough of Greenwich. The Government responded rapidly, putting forward proposals to ban foods high in fat, salt and sugar and to require schools to produce healthy, freshly cooked meals on site. This editorial was published before these plans were finalised. Its diagnosis of the problem is strongly worded and it is forceful in its urge to the Government to take action.

What's on the CD-ROM

The CD-ROM has an alternative version of the text in which the emotive, persuasive language is toned down. A detailed comparison of the two versions will illuminate how the author of the editorial has used loaded vocabulary in an attempt to catch readers' attention and convince them of the truth of the argument.

Discussing the text

● Introduce the editorial as a kind of writing found in most newspapers and read it with the children. Ask them what the journalist is doing and what their purpose is. Introduce the term 'editorial' to describe a piece that puts forward the opinion of a newspaper's editor on a current issue. Contrast this with news stories, which are generally more factual and objective.

● Re-read the text and ask the children to identify the issue. Provide background information and bring the matter up to date. Can the children identify the various participants in the story? (Jamie Oliver, the food companies, the Government, the newspaper itself.) Pursue this last point by asking the children to explain the role of the *Daily Mirror*, focusing on the fourth paragraph.

● Then assess if the children can explain the newspaper's view. Prompt them to tease this out in detail: *What does the editorial say is the cause of the problem? Who is to blame? What is the solution? Who can help put things right?*

● Focus on the style of the piece by homing in on the word *disgraceful* in the second paragraph. Ask: *Why does the writer choose this word? What effect does the writer want to have?* Draw out the idea that this forceful, evocative word is used for dramatic effect and to persuade the reader towards the journalist's point of view. In groups, challenge the children to find and record similar words and phrases, for example, *shockingly, disgusting, dished up, make a fortune, cheap rubbish, turns them off, exploiting*, then pool ideas. Note that many of these are powerful verbs. Highlight the effect by substituting less loaded, less emotive words.

● Ask the children what they notice about the layout of the editorial. Explain that the very short paragraphs are intended to make the text easier to read. Relate this to the audience and its needs: people often read newspapers in short bursts of time and in circumstances where it is hard to concentrate.

● At sentence level, focus on the connective *But* in the first paragraph. Explain how it indicates a comparison. Can the children find other connectives (*Yet, Instead, so, while, and if*) and discuss how they link ideas within or across sentences?

Talk, read and write

● Organise the children into groups to consider and discuss the effectiveness of the editorial. *Is the argument clear? Is it convincing? Why, or why not?* If appropriate, you could relate the issue to the provision of meals in their own school.

● Ask children to imagine that they are pupils at the school featured in the photographs referred to in the editorial. Divide the class into two groups and challenge one half to write letters to the editor agreeing with the story and thanking the newspaper for exposing the situation. Invite the other group of children to write letters disagreeing with and protesting against the story.

Extension

Use the story referred to in paragraph four of the editorial as a stimulus for writing a news article, with an eye-catching headline. The less able could write captions for the photographs.

4: 1: T19: to understand and use the terms fact and opinion; and to begin to distinguish the two in reading and other media

connective introduces a contrast

powerful, loaded vocabulary makes an impact and intends to persuade

very short paragraphs make text accessible

emphasises amount of money and contrast to children's 'plight' – shapes reader's attitude

emotive vocabulary

4: 1: S3: to identify the use of powerful verbs

Mirror.co.uk
THE BEST NEWSPAPER ON THE WEB

Home | **News** | Sport | TV & Film | More> |

Search The web ▾ For [   ] GO

Mirror.co.uk
THE BEST NEWSPAPER ON THE WEB

VOICE OF THE MIRROR

SERVE THE KIDS BETTER

School dinners were never considered gourmet food But at least previous generations found them edible and nutritious.

Yet years of privatised school lunches have led to a disgraceful state of affairs. It took Jamie Oliver to expose how bad they can be.

Shockingly the reality in some places is even worse than Jamie found.

Today the *Daily Mirror* publishes photographs taken in one school that reveal just how disgusting the stuff dished up for children can be.

The reason is obvious. The days when all schools had dinner ladies cooking meals on site are long gone.

Instead big companies mass-produce them – often miles from where they are served. They spend as little as possible on the food so they can make profits that run into tens of millions.

So these companies make a fortune while children are given cheap rubbish to eat.

The look of it turns them off and if they do force it down it does them little good.

Jamie Oliver woke the nation's conscience by reminding us that what people eat is almost as important as what they learn.

The government responded positively to him but it needs to do more than simply say meals should improve.

It must stop companies exploiting children and schools and insist that decent food is always served.

Heading and extract from "Voice of the Mirror" 12 May 2005 © 2005, Mirror Group (www.mirror.co.uk)

eye-catching headline with pun on 'serve'

prompts the reader to adopt the writer's attitude

links to related news story, and to newspaper's own role in the story

although 'obvious', writer explains cause of problem

connective introduces a contrast – then and now

conclusion urges government to take particular course of action

more loaded vocabulary

4: 1: T16: to identify different types of text

4: 1: T20: to identify the main features of newspapers

Why is Ellen such a star?

from *The Newspaper*

Background

This text is taken from *The Newspaper* – a print and online newspaper for young people (see www.thenewspaper.org.uk). This text is an example of a profile, a kind of biographical article often found in newspapers and magazines. The subject is the yachtswoman Ellen MacArthur, and the piece was written after her record-breaking solo round-the-world voyage in February 2005. The author includes information about Ellen MacArthur's achievements and her background, and makes their positive opinion very clear. Dramatic, extravagant language is used to emphasise the scale of Ellen's achievements and the warmth of the public's response.

What's on the CD-ROM

A simpler, more impersonal and objective version of the text is on the CD-ROM. It omits most of the dramatic language of the original and the author's view is expressed less overtly and less forcefully. Reading this version can provide a supportive introduction to the full text. Comparing the two versions will highlight the way the journalist has angled the story.

Discussing the text

● Read the headline and first two paragraphs. Ask the children to say what they think the content and focus of this piece of newspaper writing will be. Introduce and explain the term 'profile', and distinguish this kind of text from a news story that reports on a specific event.

● Read the rest of the text together. Lead the children in identifying facts about Ellen that they have learned from the profile.

● Then ask them to find points in the text where the author expresses their personal opinion. Can they summarise what this opinion is? Explain that newspaper profiles, similar to editorials, usually contain fact and opinion.

● Look back at the question posed in the headline and discuss how the author answers it: Ellen is special not just because of the records she has broken but because these were achieved 'against the odds'. In the course of this discussion, prompt children to quote extracts from the text to support their comments. Re-read paragraphs eight and nine, where the author's view is made explicit. Relate this to the structure of the text by asking: *What is the author doing up to this point?* (Describing Ellen's achievements.) *What do they do in the rest of the text?* (Describe what makes these so special.)

● Develop this discussion to focus on the style and tone of the profile. Ask the children what language is used to catch the reader's attention. Note in particular the short, dramatic opening sentence and second paragraph; the repetition of *Never once* in the third paragraph for impact and to emphasise the repeated nature of the dangers and the effort of overcoming them; the choice of powerful, even extravagant vocabulary. Focus on one of these words, for example, *blistering* in the first paragraph, and then ask children to find other words and phrases that have a similar striking effect, such as *roared on, ever-ticking clock, battled, gripped, smitten, treacherous, adore.* Note that many of these are powerful verbs. To highlight this you could show and compare the corresponding section of the version on the CD-ROM. Relate this language to the author's opinion of Ellen. Draw out understanding that they are using language to dramatise and heighten her qualities and achievements.

Talk, read and write

● Encourage children to evaluate the profile, referring closely to details in the text. Ask: *Does it give interesting information? Are there things you'd like to know about Ellen that the text does not tell you? Is it fun to read? Do you like the way the author expresses an opinion?* Focus here on the final sentence; some might see this as going too far. To explore this further, children could compare the version on the CD-ROM.

● Make available other appropriate profiles for children to read. Television listings magazines are a good source for these.

● Remind children of more fact-based news reporting and invite them to write a short news story about Ellen's arrival in port after her record-breaking journey.

Extension

Children could write a similarly enthusiastic profile of a friend or family member. Encourage them to include fact and opinion and to use powerful words.

4: 1: T18: to select and examine opening sentences that set scenes, capture interest, etc

4: 1: T21: to predict newspaper stories from the evidence of headlines

4: 1: S3: to identify the use of powerful verbs

4: 1: T16: to identify different types of text

4: 1: T19: to understand and use the terms fact and opinion; and to begin to distinguish the two in reading and other media

4: 1: T24: to write newspaper style reports

two sentences with same opening emphasise repeated effort

poignant verb choice

vivid adjective

conclusion in which author uses extravagant language to sum up view

one-sentence paragraph has dramatic effect

effective adjective

reiteration of question in headline

headline in question form to draw in reader

short, dramatic, unequivocal opening statement

powerful verb choices

turning point in text as argument changes course

summary of answer to the question

HomeNews

[Home News Index] - Microsoft Internet Explorer provided by Scholastic Inc.

File Edit View Favorites Tools Help

← Back → Search Favorites

Search the Web

Address http://thenewspaper.org.uk/home/

Front Page
Home News
World News
Health News
Earth News
Science News
Sport News
Timeout
Mailbag
Competitions
Conservation
Subscriptions
Parents
Teachers
Contact Us

Photo © Vincent Curutchet/DPPI Offshore Challenges Group

Why is Ellen such star?

Ellen MacArthur is a star. She is a yachtswoman who has, against all odds, smashed the solo, round-the-world non-stop speed record at her very first attempt. Only a year ago, Frenchman Francis Joyon had set a blistering pace by taking three whole weeks off the previous fastest time. At 72 days, Joyon's record was expected to stand for at least ten years.

Then along came Ellen.

For 71 days she had no more than 20 minutes' sleep at a time, having to be on constant lookout day and night. Alone she roared on. Up to six times a day she had to haul down and change the sails. It is heavy work. When something broke she had to fix it. Never once could she relax. Never once, until the moment her trimaran B&Q finally crossed the finishing line, could she afford to take her eyes off that ever-ticking clock.

The journey round the world took Ellen all alone through some of the most terrifying seas on earth. She battled difficult winds, mountainous waves and almost collided with a whale. One capsize would have been the end. A trimaran like B&Q, unlike a mono-hull yacht, cannot be righted once it goes over.

Yet, on the very last leg, it was the lack of wind that came close to ruining it for her. A craft with only sails to drive it goes nowhere on a windless sea.

But Ellen is not the first to sail solo around the world. She is not even the first woman to do it. So why have we all been so gripped and amazed as we look on in awe?

It could be that what Ellen does is against all odds.

Ellen MacArthur is a young woman in a man's world. A lone, long-distance sailor must handle and control a large racing yacht single-handed. He must

be brave enough to take on the worst that oceans and weather can throw at him. He is big and strong with untidy hair and beard. He is a man, in other words, and a tough one too. He is also not particularly young and will have been at sea since babyhood. Ellen, in contrast is a surprise.

First she is a very young woman, small and neat, and Ellen is from middle England. She was born and brought up in Derbyshire.

The sea is far away but, from the age of eight, Ellen was smitten by the sea. Her heroes were famous long-distance sailors, men like Sir Francis Chichester, Sir Robin Knox-Johnson and Sir Chay Blythe. She met them only in books.

The story goes on that, to get her first boat, Ellen had to save up her school dinner money. It took three years. Eight years later Ellen was taking her second boat, a 21-foot (7-metre) yacht all the way round the treacherous British coast.

Yes, Ellen MacArthur is a true star. Now the Queen is to honour her as Dame Ellen MacArthur. She will be the youngest woman ever to have been awarded this highest honour.

That we all adore her could simply be that we are in absolute awe of her utterly amazing courage, her modesty and her quite remarkable skill.

Heading and extract from "The Newspaper" http: thenewspaper.org.uk © 2005, Young Media Holdings Ltd

Screenshot reprinted by permission from Microsoft Corporation

Charlie and the Chocolate Factory

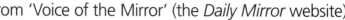 from 'Voice of the Mirror' (the *Daily Mirror* website)

Background

This is a review of a video game based on the film of *Charlie and the Chocolate Factory*. It was published in the *Daily Mirror* in August 2005, around the time the film was released. The writer assumes that readers interested in this review will be familiar with the technology and vocabulary of video games; you may need to check that everyone in class understands these, and if necessary explain technical terms such as *platforming elements* and *unresponsive controls*. The best way to do this is to draw on the expertise of other children in the class!

What's on the CD-ROM

This is a detailed plan of the review, with headings and summaries. Reading this first can help children meet the challenge of the core text. It also provides a useful model for planning reviews.

Discussing the text

● Read the title and product details. Ask the children if they can predict what kind of text will follow. The stars provide a strong clue. Confirm that it is a review. Define this term and explain that most newspapers and magazines include reviews of films, television programmes, books and so on, often on particular days of the week.

● Read the first two paragraphs. Examine the tone and how the reviewer's language links with the subject and expected readership. Note the repetition of *madcap*, the use of slang – *pretty darn fun*, and the one-word question, *Right?* If necessary, explain that the review is of a game linked to the film of the Roald Dahl novel.

● Read the rest of the review. Highlight and check understanding of the technical vocabulary. Similarly, prompt the children to attempt the meanings of other less familiar words, such as *heritage, veer, predicament, caricature,* and then confirm their meanings.

● Begin re-reading the text and ask the children to put up their hands at the point where the reviewer's opinion becomes evident. It is certainly clear in paragraph five, but look also at paragraph two: it could be argued that the implied answer to the question is *No*. Develop this by identifying what are, in the reviewer's opinion, the game's weaknesses (see paragraphs five to eight) and its strengths (paragraphs nine and ten). Children could highlight relevant points on a shared text or their own copies.

● Explain how points are organised in successive paragraphs. Draw out the idea that the text has a neat, clear structure: introduction (paragraphs one and two), factual description of the game (three and four), negative points (five to eight), positive points (nine and ten), conclusion. You could confirm this by showing the differentiated version.

● Focus now on the conclusion. Ask children to explain its purpose: to sum up the reviewer's opinion and make a recommendation. Point out that readers in a hurry could skip to the end and get the main point by reading just the four words of the final sentence. Now prompt them to say what they notice about the language. Draw out the idea that here, as at the beginning, the language is playful. Ask them to find 'lines' that rhyme (paragraph 11) and an example of alliteration (*candy caper*). Note also that this image picks up the theme of the film.

Talk, read and write

● Discuss with the children how they might respond to this review. *Would they still want to play the game? Would they want to see the film? Why? Why not?*

● Prompt them to consider the issue of audience. *Who is the author aiming this review at?* (Readers familiar with video games.) *Do you think he succeeds in interesting these readers? Does he tell them what they need to know about how the game works and its strengths and weaknesses?*

● Make other reviews available. Encourage the children to discuss similarities and differences in terms of language, structure and approach.

● In shared writing, plan a newspaper review of something the children are familiar with, for example, a favourite class book. Then compose an attention-grabbing introduction.

Extension

Ask the children to write a short review of a television programme, film, game or book, using this or the differentiated text as a model.

4: 1: T19: to understand and use the terms fact and opinion; and to begin to distinguish the two in reading and other media

playful language; jaded, cynical tone?

question involves reader and encourages reading on: anticipates answer

objective description of game

positive comments on game; commas mark grammatical boundaries – separate clause

question uses rhythm of song from film/game

figurative language picks up theme/subject of film story

4: 1: T24: to write newspaper style reports

4: 1: W11: to define familiar vocabulary in their own words, using alternative phrases or expressions

4: 1: T16: to identify different types of text

star rating (2 out of 5)

product information: hardware game is suitable for

slang, Americanised word choice

negative comments on game

technical vocabulary

conclusion answers self-asked question

alliteration

4: 1: T20: to identify the main features of newspapers

Mirror.co.uk — THE BEST NEWSPAPER ON THE WEB

Search | The web | For | GO

Home | **News** | Sport | TV & Film | More> |

Mirror.co.uk
VOICE OF THE MIRROR

CHARLIE AND THE CHOCOLATE FACTORY

★★

PS2, XBox, PC
£30
Out now

This summer sees the release of *Charlie and the Chocolate Factory*, a madcap remake by madcap director Tim Burton of a madcap movie based on the madcap book by madcap author Roald Dahl.

So a game based on such madcap heritage should be pretty darn fun. Right?

The game attempts to veer slightly from the film's familiar factory-tour plot line, instead finding Charlie Bucket rescuing the other naughty tour goers from the predicaments their greedy exploits place them in.

Charlie has to work together with teams of the iconic Oompa Loompas to free each trapped naughty child, often encountering platforming elements along the way.

Sadly the missions become repetitive, with objectives often difficult to spot.

Paired with unresponsive controls, you soon wish the game was a simple exploration of Wonka's world, which surely would be entertaining enough?

Graphically the game is inconsistent. The super-stylised character models caricature their Hollywood counterparts marvellously, but the environments they inhabit are less impressive.

The factory, so lush in the movie, appears sparse. The saturated colours often cause confusion too, leading to difficulties in navigating the gaming world.

Charlie and the Chocolate Factory does have a great soundtrack, however. Perky yet slightly creepy tunes complement the quirky settings perfectly.

There are also outstanding voice-overs from all key actors from the film, bar Johnny Depp as Willy Wonka (whose voice double does a remarkable job nonetheless).

So, Oompa loompa dompa dee do, is this game worth recommending to you?

Though children may be enchanted by the prospect of guiding Charlie around the factory, tedious tasks and poor graphics mean this candy caper may lead to an upset tummy.

Catch the movie instead.

Gerald Lynch

Heading and review from www.mirror.co.uk 2nd August 2005 © 2005, by Gerald Lynch, Mirror Group

Free book

Background
This subscription advertisement is from the back page of *Nursery Education*. It uses persuasive language and design features to emphasise the main selling points: saving money, getting something for free and the qualities of the magazine itself.

What's on the CD-ROM
This is a straightforward and purely factual description of the offer and the magazine. Comparison with the core text will help children to see how persuasive language and layout make an advertisement eye-catching and an offer appealing.

Discussing the text
● Ask the children to look at the text without reading it closely. What jumps out at them and why? The words *FREE BOOK* are big, in capitals and on a line of their own. Draw out the idea that this is the most important 'message' and so presented in a way that will grab the reader's attention.

● Now read the full advert. Ask the children to describe its purpose, what is being sold, and the intended audience. Check that they understand the idea of a subscription and that it is this rather than just the magazine that is being sold. Check also that the children know the meaning of *direct debit* and *cover price*.

● Then ask them to identify the 'selling points' – how the advertiser tries to persuade the reader to buy the product. Ask: *What are the advantages of subscribing?* Focus on saving money, receiving a free book, free delivery, and not missing any issues.

● Give pairs or small groups a couple of minutes to look for examples of how the text uses words to try to persuade the reader to subscribe; then share examples. Note in particular the use of intensifiers (adjectives and adverbs that strengthen the meaning of the word they relate to): *great reasons*, *absolutely free*, *just £39.99*. Read these phrases without the intensifiers and discuss the effect. You could extend this by asking the children to suggest other similar words, for example, *very, really, so, too, terribly, extremely*, and discuss why they are often used in marketing material.

● Given that the main pitch is financial, it is also important to consider the advertisement from a mathematical point of view. Tell the children that the cover price is £3.99 and there are 12 issues a year, and ask them to calculate the savings. (£7.89 if you pay the £39.99 subscription, £10.38 if you pay termly by direct debit.) Draw out the wider point that readers need to check advertisements that focus on saving money. You could also discuss why they think so many products cost a number of pounds and 99p!

● Switch focus to the magazine itself and the free book incentive. Can the children explain how language is used to describe these in positive and appealing terms? Note *essential*, *put the fun back into* and *loads of*.

● Return to the eye-catching presentation of *FREE BOOK*, and ask the children to identify other ways in which layout and design features are used to grab and guide the reader's attention. Look at the use of capital letters and different sizes and weights of text. Note also the use of a bulleted list to bring out the four key selling points.

● For a word-level focus, you could use the words *essential*, *professional* and *festival* as the starting point for work on the suffix -al. Explain that most words ending with this suffix (though not *festival* and *essential*) are adjectives formed by adding -al to a noun. Challenge the children to think of other adjectives in this family, for example, *musical, natural, original, digital, sensational, central*.

Talk, read and write
● Lead a class discussion on whether this advertisement is effective and well-designed, supporting opinions by referring to the text.

● Make more advertisements available for groups or pairs of children to read and comment on. Prompt them to focus on the issues raised above: key selling points; persuasive words, including intensifiers; layout and design; incentives.

Extension
Set the task of creating an advert for a comic or magazine (real or invented). Encourage them to pay special attention to identifying what will appeal to the intended audience, persuasive language and design.

4: 1: T17: to identify features of non-fiction texts in print and IT which support the reader in gaining information efficiently

4: 1: W9: to recognise and spell the suffix -al

4: 1: T16: to identify different types of text

4: 1: T20: to identify the main features of newspapers

capital letters and large type emphasise main incentive

word and punctuation convey sense of urgency

detailed information about possible savings

layout catches and guides reader's attention

intensifier to strengthen 'reasons' selling word

bulleted list emphasises and separates key selling points

words ending with suffix '-al'

appealing wording

intensifier strengthens key selling word

SCHOLASTIC

FREE BOOK
and save over £10 a year

when you subscribe to NURSERY Education today!

Pay less by Direct Debit

Great reasons to subscribe to NURSERY Education:

- **Save money** - pay just £39.99 a year or £12.50 a term by Direct Debit, saving over £10 a year off the cover price.
- **Free delivery**
- **Money back guarantee** for unmailed issues
- **Never miss an issue**

Subscribe to NURSERY Education today—it's the essential magazine for early years professionals. We will send you a copy of Chinese New Year and Dragon Boat Festival worth £15 absolutely free. Put the fun back into festivals with loads of cross-curricular activity ideas and background information to explore each festival.

How to order:
Call the Subscription Hotline on **0845 850 4411**

Order online at www.scholastic.co.uk

Yours FREE worth £15

Fill out the form below and return to us

Design and images © 2006, Scholastic Ltd

Write here right now!

by 'Brenda Harley'

Background

This letter was written in response to the editorial 'Serve the kids better' (page 111). The letter-writer draws on her experience and informed opinions to take up and develop the argument in the editorial. She agrees with some points, disagrees with others, and introduces a new issue: choice. She uses persuasive devices (for instance, *surely everyone agrees that...*) and loaded vocabulary (for instance, *so-called, ditch, nonsense*) to put her case more forcefully.

What's on the CD-ROM

The CD-ROM has a plan/framework for the letter, showing how the writer has organised her argument in paragraphs. Looking at this before reading the finished letter will help children understand the main ideas and how they are organised. It can also serve as a model for planning letters and other persuasive texts.

Discussing the text

● Display or hand out and re-read the editorial 'Serve the kids better', and explain that the text the children are going to look at now is a letter written by someone who wanted to have her say about the view expressed in the editorial. Put this in the wider context of 'letters to the editor' in newspapers and magazines and show a relevant page.

● Read the letter together. Ask: *Who wrote this? What do we find out about her? Why does she tell us about her job? What effect does this have on us reading the letter?* Draw out the idea that the writer puts herself forward as someone with special knowledge of the issue, and so worth listening to.

● Encourage the children to try summarising one of the writer's opinions or, more challenging, to summarise her argument as a whole.

● Explore this in more detail and in relation to the editorial to which she is responding. *What views in the editorial does she agree with? What does she disagree with?* (That bringing back school cooks is a complete answer to the problem.) *What new ideas does she introduce, and what is her view on them?* (Money is the most important issue; children have too much choice about what they eat.)

● Examine the structure of the letter and how the writer organises ideas in paragraphs. Ask the children to summarise very briefly the central idea of each paragraph. Discuss the effect of this clear organisation and how it helps in putting the writer's points across.

● Shift the focus to the language and tone of the letter. Organise the class into small groups and ask them to discuss the question: *How does the writer try to make the reader think and persuade them that her point of view is right?* Pool ideas. During the discussion, draw attention to the technique of drawing in the reader by asking questions; the mainly chatty, informal style; language that expresses a particular view (*so-called, scandal, proper, ditch this nonsense*); and words and phrases that assume any reasonable person will agree (*Like most people, Surely everyone agrees*).

● At sentence level, it is interesting to look at the shifts between present and past tense. Ask the children to identify sentences of each kind and to describe their functions. (The present is used to express opinions and ideas: *We need to, everyone agrees*; the past to describe earlier events: *I left my job, We all ate*).

Talk, read and write

● Prompt the children to evaluate the effectiveness of the letter. *Is it clear? Convincing? Why, or why not? What are its strengths and weaknesses?* In the course of this discussion, remind the children to refer to the detail of the text and the issues raised previously.

● Invite the children to write a letter in response to this one. Explain that 'letters to the editor' often develop debates in just this way. Alternatively, they could write a description of what they see as the ideal school meals service, including both general points and a sample menu.

Extension

● Encourage children to find and bring in interesting examples of similar letters, from members of the public to local newspapers, community magazines, newsletters and so on.

● Children could write a piece expressing their views about the meals provided in their own school.

4: 1: T19: to understand and use the terms fact and opinion; and to begin to distinguish the two in reading and other media

write here right now!

letters

★ star letter ★

Dear Sir

As an ex-school cook I read your editorial about school dinners with great interest.

Your photos are shocking, but they didn't come as a surprise to me. I know just how bad the food in many schools is nowadays. That's why I left my job. I just couldn't bear to dish out food like that any longer. I wouldn't have given it to my dog. We should all thank Jamie Oliver for exposing this scandal.

And I agree that the big so-called food companies are to blame. They're only interested in one thing: making money.

Certainly bringing back proper school cooks would be a step in the right direction. But we'd be fooling ourselves if we thought it would solve the problem on its own. No, the real issue is money. Good food doesn't come cheap. Like most people, I'd like to see every school serving tasty, nutritious, freshly cooked food. But that will cost. Are parents prepared to pay more? I'm not sure.

And another thing. We need to ditch this nonsense about choice. When I was at school, there was just one meal. We all ate the same thing, and I don't remember any grumbling.

Surely everyone agrees that this is one area where adults know best. We need to give children what's good for them, not what they want.

Yours

Brenda Harley

Text © 2007, Chris Lutrario

writer refers to her experience to support her views

disparages the companies

question encourages involvement/ response from reader

past tense to describe earlier experiences

present tense to state opinion

opening puts letter in context and states writer's 'credentials'

suggests everyone should agree

paragraph begins by agreeing with editorial, but then takes issue with it

idiom contributes to forceful expression of strongly held views

writer seeks to strengthen view by assuming shared opinion

4: 1: T16: to identify different types of text, eg, their content, structure, vocabulary, style, layout and purpose

4: 1: S2: to revise work on verbs from Year 1 Term 3 and to investigate verb tenses

Animal magic

by Tina Baker

Background

This opinion piece is taken from the listings magazine *TV Times* from October 2005. In this weekly column, Tina Baker puts forward her personal view on a current television issue. Here she comments on how natural history programmes have changed over time. She makes many references to programmes and presenters, assuming that her readers will be familiar with them. (The programme *CSI* is *Crime Scene Investigation*, a crime drama series. The style is lively and hi-tech.)

What's on the CD-ROM

This simplified version of the core text focuses on objective, factual descriptions of the different kinds of wildlife programmes mentioned. Reading this differentiated text first will familiarise children with the content and help them to meet the challenge of the more complex language in which the author presents her point of view in the core text.

Discussing the text

● Read the two headings underneath the columnist's byline and ask the children to predict where this text might have come from and what it might be about. Confirm that it is taken from a TV listings magazine and share ideas about what kinds of writing they generally include. If possible, have an example to show.

● After reading the first paragraph of the text, ask the children to explain the main point. You might need to explain that the Atkins diet is partly based around eating meat. Prompt thinking by asking questions such as: *What is Manhunters about? How is the information about these animals going to be presented?* (In a dramatic and exciting way.)

● Read the rest of the article together. Explore any challenging and interesting words used in the text. A good method would be to focus in turn on the following categories of words: less familiar words, technical words, idioms. Unfamiliar words might include *hybrid, device, genre, nostalgic* and *intervention*. Lead the children in working out meanings from the context. Technical or subject-specific terms include *voiceover, computer-generated images, visuals, docusoaps, shots, editing, storylines*. Ask the children to explain their meanings and

give examples in other contexts. Examples of idioms used are *jazz up, shake a stick at, spice up*. Discuss their meanings and their impact.

● Relate this adventurous vocabulary to purpose and audience – the writer wants to get her point over forcefully and in a way that will amuse an audience that knows a lot about the topic. (People are more likely to read the article if they are interested in nature programmes.)

● Get to the heart of the argument by asking: *How have wildlife programmes changed? What kind of programmes does the writer like and dislike? Why? When does this opinion first become clear?* Some children might think it is evident in the first paragraph. Others might point to later loaded phrases such as *jazz up* or *crocodile-tormenting tactics*.

● Examine the structure of the article, identifying the focus of each paragraph. In the first, the main idea (over-dramatised wildlife shows) is introduced in relation to a particular series. In the next three paragraphs this link is traced through previous programmes. In paragraph five the writer contrasts this with the earlier approach, and in paragraph six, sums up the present situation. In the last paragraph, a bizarre extreme pokes fun at the trend.

● At sentence-level, revise the use of commas to mark grammatical boundaries, for example, in the first paragraph, and look at the adverbs *recently* and *previously*, which are important in indicating the development of the argument.

Talk, read and write

● Ask whether the children agree with the writer's view on modern wildlife programmes. Share ideas about how these programmes should be presented, prompting children to draw on their own television experiences.

● Use shared writing strategies to compose a similar opinion piece that expresses a positive view of exciting, dramatised wildlife shows. Help the children to use powerful language to keep the reader interested and entertained.

Extension

Invite children to write a short review of a television programme they particularly like or dislike. To provide an extra challenge, you could ask them to write more generally about a genre, for example, soap operas or cartoons.

Annotations (right/top): title of article · commas mark grammatical boundaries and aid reading · striking idiom makes text more interesting, adds emphasis · new, media-specific term combining 'documentary' and 'soap opera' formats and terms · references to other programmes aids understanding if reader is familiar with them · inverted commas show this is not the writer's phrase, nor her view

Annotations (left): byline: journalist's name · title of weekly column · paragraph introduces theme of article · powerful words entertain reader and hint at writer's possible disdain · well-known TV personalities · choice of words hint at writer's personal view · grand claim of knowledge – presents opinion as fact · conclusion in which writer mocks the trend by taking it to ridiculous extreme

TINA BAKER

HER PERSONAL TAKE ON TV

Animal magic

BBC2's forthcoming new series, *Manhunters*, dramatises tales of creatures partial to the Atkins diet chasing their version of fast food – fleeing humans. The drama element is the latest take on natural history because it seems straightforward pictures of wild beasties just aren't exciting enough anymore.

Recently, we had the strange wildlife-meets-CSI hybrid, *Animal Crime Scene* – where investigations of animal 'murder mysteries' were used as a device to jazz up a nature programme. Along with an authoritative voiceover from that nice Mr Attenborough and more experts than you could you shake a stick at, this series also used sophisticated computer-generated images to spice up the visuals.

Before that, there was the wildlife-as-wrestling-fodder genre, using the likes of Steve Leonard to poke, provoke and leap upon unsuspecting species and writhe around on the ground with them a bit. Steve Irwin even made a career out of his enthusiastic crocodile-tormenting tactics.

And, previously, there were the animal docusoaps like *Vets in Practice* and *Animal Hospital*. Human interest was the added element here. When Rolf Harris dabbed his eyes and placed a consoling arm around a bereaved pet owner, the nation sobbed in unison.

All these new improved animal programmes make me quite nostalgic for the days where they'd point a camera at a wildebeest and just see what it did. The most intervention viewers experienced then was Johnny Morris adding daft voices to shots of zoo animals getting on with their everyday business.

But now wildlife shows are like the last series of *Big Brother* – it's all about manipulation. Either the creatures themselves are prodded into a reaction, or we the audience are cajoled into a response thanks to clever editing and emotive storylines.

Perhaps I should start training my cats to juggle – it can only be a matter of time before 'Pet X Factor' is the next big thing.

Extract from 'Animal Magic' by Tina Baker from "TV Times" 1–7 October 2005 © 2005, Tina Baker/TV Times/IPC+ Syndication (2005, IPC Media); photo courtesy of the TFA Group www.tfa-group.com

School thinner from the *Daily Mirror*

Background

This news report is taken from the *Daily Mirror* in September 2005. It concerns not a specific event but the latest developments in an ongoing story – the campaign for better school meals (see 'Serve the kids better' on page 111). This report was written at the point when the Government had made initial proposals and set up a review panel. As is evident in the last paragraph, the *Daily Mirror* itself was taking a stand on the issue. The Caroline Walker Trust is a charity founded to continue the work of the nutritionist Caroline Walker.

What's on the CD-ROM

This simplified version of the report lists the different foods and whether they are to be promoted, rationed or banned. It omits the more complex description of the political background and the various organisations and people involved. It can be used as an introduction to the core text or an alternative to it for less able readers.

Discussing the story

● Start by reading just the headline. Ask the children if they can work out what the story will be about. Identify the word play (the rhyme of *thinner* and *dinner*), and discuss why this is often a feature of news headlines.

● Next read the 'strap line' alongside the newspaper's campaign logo. Introduce this journalistic term and ask the children to explain the purpose of this part of the text: to present the gist of the story in an eye-catching form. Note how concisely the point is expressed and how it is more in the style of a heading than a full sentence; a full version might begin, *The Government has put forward a rationing plan to cut... .*

● Identify the byline giving the journalist's name and her post on the newspaper.

● Read the opening, or 'lead', sentence of the report. This confirms and slightly expands the strap line by referring to school dinners and the Government.

● Bring the story up to date, and, if appropriate, relate it to the other texts on the topic. Then read the rest of the report together. Check that the children understand the less familiar vocabulary and the more complex sentences. Ask questions to help the children understand and begin to interrogate the content of the report: *What has happened? What is going to happen? What might happen?*

● Extend this by prompting the children to identify the 'key players' in the story (the Government, the School Meals review panel, the National Health Forum, the Caroline Walker Trust, Jamie Oliver, the newspaper itself) and to describe the part that each plays. Note that for the most part the story involves organisations rather than particular people, and explain that this is often a feature of political stories where the actions of individuals can be of relatively little importance.

● Can the children identify other characteristic features of newspaper stories, for example, the use of quotes from participants, short paragraphs, the placing of background information at the end of the story?

● For a word-level focus, list or highlight, without explaining why, all the two-syllable words with double consonants (*thinner, dinner, fizzy, twizzlers, nuggets, happen* and *banned*). Ask the children what they have in common. Then ask for suggestions of other words with this spelling feature. Challenge the children further by asking them to try doubling all the consonants in the alphabet in order. Which ones can't be doubled? (H, J, K, Q, V, W, X, Y.)

Talk, read and write

● Note that this is a complex news story and ask the children if the writer has made it clear and interesting. *What are the best things about the report? Do they see any weaknesses?*

● Challenge the children to write a simplified version of the report for readers of their own age or younger. Encourage them to start with a new headline and strap line and to use other news features, such as an attention-grabbing first sentence. If possible, set this up as an ICT task and encourage children to experiment with a variety of text sizes and features, as used in newspapers.

Extension

Children could create a poster advertising the new school meals. How will they make the dishes appear tasty, varied and nutritious?

4: 1: T20 : to identify the main features of newspapers

4: 1: T24: to write newspaper-style reports

4: 1: W5: to spell two-syllable words containing double consonants

strap line gives gist of story in eye-catching way

short paragraphs divide text into small bites

paper's own role in story is high

SCHOOL THINNER

Chips rationing plan to cut fat in pupils' food

By ROSA PRINCE
Political Correspondent

CHIPS could be rationed in school dinners under Government plans to improve pupils' diets.

Other fried foods such as turkey twizzlers and chicken nuggets may be kicked off the menu altogether if they exceed new fat or salt content limits.

The ideas are being considered by the School Meals review panel, set up in the wake of the *Daily Mirror* campaign to improve pupils' dinners along with TV chef Jamie Oliver.

Panellists are due to report back to Education secretary Ruth Kelly this month and have been ordered to view the proposals favourably.

A Department for Education spokeswoman said: "Part of the panel's brief was to consider rationing or eliminating altogether unhealthy food from school menus.

"They have not reported back yet and we do not know what they will recommend. But certainly it is not unlikely at all that this will happen."

The rationing plan was first suggested by the National Health Forum and Caroline Walker Trust. They demanded salt be banned altogether

from school menus and chips rationed to one portion a week.

Fat content would be limited to 10 per cent – so products such as beefburgers, which have up to 19 per cent fat, nuggets, 17, and twizzlers, 21 – would join a food blacklist. Some favourites, such as chips, would be rationed rather than rejected as nutritionists agree children need occasional treats.

But rather than greasy thin fries, dinner ladies will serve relatively low fat chunky

chips with skins for extra nutrition.

Cakes and ice-cream will always be accompanied by fruit and caterers will receive training in healthy food preparation. Oily fish – especially beneficial for growing youngsters – is to be served at least once a week. Out go mushy peas and boiled cabbage. In come lentils, rice, salads and lean cuts of meat.

The Government is also considering banning fizzy pop from schools, with water from fountains or kiosks available all day.

The Department of Education has set aside £90 million over the next three years to improve school kitchens. Many only have facilities to reheat, boil or microwave pre-processed meals, but ministers want all pupils to benefit from fresh ingredients cooked on the premises.

There are now about a million obese children in England.

Ministers were prompted to take action over the poor quality of school meals by Channel 4's *Jamie's School Dinners*.

The *Mirror* also campaigned for an increase in the amount spent on pupils – and we reported last week how it is set to rise from 37p per pupil to between 50p and 60p by 2007.

'School Thinner' by Rosa Prince from "Daily Mirror" Monday 5th September 2005 © 2005, Mirror Group; photo © 2006, Jupiter Images Corporation

pun as eye-catching headline

byline

lead sentence reiterates main point

two-syllable words with double consonant

direct quote from someone involved in story

4: 1: T18 : to select and examine opening sentences that set scenes, capture interest, etc

4: 1: T21: to predict newspaper stories from the evidence of headlines, making notes and then checking against the original

Brush and ink paintings by Fiona Watt

Background

These instructions for making delicate pictures are taken from *The Usborne Book of Art Ideas*. In the original, they depend heavily on the illustrations, which show the effects aimed for and how the final picture is built up. Unusually, they combine general advice on technique with guidance for painting a specific subject. Although the familiar device of numbered steps is used, this set of instructions is in many ways notably informal and personal in style.

What's on the CD-ROM

This version of the instructions is largely visual and presented in the form of a cartoon strip, with short captions and labels. Looking at it first will help children with comprehension of the full text. A comparison of the two versions will prompt children to consider different ways of presenting information in instructions and their relative strengths and weaknesses. This will also contribute to children's visual literacy.

Discussing the text

● Present the text without comment. Ask the children to begin reading it and to put their hands up when they know what kind of text it is and can explain how they can tell. (This may take a while as the first few sentences are not in the style most typical of instructions.) When a good many hands are up, ask someone to identify the text type and give reasons. Ask others if they agree, and if so to expand on or give other reasons, or, if not, to give reasons why not.

● Read on together to confirm that this is an instructional text and to establish its exact purpose.

● Now begin to examine the language and structure of the text in more detail. Ask the children to identify similarities with other instructional texts they know. Note in particular the many sentences beginning with imperative verbs and the sequence of numbered points.

● Move on to discuss ways in which it differs from other more typical instructional texts. Note the lack of a full list of equipment and materials needed; the unnumbered points in the picture boxes (consider how these differ from the numbered points); and the friendly, personal tone, indicated in part by the use of

you and *your*. (Most instructions use just the imperative, and *the*.)

● Discuss the role of the illustrations. *How do they help? Would the written instructions work without them?*

● For a word-level focus, draw attention to the repeated adverb *lightly* in step five. Ask the children what word this goes with (*press*) and why it is important. Introduce the term 'adverb' and note the typical structure of the words (adjective plus *ly*). Can they suggest other adverbs that might be useful in art instructions (*slowly, gently, carefully*) and explain why adverbs are often important in instructions?

Talk, read and write

● Discuss whether these instructions make the children want to paint a picture like this. List reasons why the text is or is not appealing.

● Raise the issue of general instructions for a technique versus instructions for a specific picture. Which do they prefer? Why? Is the latter too restrictive or does it give good initial practice in the technique?

● Ask the children to evaluate the instructions. (It may help if they re-read and imagine that they are following them.) *Are they easy to follow? Do they tell us everything we need to know?* Some children might feel that the instructions are incomplete or sometimes unclear; others might like the detailed advice and the friendly tone. Whatever their view, encourage children to support it by referring to the details in the text.

● Children who thought there were shortcomings could write a new, improved version. Others could look at other books including instructions for art techniques and report to the class on how they were organised and presented. Prompt discussion of particular issues for instructions of this kind, such as the pros and cons of prescriptive and open-ended approaches and the different assumptions made about the reader's experience and skill.

Extension

Ask children to write instructions for making pictures or 3D objects using an art technique that they enjoy. They will need to choose whether to make this general or specific to a particular subject.

unnumbered points give additional guidance

adverb telling how the action should be done

Brush and ink paintings

ANY THICK WHITE PAPER

The best kind of brush to use for pictures like these are soft-haired brushes which have a pointed tip. Chinese or Japanese lettering brushes are ideal for these techniques.

Mixing the inks

To do the paintings on these pages, you need to use three shades of one colour of ink. Use ink from a bottle or snip the end off an ink cartridge.

Add a few drops of ink to water in a small container to make a watery ink.

Mix a medium shade by adding more drops of ink to water in another container.

Undiluted ink. Use straight from a bottle or squeeze the ink from a cartridge into a container.

Use a soft brush with a pointed tip.

Bamboo

Practise on scrap paper before doing a large picture.

Use the width of the bristles to paint.

1 Dip your brush in the watery ink, then dab the bristles on a paper towel. Paint a section of a stem.

2 Paint another two sections above the first one. Leave a small space between each section.

Don't put more ink on your brush.

3. Using the medium ink and the tip of your brush, add branches coming out from the stem.

Use the tip of brush to begin with, then increase the pressure.

4 Add twigs onto the branches. Leave a small space between one twig and the next one.

5. For a leaf, press lightly on the tip of the brush, then press a little harder, then press lightly again.

Use undiluted ink.

6 Use the tip of the brush and undiluted ink to paint grass and lines at the joints on the stem.

Press lightly.

begins with advice and information about materials, but lacks lists typical of genre

subheading alerts reader to content of this section

addresses reader directly ('you' usually omitted in instructions)

numbered points make sequence of steps clear

precise verb

sentences begin with imperative verbs

Down the slippery slope by Chris Lutrario

Background

This text gives detailed instructions for carrying out a science investigation. The topic is friction and the instructions lead us step by step through the investigation of the slipperiness of different surfaces. In the course of this, it highlights some important general issues in science, for example, fair testing, recording results and drawing conclusions. It has many features typical of instructional writing, but also has some interesting differences. In particular, it is more open-ended than most.

What's on the CD-ROM

The text on the CD-ROM is a report of an investigation carried out following the instructions. It consists of an account, a table of results and a conclusion. It differs from the core text in purpose and language. It is written in the past tense and in a more personal style. Looking at both texts raises questions: *Did the report-writers follow the instructions accurately? Did they do anything else?* Note that the report says the children made a mark on the plank. This is not included in the instructions but is a response to the need to always start from the same point.

Discussing the text

● Introduce the text by explaining its purpose and the context in which it would be used.

● Focus on the first subheading, *Aim*. Ask the children where they have seen this included in other instructions. *Why is it especially important here?*

● Read the equipment section. The children will be familiar with this as an element of instructions. Can they describe what is special about this list? Note where the reader is given some choice and where there is precise detail, for instance, about the size of the block and plank. Note also the *IMPORTANT* flash. *Is this effective? What if, instead, the author had just continued the list with 'large building blocks or bricks of the same size'?*

● Move on to the next section, and ask: *What do you notice about how this is organised and presented?* Point out the use of bullet points to indicate different stages and again the *IMPORTANT* flash. *Is the end the best place for this?* Discuss where it would be most helpful

for the reader. Ask: *Can you see a way that these instructions could have been divided into two parts? What headings could have been used? Would this have been better?* (Arguably, the first three points could be grouped under a heading such as *Preparation* and the rest under a heading such as *Carrying out the investigation*.) Discuss the meaning of the instruction *Repeat for the other surfaces. What is the investigator being asked to do? Is he or she given enough information here?*

● Focusing on the language and structure of the text, note the typical positioning of imperative verbs at the start of sentences. Ask the children to identify the main verbs in sentences where they do not come first (*If it moves, write…. Always put…*). Note the use of commas to separate clauses in the four sentences beginning *If*. Ask children to write and punctuate sentences beginning with sub-clauses starting with *if*.

● Read the last two sections. Ask the children to describe how these differ from the earlier sections. *Are these instructions? Why not? Why do you think the author has used questions here? Why is it more personal?* (Note the use of *your* and *you*.)

Talk, read and write

● If possible, carry out this investigation in a science lesson. Then, in a literacy lesson, evaluate the instructions 'for real', asking key questions such as, *Were things in the best order? Was it clear? Was there anything else you needed to know?* Prompt the children to identify strengths and weaknesses and to suggest improvements. Extend this by showing the alternative text and asking the children to compare the two versions.

● Challenge the children to write an improved version of these instructions, and/or one that is different in form, for example, more visual.

● Invite the children to find and read other instructions for science experiments and compare them with this text.

Extension

Set the task of writing instructions for a fantastical scientific experiment or process, for example, to turn stones into gold or to make a paint that makes things invisible.

4: 1: T22: to identify features of instructional texts

statement of aim, especially important when there is no single, obvious outcome

instructions begin with imperative verbs

what to do next depends on outcome so far

flash highlights crucial point

Friction

Down the slippery slope

Aim
To investigate the slipperiness of different surfaces.

How to carry out the investigation
- Draw up a two-column chart. Give the left-hand column the heading 'Surface'. Give the right-hand column the heading 'Number of bricks'.
- Choose one of the materials and cover the plank with it. Write the name of this material in the 'Surface' column.
- Lean the plank against one of the bricks to make a ramp.
- Place the small wooden block at the top of the ramp, and let go of it. If it moves, write 1 in the 'Number of bricks' column. If it does not move, add another block to the pile to make the ramp steeper. Put the small block at the top again, and let go. If it moves, write the number 2 in the 'Number of bricks' column. If it does not move, keep adding blocks to the pile until it does. Record the number of bricks.
- Repeat for the other surfaces.

IMPORTANT Make sure the test is fair:
Always put the block down at the same point on the plank. Don't push the block. Just let go.

Text © 2007, Chris Lutrario; illustration © Garry Davies

Draw your conclusions
Which surface is the most slippery? The least slippery? You could list the surfaces in order of slipperiness.
What do you notice about the slippery surfaces? What do you think makes them slippery? Do they have anything in common?

Take the investigation further
Did some surfaces take the same number of blocks before the small block moved? How could you find out which of these surfaces was the most slippery?

Equipment
- a small block of wood, about 10cm by 5cm
- a plank of wood, about 20cm wide and 1m long
- large building blocks or bricks

IMPORTANT The blocks must all be the same size
- different materials for covering the plank, for example, carpet, aluminium foil, sandpaper, newspaper, sheet of rubber, shiny paper, cloth
- pencil and paper for recording

SURFACE	NUMBER OF BRICKS				
Newspaper	3				

fairly precise measurements important to success of investigation

bulleted list of steps to follow

rather than specify, writer explains general idea and gives examples

bulleted list to separate items of equipment

questions, rather than imperative sentences, show shift in emphasis to interrogating evidence

4: 1: S2: to revise work on verbs from Year 1 Term 3 and to investigate verb tenses

4: 1: T17: to identify features of non-fiction texts in print and IT which support the reader in gaining information efficiently

4: 1: T25: to write clear instructions using conventions learned from reading

4: 1: T26: to improve the cohesion of written instructions and directions

Pancakes

by Sam Stern

Background

This recipe is taken from *Cooking Up a Storm* which Sam Stern wrote when he was just 14. The youthful, enthusiastic tone and the informal style, with use of slang, give the recipes a very distinctive voice, although they also have the necessary detail and precision. The book is intended to appeal to a young audience and to convince them that cooking is fun. The recipes are organised in sections and preceded by an introduction that describes the author's approach to cooking – and eating.

What's on the CD-ROM

The differentiated text is the introduction to 'Brilliant Breakfasts', the section of the book containing the pancakes recipe. With its description of breakfast time in the author's house and of his tastes and preferences, this sets the recipe in an interesting personal and social context.

Discussing the text

● Look at the title and ingredients and ask what kind of text this is. Confirm that it is a recipe and briefly discuss what is especially important about this kind of instructions, focusing on precision, clarity and sequencing.

● Read the introductory paragraph and the first two steps of the method. *What is unusual about this recipe?* Who do the children think it is written for? Focus on the friendly, chatty style, the enthusiastic tone and jokey, 'youthful' language in phrases such as *early morning juggling* and *a good glug of milk*. Note how the first sentence draws the reader in.

● Provide background information about the author and draw out understanding that his aim is not just to describe how to cook pancakes but also to make it fun. Consider the kind of relationship that the author is trying to build up with the reader, noting the use of *you/your* and the encouraging tone (*you're not a failure*).

● Read the rest of the method. Ask the children to look for features that it shares with most instructional texts, for example, the numbered list of steps and imperative verbs.

● Focus on the phrase *whip the pan off the heat* in step six. Check understanding and ask the children to suggest more ordinary words that might have been used instead of *whip*

(*take, move, lift*) and why the author chose *whip*. Ask them to find examples of other interesting word choices (for example, *team them, chucking* and *chuck, glug, blitz those blobs*). Note that several of these are powerful verbs.

● Read the second sentence in step four and discuss its purpose. Find other places where the author provides additional advice and encouragement.

● Study the *Eat with* and *Variation* sections. Discuss their purpose and how they fit in with the main text.

● Organise the children into small groups and give them one minute to find and list the adverbs in the text. Then ask each group to say how many they have found. Starting with the group claiming the fewest, begin to record the adverbs, then ask other groups to suggest more. Confirm that there are six adverbs, two of which are repeated: *gradually, furiously, slightly, entirely, lightly* (twice), *immediately* (twice). Identify the words they modify, noting that all but one of these (*smooth*) are verbs. Discuss their function and why adverbs can be especially important in instructions because they indicate how an action is to be carried out.

Talk, read and write

● Ask questions that prompt evaluation of the text: *Would this recipe make you want to cook pancakes? Why?/Why not? Does it sound easy? Do you think the author tells you everything you need to know? Is it clear? Do you think it works for a young audience?*

● Work together to compose a more straightforward version, for example, by removing or replacing the fun words and deleting phrases containing *you*.

● In contrast, ask the children to write a recipe in a similar persuasive, enthusiastic style for something that they know how to make, such as a cup of tea, a milkshake, a sandwich.

Extension

Encourage the children to bring in a recipe book from home. Organise a display and ask contributors to write a guide card for their book, describing the style, tone and intended audience.

4: 1: T26: to improve the cohesion of written instructions and directions

numbered steps of what to do

4: 1: S4: to identify adverbs and understand their functions in sentences

encouraging, supportive

intriguing question to 'hook' reader

reader addressed directly

Pancakes

Fancy a bit of early morning juggling? Then try pancakes. These treats tick all the boxes. They're tasty, popular, quick to prepare and make easy eating. Team them with whatever extras take your fancy (if you like) make your mix the night before. Store in the fridge in your measuring jug. Just before you're ready to cook, give the mix a couple of good whisks with a fork. Now it's ready to pour into your pan. Warning: the first pancake of the batch often sticks and needs chucking away. If this happens to you, you're not a failure.

Makes 8
Ingredients
100g/4oz plain flour
Pinch of salt
1 egg
300ml/½ pint milk
Butter for cooking

Eat with:
SWEET: Maple syrup, freshly squeezed lemon or orange juice, and sugar.
SAVOURY: Grated cheese and cooked ham.

list of foodstuffs needed, with quantities/ measures

sentences begin with imperative verbs

informal, eye-catching word choice; precise measurement not needed

adverbs add precision to actions

additional advice

powerful verbs make meaning clear

chatty, informal style

Method

1. Sift the flour and salt into a bowl. Make a deep dent in the flour. Crack the egg and drop it into this hole.
2. Tip a good glug of milk on to the unbeaten egg. With your wooden spoon, start to beat the egg and milk together in a circular movement without mixing in too much of the flour at first.
3. Gradually mix in the rest of the flour and start to beat everything furiously. Hold on to the bowl with one hand as you do this. Tip the bowl to one side slightly if it helps. The aim is to build up some real wrist action to make sure that the batter becomes smooth while it's still very thick.
4. Add the rest of the milk bit by bit, beating until you have a lovely smooth thin batter. If it's not entirely smooth you can always use a balloon whisk to blitz those blobs out.
5. Heat a pancake pan or small frying pan. You want it hot enough to make the butter sizzle when you chuck it in.
6. Use a little knob of butter to coat the pan very lightly. If the butter starts to go brown it's beginning to burn and starts to taste bitter, so whip the pan off the heat if this happens.
7. Pour 2–3 tablespoons of batter into your pan and swirl it round immediately so that it coats the entire surface.
8. Now cook until you think the underside is done. Check by flicking up the edge of the pancake with your spatula. If it's cooked it is lightly browned and it doesn't stick.
9. Tossing time! Or play it safe and use a fish slice or spatula to turn the pancake over.
10. Cook second side till light brown and serve immediately.

Variation
At STEP 6, toss a handful of blueberries into the pan till they're softening and oozing juices, then pour in batter mix. Cook. Don't toss – turn with a spatula.

Extract from "Cooking up a storm" by Sam and Susan Stern © 2005 Sam Stern and Susan Stern; photos © 2005, Trish Gant (2005, Walker Books Ltd)

4: 1: T22: to identify features of instructional texts

4: 1: T25: to write clear instructions using conventions learned from reading

4: 1: S2: to revise work on verbs from Year 1 Term 3 and to investigate verb tenses

4: 1: S3: to identify the use of powerful verbs

Lewes town walk by Chris Lutrario

Background

This extract from a town walk leaflet provides an example of directions – an important and distinctive kind of instructional text. It has two related purposes: first, to guide the reader along a route through the town; second, to point out and provide brief information about interesting places along the way. The text accompanies a map on which the route is clearly marked.

What's on the CD-ROM

The map provides a graphic representation of the walk. The route is shown by a dotted line, and points of interest are labelled. Talking through the route ('*You have to turn right at the end of Keere Street*') before reading, will establish the purpose of the core text and introduce its language. Comparing the two versions can increase children's awareness of the relative strengths and weaknesses of written and graphic texts, and contribute to the development of their visual literacy.

Discussing the text

● Introduce the text as a special kind of instructions and begin to glance over it with the children. Ask them who would use it, when, where and why. Go on to note that, as with most instructions, it is intended for immediate, practical, on-the-spot use.

● Introduce and define the word 'directions', and encourage the children to suggest other examples they have come across.

● Read the text together. Ask the children to explain the numbering and discuss why order is of crucial importance in directions.

● Identify the two different sections within each numbered stage. Note the use of a second paragraph to pick out main sights along the route, the places where the walker stops and looks. Then organise the class into two 'teams', one to look at the instruction and the other to look at the description. Give them a few minutes to identify how these different texts work and how they use verbs. Tell them to be ready to report back. In the ensuing discussion, establish the use of the first paragraph to give directions, and the second to provide information about some significant places along the route. Note that verbs in the first part

are mainly in the present tense, and many sentences begin with imperative verbs, as is typical of instructions; in the second part, verbs in the present tense describe what you can see (*stands Southover Grange*) while verbs in the past tense describe the history of places (*Tom Paine once lived*).

● Remind the children of the function of prepositions. Identify one in the text, for example, *at*, and ask them to search for more. When several have been found, discuss why there are so many in this text, and in directions generally: it is important to indicate the positions of places (*at the top, to the right of*) and the direction of movement (*through, up*). Develop this by asking pairs of children to give each other oral directions for getting from one place to another in the school; ask listeners to put their hands up when they hear a preposition.

Talk, read and write

● Prompt the children to evaluate the text. Ask: *Do you think these directions would be easy to follow? Why? Why not?* (You could note the detail included at intervals to help the reader, for example, *just to the right of the house, soon you will reach.*) *Do you think the information is interesting? Would it make the walk more enjoyable? Where in the walk would you most like to stop and look? Why?*

● Invite the children to write a walking tour of the local neighbourhood, for example, the park, main street, shopping precinct, using this text as a model and including both directions and information on sights.

● Explain that this walk is part of a leaflet for tourists. Ask the children to write a front page for the leaflet that sets out to attract people's attention and persuade them to come to the town. They will need to develop the information included about the walk to do this.

Extension

● Ask children to bring in other examples of walk guides, for example, collected from tourist information offices on holiday.

● The children could write directions and/or a map for walking from home to school, using the core text as a model.

Lewes town walk

The walk begins at the railway station, and takes about an hour and a half

1 Turn right out of the station and then left down Southover Road. After about 200m you will see on your left a gate in a flint wall. Walk through into Southover Grange Gardens. At the far end of the gardens stands Southover Grange. This house was built in 1572 from stone taken from the ruined Priory. In front of the house is an ancient mulberry tree, planted at least 400 years ago.

2 Leave the gardens through a narrow doorway in the wall just to the right of the house. Turn left then right up Keere Street. There is a story that the Prince Regent once drove a coach and four down this steep, narrow, cobbled street for a bet.

3 At the top on the left is the half-timbered 15th-century bookshop. Notice the milestone set high up on the front of the building.

4 Turn right and walk down the High Street. Soon you will reach on your right Bull House, another 15th-century building. The writer and revolutionary Tom Paine once lived in this house. Notice the carved wooden figures holding up the roof.

5 Continue on down the High Street until you reach St Michael's Church. Notice the unusual round tower and the modern statue of St Michael.

6 Turn left into Castle Gate. In front of you is the huge flint outer gateway (or Barbican) of Lewes Castle. The Barbican was built early in the 14th century. The grooves for the portcullis can still be seen.

7 Walk through the gateway and on up the hill. On your right is the bowling green. Tournaments and jousts used to be held in this large open space. A special kind of bowling using wooden disc-shaped bowls has been played here since at least 1639.

Map labels: LEWES RAILWAY STATION · STATION ROAD · SOUTHOVER ROAD · STATION STREET · HIGH STREET · SOUTHOVER GRANGE GARDENS · SOUTHOVER GRANGE · FIFTEENTH CENTURY BOOKSHOP · BULL HOUSE · ST. MICHAEL'S CHURCH · LEWES CASTLE · THE BARBICAN · BOWLING GREEN

Text © 2007, Chris Lutrario; map from The Map for the Lewes Chamber of Commerce, design and illustration © 1996, Andy Gammon andygammon@esprapex.com www.leweschamber.org.uk)

Annotations:

4: 1: T25: to write clear instructions using conventions learned from reading

general overview of walk, including time, helps reader decide if it's suitable

plain text gives directions

present tense verb: building, and reader, in the here and now

past tense verb for something that happened in the past

4: 1: S2: to revise work on verbs from Year 1 Term 3 and to investigate verb tenses

interesting subject-specific vocabulary

numbered sequence of stages in walk

prepositions showing direction of movement

prepositions indicate place

considerable detail to help find a place easy to miss

4: 1: T16: to identify different types of text

4: 1: T22: to identify features of instructional texts

4: 1: T26: to improve the cohesion of written instructions and directions

Albert Park
by Chris Lutrario

Background

This notice advises park visitors how to behave. Rules are a kind of instructions which children will be familiar with in many different contexts. As is often the case with rules, these are written mainly in the form of prohibitions.

What's on the CD-ROM

This text is a visual version of the rules, in which symbols show the kinds of behaviour forbidden in the park. Talking through this first can familiarise children with the content and vocabulary of the core text. Children can consider the pros and cons of verbal and visual communication. In particular, it is interesting to note what is missing in the diagrammatic form (the reasons and additional detail included in some of the prohibitions), and that the positive guidance in the written version of 'Be considerate' is turned into prohibitions.

Discussing the text

● Read the first part of the notice together. Ask children to describe its purpose, where they would see it, and the intended audience (visitors to the park).

● Explain that the notice is an example of a particular kind of instructional writing, and ask them to say how it differs from others: it tells the reader what *not* to do. Point out the key phrase *DO NOT*; then cover it up to show how its omission reverses the sense of the instructions.

● Examine the organisation and layout of the text. Consider the bullet points, the use of capitalisation for emphasis, and the function of the headings. Note how these group similar items together and are stated positively in terms of what *to* do. Focus on the second sentences in rules four and five. Ask the children what these add: in four some positive advice, in five a reason for the rule.

● Ask: *Does the order of the rules matter? Why not?* Compare this with most other instructions in which correct sequencing is vital. Relate this to the use of bullets rather than numbers.

● Now confirm these points in relation to the rules in the second section.

● Read the third section and ask the children to say how these rules differ from those in the

previous two sections: they tell the reader what to do rather than what not to do. Think about possible reasons for this change, for example, it is more appropriate to the idea of being considerate; these rules are more open-ended and flexible; it is easier to express these in a positive way.

● Ask the children to identify the verbs in these three rules: *make sure* (twice) and *Keep*. Note that they are in the imperative form, as is characteristic of instructions, but not always at the beginning of the sentence.

● Revisit the issue of audience. Elicit that this notice will be read by all sorts of people and that they won't want to stand around reading. Discuss how this affects the style and organisation of the text, noting that the rules are short and simple, and clearly laid out with careful use of emphasis.

Talk, read and write

● Discuss whether these rules are good ones for behaviour in a park. *What would they take away or add?* If possible, relate this to rules in the children's local park. Consider the tone in which the rules are expressed. *Is it friendly? Reasonable? Helpful?*

● In shared writing, add explanatory sentences to the rules that do not have them.

● Experiment with turning the positive rules in the last part of the notice into prohibitions, and perhaps reordering the sentence, for example, *DO NOT leave a mess after you have had a picnic.* Consider which is clearer and more forceful. Conversely, try expressing the rules in the first two parts in a positive form – virtually impossible in some cases!

● Find rules or codes of conduct in the classroom and around the school. Compare them with those for Albert Park, considering presentation, style/tone and approach (positive or negative).

Extension

Ask children to write a conversation between two children in the park: one wants to ignore a rule, the other wants to obey it. Alternatively, children could write a story with a moral about someone who breaks a park rule and comes to regret it.

4: 1: T17: to identify features of non-fiction texts in print and IT which support the reader in gaining information efficiently

4: 1: T22: to identify features of instructional texts

4: 1: T16: to identify different types of text

4: 1: S2: to revise work on verbs from Year 1 Term 3 and to investigate verb tenses

4: 1: T25: to write clear instructions using conventions learned from reading

ALBERT PARK

Look after your park

- DO NOT light fires.
- DO NOT pick flowers.
- DO NOT walk on the flowerbeds.
- DO NOT ride your bike on the grass. Keep to the cycle paths.
- DO NOT feed the pigeons. They make a mess and cause a nuisance.

Look after yourself

- DO NOT climb trees.
- DO NOT paddle or swim in the boating lake.
- DO NOT climb on the bandstand or any other buildings.

Be considerate

- If you have a picnic, make sure you tidy up afterwards.
- If you use a radio, CD player, etc, make sure it is not too loud.
- Keep your dog on a lead and clean up after it. Bins for dog mess can be found at many different points throughout the park.

text © 2007, Chris Lutrario; photos © 2006, Jupiter Images Corporation

Annotations:

heading states general rule in positive form

prohibition emphasised by use of full caps

bullets separate items (numbers not needed as there is no sequence)

stated in positive form (rather than negative as above), telling reader how to behave/what to do

commas mark conditional clause beginning 'If…'

Race to 100

by Chris Lutrario

Background

Children are likely to be familiar with instructions for games. This text, which explains how to play a simple number game, provides a good example of this common form of instructions. The educational aim of the game is to provide an entertaining context for practising number bonds. Full instructions for the main game are followed by brief instructions for two, increasingly challenging variations.

What's on the CD-ROM

This abridged and simplified version of the text gives instructions for the main game only. The text is organised in a sequence of shorter numbered steps. It can be used to provide a supportive way into reading the core text. Identifying differences between the two texts can increase children's understanding of different ways of writing and organising instructions.

Discussing the text

● Read the title and the *What you need* section. Ask the children what these instructions are for and how they can tell.

● Read just the subheadings from the rest of the text, and ask the children to describe the information they would expect to find under each. Help them to focus on the structure of the instructions: *Why has the author divided it up into these sections? Are the sections in the best order?*

● Read the text of *Getting ready.* Ask the children to imagine following these instructions, perhaps acting out the shuffling, dealing, and so on. *Are the instructions clear? Do they tell you everything you need to know? Are they in the right order?*

● Repeat for *Playing the game.* In addition, ask: *Why hasn't the author given every 'action' a number? Why, instead, has he grouped some together?*

● Read the final two sections, describing variations of the basic game. Discuss their purpose and how they differ in style from *Playing the game.* Draw out the idea that they do not stand on their own but require that the reader knows how to play the basic game. Ask the children why they think the author gives a detailed example in the second variation. (It

helps the reader to understand the more complex instructions and alternatives in the sentence beginning *Add...*)

● Focus on language. Play 'Hunt the verbs', and note their position at the start of sentences. Re-read the two sentences beginning *If...* in *Playing the game.* Note the use of the comma to mark the conditional clause in each. Read out an alternative version in which the sentences begin with the main clauses: *Move on 10 steps... Go back...* and ask why the author chose the first way? (The important thing to know first is in what situation to carry out these actions.)

● Support the children in identifying significant presentational features (such as headings in bold, the bulleted lists, numbered sections, capital letters to stress certain words) and in describing their functions. Consider a game-playing situation and think about how these features help the reader/player.

Talk, read and write

● Play the game, or one of the variations, in a maths lesson. Then follow this up as soon as possible in a literacy lesson in which children can evaluate the instructions having used them. Revisit the issues raised in the discussions of layout and organisation above, and encourage the children to suggest improvements.

● Generalise from this by asking the children to suggest criteria for good games instructions. Draw up a checklist. Encourage children to refer to it when they next play a game with written instructions.

● Ask the children to write full instructions for one of the variations of Race to 100, using the original text as a model and referring to the checklist.

Extension

Challenge the children to write instructions for a simple game they play at home. Encourage them to choose one that doesn't take long to play or require special equipment. Organise a session in which they can share these games and put their instructions to the test. Ask them to bring in other examples of games rules. Organise a display. Depending on ability, children could write labels that describe or evaluate the instructions.

4: 1: T22: to identify features of instructional texts

4: 1: T26: to improve the cohesion of written instructions and directions

4: 1: S5: to practise using commas to mark grammatical boundaries within sentences

numbered instructions – sequence is crucial

punctuation shows this is intended to be a fun challenge, something special

Text © 2007, Chris Lutrario; photos © 2006, Jupiter Images Corporation

Race to 100

(for 2 to 4 players)

What you need
- number cards 10–100
- a number line
- felt-tip pen
- 2 small counters
- 2 dice

Aim of the game
To move your counter from 1 to 100

Getting ready
Shuffle the number cards, and deal out 12 of them. Write the word UP above each of these numbers. Put these cards to one side. Shuffle the remaining cards, and deal out 12 more. Write the word DOWN above each of these numbers.

Playing the game
1 Put your counters on 1. Decide who will start.

2 Roll the dice. Add the numbers shown together. Move your counter on that number of steps. If you land on an UP number, move on 10 steps. If you land on a DOWN number, go back 10 steps.

3 Take turns to roll the dice and move the counters until one of you passes 100. That person is the winner.

NOW make the game harder – and faster! Roll 3 dice each time. Choose two of the numbers to add together. Try to land on an UP number. Make sure you don't land on a DOWN number.

NOW make the game even harder! Roll 3 dice. Choose two of the numbers. Add, subtract, multiply or divide them to get the number that lets you move on the most steps. Try to land on an UP number. For example, if you rolled 6, 2 and 5 you could:
- add 6 and 5 to move on 11 steps
- subtract 5 from 6 to move on 1 step
- multiply 6 by 5 to move on 30 steps
- divide 6 by 2 to move on 3 steps.
You should be able to reach 100 very quickly!

reader needs this information immediately

bulleted list of equipment needed to play

statement on how to win; rest of reading will have this in mind

short sentences begin with imperatives, indicate key actions

brief, simple instructions for playing a variation

detailed worked out example to clarify and develop brief preceding instructions

4: 1: T17: to identify features of non-fiction texts in print and IT which support the reader in gaining information efficiently

4: 1: T25: to write clear instructions using conventions learned from reading

4: 1: S2: to revise work on verbs from Year 1 Term 3 and to investigate verb tenses

Feng-shui for your bedroom

from *Poppi Extra!*

Background

These guidelines for applying the principles of feng-shui come from a 2005 edition of the children's magazine *Poppi Extra!* The magazine is aimed at 'glam girls who love to have fun' but the ideas in this article are of wider interest. Unusually, the sections, though numbered, do not follow a time sequence and could be reordered without affecting the outcome. The tone of the piece is casual and friendly.

What's on the CD-ROM

This is a plan of a child's bedroom that follows feng-shui guidelines. Labels indicate key principles, such as the separate work area. This visual version can be used to support children's reading of the core text or as an alternative to it. The texts show how similar information can be presented in different ways.

Discussing the text

● Read the title. Who has heard of feng-shui? Encourage children to share ideas.

● Read the first paragraph and discuss its purpose: to provide background about feng-shui and to present the aim of the following 'tips'. Ask the children to explain why the writer starts the last sentence with the phrase *Why not* – to draw readers in and get them thinking about acting on the tips.

● Read the first tip. Establish how the information is organised – a heading followed by a paragraph giving more detail. Ask the children how they can tell that this is a kind of instructions. Note the verbs at the start of some sentences. But what makes it different from most instructions? It not only tells the reader what to do but also explains why and what the outcome will be. Identify examples of these functions. Draw out the idea that explaining outcomes is important here, as nothing definite happens as the instructions are followed.

● Finish reading the tips. Revisit the points above, focusing on language features and the inclusion of both 'what to do' and 'reasons why'. Ask the children to identify the tip that is the odd one out: three, because it focuses on what *not* to do.

● Consider the order in which the five sections come. Does it matter? Re-read two tips at random and draw out the idea that the tips

are not steps: they do not have to be followed in sequence. Contrast this with most other instructions where the order is crucial. Ask the children to explain how the sections *are* organised – each is focused on a particular idea or theme.

● Read the section *Things to avoid*, and discuss its function. Note that it focuses on objects that go against the principles of feng-shui, and (like section three) tells the reader what not to do.

● Now encourage the children to comment on the style of the text. *Is it written in a friendly way? Is it trying to be helpful?* Focus attention on the encouraging, supportive approach, as in *Try not to…* and *Remember to…*, the use of *you* and *your*, and informal phrases like, *is okay* and *blue is also great*.

● A natural sentence-level focus is provided by the frequent use of connectives. Highlight one and establish its function in the sentence. Then ask the children to find others. Concentrate in particular on the repeated use of *so* and *so that* leading to the outcome of particular actions – an important issue in this context.

Talk, read and write

● Encourage the children to share ideas about the effectiveness of the text: *Does the writer make it interesting? Do they make you want to try it out? Why? Why not? Do you think feng-shui is a good idea?*

● Use shared writing strategies to compile a list of feng-shui dos and don'ts, drawing on information in the text and any further details children know.

● Discuss other areas in which instructions of this kind (where sequence does not matter) could be written, for instance, taking exercise or eating a balanced diet.

Extension

● Ask children to bring in examples of 'advice-type' instructions where sequence does not matter.

● They could also write an 'assessment' of how closely their bedrooms follow feng-shui principles or draw a plan of an ideal feng-shui bedroom, with captions to indicate the main points, such as *pastel colours for calming effect.*

numbered action points also work as subheadings

helpful, encouraging tone

section briefly listing items not to include

sentence begins by explaining reason for instruction above

paragraph gives background and aim of text

Chinese vocabulary with pronunciation guide

informal language

rhetorical question encourages reader's involvement and action

connective indicates outcome or purpose

connective indicates reason

sentences beginning with imperatives typical of instructions

FENG-SHUI FOR YOUR BEDROOM

Feng-shui (pronounced foong shway) is an ancient Chinese art. Feng means wind or air and shui means water. According to the Chinese, wind and water carry an invisible life energy called ch'i, and you can bring good ch'i into your life by decorating your house in certain ways or positioning your furniture in certain ways. Why not try these five feng-shui tips to make your bedroom an oasis of calm and tranquillity?

1 Think about where you position your bed.
For good ch'i you should be able to see the door from your bed but you shouldn't be facing it. And the head of the bed should always be placed against a wall so that you feel secure when you sleep. Try not to put your bed by or facing a window as this allows the ch'i to flow out of the room too quickly. If you can't avoid this because of the size/shape of your bedroom then hang a wind-chime over the window to disperse the ch'i evenly.

2 Declutter your room.
One of the basic rules of feng-shui is to get rid of clutter. Clear out everything that you don't use or need. Try to leave the centre of the room clear and unobstructed so that the ch'i can flow through uninterrupted.

3 Don't leave any electrical equipment...
The electro-magnetic fields from TVs, DVD players, stereos etc cause bad ch'i, so always switch off (by the wall socket) anything electric before you go to sleep. Remember to switch off your mobile too, and don't sleep with it by your pillow.

4 Go for soft colours.
Pastel colours or light blues and light greens encourage a sense of calm in your room which will help you rest better. The occasional splash of a vibrant colour such as red, perhaps as a lampshade or cushions is okay. Colours like red or gold are particularly good for energy and stimulation around your desk or study area, but avoid having these colours by your bed.

5 Keep your study area separate from your sleeping area.
Your bed and sleeping area should be a cosy, restful haven so if you have a computer or desk in your bedroom, keep them well away from your bed. Set aside a special study area, with no distractions and don't forget your 'smart' colours such as red and gold to promote energy. Blue is also great in a study because it aids concentration.

Things to avoid:
Fans in your bedroom can disrupt the flow of ch'i, as can water such as fountains or aquariums and more than three potted plants.

Characters and text extract from "Poppi Extra!" © 2005, Toontastic Publishing Ltd and Mr. Lucky Bags Ltd

Daily life

by Andrew Solway

Background

Peter Connolly's information book *Ancient Greece* is divided into sections focused on particular aspects of the life and culture of the Ancient Greeks. The text here is the beginning of the section entitled 'Daily life' by Andrew Solway. After a short introduction about how the society of the Ancient Greeks was organised, it focuses on the lives of babies and children. The thematic organisation (signalled by a heading and subheadings) and the generalised nature of the information are typical of non-chronological reports.

What's on the CD-ROM

The concept map on the CD-ROM shows how information on different topics is clustered at different levels. You could present this as the author's (imagined) plan, and discuss how information is organised, and how it is developed in the full text. This concept map can also serve as a model for children's own planning of non-chronological reports.

Discussing the text

● Focus on the main heading/title, *Daily life*, and ask the children what topics they would expect to find. Go on to explain that this extract focuses on childhood in Ancient Greece (which the children may have mentioned as one of their predictions).

● Read the first paragraph and ask what its purpose is. Help the children to see that it is not about any specific aspect of daily life; instead it serves as a general introduction and makes some important broad points. Identify the text as a non-chronological report and explain that these texts often begin with an introduction like this.

● Look at the subheadings and explain that they structure the information by topic. Contrast this with the chronological organisation of other non-fiction texts, such as recounts and instructions.

● Pose a question which the text will answer: *What leisure activities did children enjoy?* Before anyone answers, ask first: *Which section will have the answer?* Ask the children how they knew. (By the subheading.) Read the relevant section together and pick out the key points.

● Read the rest of the text in full and discuss its content. Consider any similarities and differences between life for children in Ancient Greece and life for children in the UK today.

● Now switch the focus to the language of the text by asking questions that spotlight significant features of non-chronological reports: *Does the author express an opinion?* (No, it is impersonal and objective.) *Is it about particular children or all children in Ancient Greece?* (Information, and participants, are general rather than specific.) *What new, special words do you meet?* (*Citizens, slaves, dowry, chariot, fables, paidotribes.*) Encourage the children to develop their answers by reference to specific details in the text and note that the features they are identifying are typical of non-chronological reports.

● Re-read and examine some of the sentences in which commas are used to mark grammatical boundaries (for example, the first sentence, which contains a list, and the third sentence, which breaks the sentence before a connective and additional clause). Note how the commas help the reader and show how the sentences work.

● Focus on the sentences that include connectives. Discuss how they link ideas. In particular, note *but* (*Poor women... but many mothers...*) and *while* (*Women... while slaves...*) and how they are used to contrast the lives of different people.

Talk, read, write

● Ask everyone to choose the fact from the report that they find most interesting or surprising. Share and discuss ideas.

● Evaluate the text. *Is it clear? If not, what needs more explanation? Could the information have been arranged in a better order?* If it was not interesting, ask how it could have been made more interesting, for example, by developing some facts more or by using language in a more lively, personal way.

● Ask children to re-present selected information from the text in the form of a two-column comparison chart.

Extension

Children could choose a subheading and write about this aspect of life in the UK today.

Text extract from "Ancient Greece" by Peter Connolly, text by Andrew Solway © 2001, Oxford University Press (2001, OUP); images © 2006, Jupiter Images Corporation

Daily life

Life in Athens was very different for men and women, the rich and poor, free citizens and slaves. Only wealthy Athenian men could really enjoy the freedom and cultural life that the city could offer. Women were expected to spend almost all their time looking after the home and the children, while slaves had no freedom at all – they were at the command of their masters.

A new birth

Athenians did not have large families. Boys were valued much more than girls. Girls also had the disadvantage of needing a dowry (money paid to the bridegroom's family) when they married. Unwanted babies were left out in the open to die: this was not a crime in Athens. Sometimes a family who could not have children would rescue an unwanted baby.

When a new child was born, its father proclaimed the birth by hanging an olive branch by the front door. About ten days after the birth there was a celebratory meal, and the family gave presents to the new baby. Poor women had to care for their own children, but many mothers had a slave to help nurse the baby.

Childhood games

Until the age of about 7, boys and girls were brought up at home. They played with dolls and balls, and may even have had a toy chariot to ride in. Mothers would tell their children stories and rhymes – they would for example have known Aesop's fables, stories about animals that you can still read today. At the age of about 7, girls began to help around the house – but boys were sent to school.

School

All but the poorest boys in Athens went to school from about 7 years old. They were put in the charge of a slave, known as a paidotribes, who took them to and from school, tested them on their work, and made sure they behaved. School was held in the house of the teacher. Boys learned to read and write, and to do arithmetic. They learned history from Greek writers. And as they got older, they learned to sing and play the lyre or flute.

Annotations:

- 4: 1: **T19:** to understand and use the terms fact and opinion; and to begin to distinguish the two in reading and other media

- introductory paragraph describes general aspects; provides context for following information

- generalised information about all boys and girls in Ancient Greece

- comma before subordinate clause

- subheads say what's in the sub-sections

- subject-specific vocabulary given in Greek

- 4: 1: **S55:** to practise using commas to mark grammatical boundaries within sentences

- 4: 1: **T16:** to identify different types of text

- 4: 1: **T17:** to identify features of non-fiction texts in print and ICT which support the reader in gaining information efficiently

- main subheading shows focus of this section of book

- connective signals contrast

- subject-specific vocabulary explained in following brackets

- impersonal, remote tone; author does not express an opinion

- comma after subordinate clause

- connective signals contrast

- 4: 1: **T27:** to write a non-chronological report, including the use of organisational devices

Rivers

by Andrew Taylor

Background

This text explains how a river's characteristics change as it moves from source to mouth. The explanation genre is signalled clearly by the use of questions as subheadings.

What's on the CD-ROM

The CD-ROM text presents the same information through a simple labelled diagram, highlighting the different forms explanation texts can take, particularly when explaining a process. It also provides a model of note form.

Discussing the text

● Before reading, ask the children to talk in pairs about what they know about rivers, making notes on whiteboards.

● Highlight the subheadings in the text and ask children to classify any rivers they know under the headings. Alternatively use images of rivers for the class to classify. Ask the children to explain why they would place a river in a particular category.

● Encourage prediction about the text, demonstrating how to use the title and the subheadings as clues.

● Read the text and ask the children to add to their whiteboard notes any new information they have gained.

● During a second reading, clarify technical vocabulary such as *source*, *mouth* and *meander*. Model how to re-read or use context to understand word meanings. Reinforce dictionary skills where necessary.

● Model how to begin a summary by making quick illustrations and brief notes of the main information. For example, under *Young river*, write *Water moves very quickly*. Alternatively, organise groups of three and ask them to make notes on the different stages in a river's life. Ensure that each stage is covered. Then reorganise the groups to share knowledge.

Talk, read and write

● Remind the children how the opening paragraph summarises the rest of the text. Use the first sentence to draw a flow diagram of the river journey from source to mouth. Then re-read the paragraph. Can the children add any more information to the diagram? The rest of the paragraph adds detail and examples.

● Discuss how explanation texts usually develop in a logical order: each paragraph or section gives more detail until the whole process is complete. Point out how subheadings organise this text into sections – each introduces another stage in the river journey. Add labels to the diagram, using the subheadings as a guide. (You could compare the diagram with the example on the CD-ROM.)

● For a word-level focus, pick out one or two verbs in the text. Elicit that the text is written in the present tense, characteristic of explanations. Ask the children to find other examples of present tense verbs.

● Identify the time connectives used. Explain that the subheadings also act as time signals. There are also examples of causal connectives which help to link the explanation together.

● At sentence level, highlight the use of commas to separate clauses, for example, *Near the source, streams usually move quickly.* Explain that commas help readers to break up a sentence to help comprehension. Clauses mean that a sentence can contain a lot of information without confusing the reader. Practise reading the sentences aloud to illustrate this. You could develop this into work on subordinate clauses and adverbial phrases.

● Ask groups to use the text to prepare their own labelled diagram of the flow of a river.

● Other groups could identify examples of explanation genre features, using a table:

Features of explanation texts

Explanation texts often have or use	Examples from the text
A general opening which gives an overview of the text	
Paragraphs which develop ideas logically	
Verbs in the present tense	
Time connectives	
Causal connectives	

Extension

Ask children to collect pictures of rivers from various sources. Using the information in the core text, ask them to identify what stage of the river's life their pictures show. They could use sticky notes to label the picture and give a reason for their ideas.

4: 2: T19: to identify how and why paragraphs are used to organise and sequence information

4: 2: S4: to recognise how commas, connectives and full stops are used to join and separate clauses

paragraphs beneath subheads answer the questions; paragraphs sequential in explaining process

causal connectives

common words but used in subject-specific sense here

Rivers

Photo © Donna Murillo

Photo © Michelle Block

During its journey from source to mouth a river changes both its look and nature. Rivers begin as narrow, fast flowing streams in the mountains or hills, but by the time they reach the sea or a lake, they are wide and slow moving. At each stage the river supports different sorts of plants, birds and other wildlife.

What are young rivers like?
Near the source, streams usually move quickly, tumbling over boulders and cascading across moorland or through woods. The water will cut deep channels into the rock. If the water looks white it indicates that the bed or floor of the river is rocky.

What makes a river middle aged?
Gradually, these fast-moving streams will join up with others. The flow of the current begins to slow down and the river begins to get wider. The channels cut by the river get shallower. It is at this stage that this stretch of moving water can be called a river – a river is defined as a stretch of water more than five metres wide.

A middle-aged river often winds or meanders from side to side. Sometimes it will cut several channels in the land and create islands. Rivers at this stage do not often flow over a rock bed so it is rare to see any white water.

What is a river like in old age?
In the final stage of a river's life it moves slowly towards the sea. The course it runs is almost flat and the river banks spread out to form an estuary, or mouth. As the banks get wider they start to form the seashore.

Many rivers are tidal in their estuaries. This means that seawater rushes into the mouth and up the river as the tide comes in.

Text © 2007, Andrew Taylor

A stream

A middle-aged river

An estuary

Photo © Bjorn Lotz

opening paragraph summarises whole text

adverbial phrases begin to answer the 'where' and 'when' questions

questions used as subheadings to organise text

time connectives

verbs in present tense, typical of an explanation

4: 2: T16: to prepare for factual research by reviewing what is known, what is needed, what is available and where one might search

4: 2: T20: to identify from examples the key features of explanatory texts

Tornadoes

by Andrew Taylor

Background

This explanatory text was inspired by a tornado that occurred in Birmingham in July 2005. The main emphasis in this unit is on children writing an explanation, but it is important to establish prior knowledge, encourage prediction and clarify unfamiliar language, as part of the reading process.

What's on the CD-ROM

The text on the CD-ROM is a simplified version of the core text. It can be used as an easier introduction to the subject.

Discussing the text

● Discuss the topic of tornadoes and other extreme wind conditions. Read the text and establish new knowledge about tornadoes.

● Ask pairs to analyse the features of the text using a chart as in 'Rivers' on page 42. Examine the evidence collected as a class and discuss why explanation texts include these features.

Talk, read and write

● Decide on a topic for explanatory writing. You might use the tornado text as a basis, or a familiar topic from another curriculum area. Work together to collect the basic information you want to explain, perhaps as a randomly ordered list of bullet points.

● Explain how, in writing an explanation, it is useful to focus on three main aspects: *knowing* the information, *organising* it and *'selling'* it (making it interesting, engaging, accessible).

● Discuss the importance of the title – it should state clearly, succinctly and precisely what the text is about. Using a question word such as *How* or *Why* can help. Agree on a good title for the shared writing.

● Now work on the opening paragraph. Go back to the table of genre features and the core text and point out how the first paragraph gives an overview of the whole text. Explain that it is also important that the first paragraph 'wakes up' the reader so that they are interested in the topic. Re-examine the first few sentences of the tornado text. Can the children suggest a more exciting opening sentence? For example, *Twisters or tornadoes are hugely powerful, spinning funnels of air that cause enormous damage.*

● Using the information collected, write a few alternative opening sentences that give an overview and interest the reader. Use questions, exclamations and short sentences. Then challenge the children, in pairs, to write their own opening sentences.

● Now talk about the 'body' of the explanation. The features table identifies paragraphs that explain the process point by point and organise information into chunks (the paragraphs). In the tornadoes text, the second paragraph describes what happens as a tornado begins to form, the third paragraph how the tornado gets bigger and more destructive.

● Look at the information collected and categorise it under different titles. Ask: *What happened first? What happens next?*

● Once the information is organised, demonstrate how to convert it into interesting prose. Model the first few sentences. Highlight time connectives, such as *first*; show how to extend the sentence using causal connectives, such as *because* and *so*; and introduce lively ways of expressing ideas. Ideally read and revise one of your sentences to make it more interesting and precise. Ask the class to write the next paragraph in pairs, reminding them to focus on linking sentences and expressing ideas in ways which will attract the reader.

● Finally, discuss how to end an explanation. Ideally the ending should relate to the reader in some way and be more direct than the main explanatory text. Remind the children of how this is done in the tornadoes text, through the use of a remarkable story presented briefly and in a way that would interest the reader. Ways of doing this include ending with a question or a challenge, for example, *Why don't you find out about extreme weather conditions in your local area?* Share good examples.

● Encourage the children to write their own explanations independently, using the work developed in class as the basis. Use guided writing to support less confident writers.

Extension

Children could research other types of violent winds such as hurricanes and cyclones, as well as tornadoes, and identify similarities and differences between them, presenting their information as a comparison table.

Tornadoes

A tornado is a strong, violently destructive wind made up of a spinning funnel of air. Tornadoes are sometimes nicknamed 'twisters' because of the way the air moves in a twisting spiral shape. Air speeds inside a tornado can reach up to 250 miles per hour.

Tornadoes form beneath thunderclouds. Warm and cool air meet and create strong downdrafts of spinning air. This rapidly spinning air appears as a funnel-shaped cloud, stretching down beneath the storm cloud. As more and more air is sucked in, the funnel gets larger and may touch the ground. If this happens, the winds can cause devastating damage – uprooting trees, ripping buildings apart and lifting cars into the air. As the funnel sucks up the dust and debris in its path, it gets darker. It moves across the ground, following the path of the thundercloud above it.

When a tornado forms over the sea, water is sucked into the funnel of air. This is called a waterspout. A tornado that happens over an area of desert sucks up sand and is called a dust devil.

Tornadoes can happen almost anywhere in the world, although they are much more common in some places, for example America, than in others. The mid-west states of the USA are known as Tornado Alley because there are so many tornadoes there each year. Tornadoes are much less common in Britain, although they do occur from time to time. On 27 July 2005, for example, a tornado badly damaged houses and cars in a suburb of Birmingham. One passerby described how the tornado in Birmingham picked up a ten-year-old boy, sending him flying through the air. He was lucky to land on his feet!

Photo © Lauren Stephens

Photo © Edward Warek

Photo by Ian Dunsford © 2005, Birmingham City Council www.birmingham.gov.uk

Text © 2007, Andrew Taylor

present tense verbs

powerful adjectives

general opening statement introduces topic

causal connective

general information is developed

time connective

specific facts introduced

causal connectives

examples and anecdotes to support information above

dramatic event; sounds slightly comic, but demonstrates potential danger of tornado

4: 2: T19: to identify how and why paragraphs are used to organise and sequence information

4: 2: W13: to know a range of suffixes that can be added to nouns and verbs to make adjectives

4: 2: T16: to prepare for factual research by reviewing what is known, what is needed, what is available and where one might search

4: 2: T20: to identify from examples the key features of explanatory texts

4: 2: T25: to write explanations of a process

Mummies

by Andrew Taylor

Background

This is a short explanatory text from a made-up website (although, uncharacteristically, much of it is in the past tense) that answers a question about how and why something was done in the past. There are many good websites where you could find supporting images and information such as www.nationalgeographic.com.

What's on the CD-ROM

This basic version of the core text includes a numbered list to distinguish the different ways that mummies are made.

Discussing the text

● Begin by establishing the children's prior knowledge of the topic. It is likely that some will link mummies with horror films and will need to be persuaded that there is nothing intrinsically horrible about a preserved body!

● Before reading the text use the title and subheadings to pin down the structure. The first section gives a general overview of the topic; then the paragraphs under *Natural mummies* and *Man-made mummies* extend the explanation further, covering material indicated by the subheadings. Then read the text in full.

● Depending on how familiar they are at investigating explanation texts, you could ask the children to work in pairs to identify common features, for example, the use of connectives. If the children are less familiar with these features, highlight examples and encourage them to identify others.

● Now point out the sentences containing …*but mummies were also made by the Incas of South America*… and *Often mummies are made*… These clauses are written in the passive voice. Explain that this is a quite formal way of writing, a feature of many explanation texts. Point out how those who committed the action (the Incas) are 'hidden' later in the sentence and made less important. Write up the active form of the first example: …*but the Incas of South America also made mummies*… and compare the two versions. In the sentence *Often mummies are made*… the passive is used because the making of the mummy is more important than the people who did it, or this information is not known. The passive focuses attention on the action not the person doing the action. Practise turning some simple active sentences into the passive voice.

Talk, read and write

● Ask a question that involves the children reflecting on a familiar event, process or phenomenon. For example, how do they prepare themselves for a special occasion such as a wedding or Divali celebration? Ask them to talk in pairs, then collect ideas as a class list. If you are using an interactive whiteboard, move text around to group similar information, such as about washing or putting on particular clothes, or use colours to indicate this.

● Look at the information you have organised. Model linking a group of points in a paragraph, using causal and temporal connectives such as *so*, *because*, *first* and *next*. Read the text, check for accuracy and completeness and think of a subheading for the paragraph. The children could then complete the same task for the next group of information.

● Read an example, responding positively to it, picking out ideas that are well expressed and well organised and the effective use of connectives.

● Now pretend that you know nothing about the particular special occasion and why you should dress up for it. Talk in role, making clear your confusion! Then ask the children to discuss in pairs how they could introduce the topic to you. Collect ideas before demonstrating how to rework them into an introductory paragraph, along the lines of: *In Britain, weddings are special occasions and friends and family gather to celebrate the event. Special clothes are worn and everyone takes great care over their appearance.* Check whether the drafted paragraph links well with the example work you had examined, editing if necessary. Then ask the children to work on introductory paragraphs for their pieces.

Extension

In order to apply their knowledge of explanation texts to the historical context, ask children to research and then explain the process by which the Ancient Egyptians mummified bodies. Ask the children to draft introductory paragraphs of two or three sentences, giving an overview of mummification.

4: 2: T19: to identify how and why paragraphs are used to organise and sequence information

4: 2: S3: to understand the significance of word order

passive voice 'hides' subject (the Incas) towards end of sentence

noun from verb 'mummify' from original noun 'mummy'

subheadings act as signposts, indicating information ahead

overview of topic, mentioning the two areas that will be expanded on below

4: 2: T16: to prepare for factual research by reviewing what is known, what is needed, what is available and where one might search

passive voice – who made the mummies isn't, at this point, important

causal connectives

Address: http://www.mummiesfromegypt.co.uk

File Edit View Favorites Tools Help
Back · · · Search Favorites · Go Links · Internet

Photo © Rob Kiser

Man-made mummies
Many societies and cultures used mummification to preserve a body. The most famous mummies are those made by the Ancient Egyptians, but mummies were also made by the Incas of South America, by burying bodies in frozen ground high in the mountains. Often mummies are made for religious reasons, so that a person has their body in the afterlife.

Mummies
A mummy is the preserved body of a person who has died. Some mummies occur naturally, because for some reason the normal processes of decay, which break a body down, cannot happen. Other mummies are made deliberately in order to preserve the dead.

Natural mummies
There are examples from across the world of bodies being preserved or mummified by natural conditions. Perhaps the dead body fell into a bog, or a person died on an icy mountain. In these cases the conditions meant that the body did not decay as it would normally. In 1991, for example, the frozen remains of a man were found under the snow on the Italian Alps. When it was examined, the body was found to be over 5,300 years old. The man's body was so well preserved that a tattoo was still visible on his arm, and scientists could tell what he had eaten for his last meal.

Photo © 2006, Jupiter Images Corporation
Text © 2007, Andrew Taylor

Screenshot reprinted by permission from Microsoft Corporation

---

4: 2: T24: to improve the cohesion of written explanations

4: 2: W3: to use independent spelling strategies, including building from other words

RSPCA

by Frazer Swift

Background

This text answers two of the questions it uses as subheadings – *What does the RSPCA do?* and *How does the RSPCA help?* All of the royalties from the original book, *RSPCA* by Frazer Swift in Heinemann's *Taking Action* series, are donated to the organisation. The text is written from a point of view that supports the RSPCA. This extract discusses the perhaps less well-known role that the RSPCA has in fighting cruelty.

What's on the CD-ROM

This extract is from the same source. It is really a list of ideas or action points that suggest how children can support the RSPCA in its core purpose of preventing cruelty to animals. It is written in bullet-point form, so is also useful for considering how to take notes and how to present explanation or information texts.

Discussing the text

● Ask what the children know about the RSPCA. Allow paired discussion and then take feedback. Begin a KWL grid (What I *know* about the RSPCA, What I *want* to know, What I've *learned*).

● From the discussion fill out the K column and ask the children what more they would like to find out. Add this to the W column. Retain the grid for later in the lesson.

● Point out the two questions used as subheadings. One test for an explanation text is that it should answer a question, or questions, for example, on what something or someone does, how something happens or how something works.

● Prepare a glossary page on the board to collect unfamiliar vocabulary as you read the text. Words and phrases you may need to clarify or use as a basis for dictionary work include: *cruelty, charity, donations, welfare organisation, laboratories, alternatives, experiments, inspected, proper living conditions, mistreating.* Encourage discussion about and interaction with the vocabulary.

● Read the text and ask the children what they have learned about the RSPCA. Structure oral feedback by suggesting a 'speaking frame' for contributions, for example, *I didn't know that the RSPCA…*

● Return to the KWL grid at this point, focusing on the L column. Ask the children to share what they have learned. Mark the text, underlining the points children suggest. Then demonstrate how to summarise the information into note form and add it to the L column. For example, the first sentence of paragraph two could provide: *Cares for animals needing help; Encourages kindness to animals.*

● Briefly revise generic features of explanations and then go through the text a paragraph at a time to find which features are evident, for example, general introduction, use of present tense, paragraphs that group information. Identify how the opening paragraphs introduce the topic, by tuning the reader into what this extract is about.

● Discuss why there are no time connectives in the piece. (Largely because it is explaining an organisation rather than a process, so there is no particular time order to the points raised.) There are few causal connectives too, because most paragraphs stand alone, with little connection with the one before.

Talk, read and write

● Return to the KWL grid and revisit the W column. Are there still questions unanswered or aspects of the RSPCA's work unexplained? If so, allow children to research the topic, for example by using the RSPCA's website (www.rspca.org.uk).

● You might also ask some children to complete the L column of the grid as an independent activity, either from this text or after researching more information .

● Give groups copies of the text and ask them to identify generic features of an explanation, drawing on the discussion at the start of the lesson.

Extension

Ask children to prepare for a discussion about whether we spend too much time, money and energy on caring for animals and not enough on caring for children. Ask them to list three ideas on either why we should care more for animals or on why children are more deserving of our help.

4: 2: T17: to scan texts to locate key words or phrases, useful headings, words or sentences

4: 2: T20: to identify from examples the key features of explanatory texts

these subheadings indicate text written from point of view that supports RSPCA

written with a positive 'bias' towards the RSPCA; promotes its work – almost persuasive in tone

RSPCA Merthyr Tydfil Animal Clinic © Andrew Forsyth/RSPCA

Text extract from "Taking Action: RSPCA" by Frazer Swift © 1997, RSPCA (1997, Heinemann)

RSPCA

WHAT DOES THE RSPCA DO?
The Royal Society for the Prevention of Cruelty to Animals (RSPCA) cares for animals that are in need of help and encourages people to be kind to animals. The Society is a charity and does not receive any money from the government. It depends on donations from the public to enable it to do its work.

COMMITTED TO CARING
The RSPCA was set up in London in 1824 and is the oldest animal welfare organisation in the world. With a team of over 300 inspectors throughout England and Wales, it is also the largest. The Society is so big that it has been split into 10 regions throughout the country, each one with smaller branches run by volunteers.

Lots of people know that the RSPCA helps pets, but the Society is concerned about cruelty to all animals – pets, wildlife, farm animals and animals used in laboratories.

HOW DOES THE RSPCA HELP?
The RSPCA provides advice and training for animal welfare organisations in other countries. It also encourages scientists to find alternatives to animal experiments and asks farmers to improve conditions for their animals.

KINDER FARMING
Freedom Food, the RSPCA's animal welfare food-labelling scheme, is another way the Society is improving animals' lives. Freedom Food farms are inspected to make sure that the animals have proper living conditions and are well cared for. So shoppers buying Freedom Food meat, eggs and dairy products can be sure that the animals had a good life.

The RSPCA works with the police to take people to court who have been cruel to animals. It also persuades the government to improve the law to stop people mistreating animals.

RSPCA Animal Collection Officer © Alban Donohoe

use of questions for main subheadings helps reader to know what text is about

general introduction

present tense verbs

brief history of Society adds to its credentials

4: 2: T16: to prepare for factual research by reviewing what is known, what is needed, what is available and where one might search

4: 2: T18: to mark extracts by annotating and by selecting key headings, words or sentences

4: 2: T19: to identify how and why paragraphs are used to organise and sequence information

Detectives of the past

 by Andrew Taylor

Background

This text explains why archaeologists look for certain clues and what artefacts can tell them.

What's on the CD-ROM

This is a simplified version of the core text, useful for the less able and as a writing model.

Discussing the text

● Share existing knowledge of archaeology and then point out that this writer suggests that archaeologists are like detectives.

● Read the text and ask how, according to the text, archaeologists are like detectives. Prompt children to give specific examples.

● Discuss how the text explains what an archaeologist does. Highlight the first paragraph. This attracts and 'tunes in' the reader, using an intriguing hook (*archaeologists are like detectives*). It also makes clear what the rest of the text will be about.

● Highlight the subheadings. Elicit that they act as titles for the paragraphs. For example, the subheading *Traces of buildings* tells the reader that the following paragraph is about building remains. This text is a good example of how an explanation text can be organised; information on a specific point is gathered together and built up in stages, rather than scattered across the text. Subheadings help the reader to identify where to find information on particular topics.

● The buildings section is a good example of an explanatory paragraph. Point out how the sentences build on the opening sentence, giving extra details about how archaeologists find out about different sorts of buildings. Show how the connectives *If* and *But if* play an important part by linking one sentence to another. Reinforce the children's understanding of these connectives by challenging them to use them in sentences of their own.

● Remind the children that the text suggests that archaeologists are like detectives. Having read the text, do they agree? Encourage a flowing discussion on why or why not.

Talk, read and write

● Recap on some of the genre elements of an explanation text you have identified: the overview opening paragraph, the use of paragraphs and subheadings to organise information, connectives to link ideas and sentences within a paragraph. Help the children to apply these ideas to their own writing.

● Agree on a topic or question for explanation, for example, from work being covered in science or history. Gather as much information as possible in note form from the children about the topic. Then demonstrate (for example using different-coloured linking key lines, or moving text around on an interactive board) how to organise it under different headings. Show that if the explanation is of a process, the order of these subheadings and paragraphs will be particularly important.

● Remind the class that the first paragraph in an explanation text gives an overview of the whole text. Stress too that it also needs to encourage the reader to read on. Draft together some opening sentences and discuss effective ones. Then use the subheadings you have developed to inform the rest of the paragraph: the paragraph should generalise the information covered in the text, so the subheadings are helpful for creating an overview.

● Choose one of the other subheadings you have listed and work together to compose a paragraph about it. Remind the children of the importance of an introductory sentence and ask them to have a go at writing one. Compare the children's work. Then talk about what else needs to be included in the paragraph and ask the children to compose three or four sentences that build up the details they want to convey.

● Now draw attention to the language used in one or two examples. Ask the class to check the tense and the use of connectives. Rework one or two sentences, so that they link better with the rest of the paragraph.

● Finally ask the children to work in pairs to read each other's work. Ask them to pretend they know nothing about the process or subject being explained. *Does the explanation make sense and is it complete? Is it interesting?* Ask them to work together to review word choices.

Extension

Children could interview someone about their job, identifying the main things involved and how they set about doing it.

4: 2: T19: to identify how and why paragraphs are used to organise and sequence information

4: 2: T25: to write explanations of a process, using conventions identified through reading

4: 2: S4: to recognise how commas, connectives and full stops are used to join and separate clauses

4: 2: T20: to identify from examples the key features of explanatory texts

4: 2: T24: to improve the cohesion of written explanations

unexpected simile, intended to engage the reader

focus of paragraph: tools

focus of paragraph: things people made in the past

causal connectives – there are more causal connectives than temporal connectives in this text

focus of paragraph: human remains

opening paragraph tunes reader in to topic and gives overview of whole topic – a common feature of explanation texts

focus of paragraph: houses

information organised into discrete paragraphs

Detectives of the past

Archaeologists are like detectives. But instead of solving crimes, they piece together scraps of evidence – metal objects, stone, pottery, leather, building foundations and bones – to understand how people lived long ago.

Metal and stone tools

Archaeologists often find tools made from metals such as bronze and iron, or from rocks such as flint. As well as finding the tools themselves, sometimes they can tell from other objects what kinds of tools were used to shape them. The basic design of many simple tools – including axe-heads and knives – has hardly changed for thousands of years.

Photo © Tom Denham

Pottery and crafts

Archaeologists also search for evidence of crafts to build up a picture of life long ago. From even a fragment of pottery, experts can often work out exactly what sort of a cup, plate or dish it was originally part of. Scraps of leather or pieces of woollen cloth provide clues to the history of shoe-making, weaving methods, and the dyes used for colouring yarn and cloth.

Photo © Fons Reijsbergen

Traces of buildings

Among the most important discoveries are traces of the kinds of homes people built long ago. If a building was made of stone, the foundations or even the walls may survive in their original state. But if it was built of wood, there is usually more detective work to be done. The only clues to how it was built may be dark marks in the soil. Sometimes archaeologists find round, dark 'post holes'. These show where the main uprights were sunk into the ground, and so reveal what size and shape the house was.

Photo © Vicky S

Human bones

Human bones provide clues to how long people lived, and sometimes even of the diseases that they suffered or died from. But some, acidic soils decay bones, so archaeologists have developed special techniques for identifying where bones once lay even if they are no longer there. On the famous Sutton Hoo dig, archaeologists discovered that the shapes of buried bones showed up as dark lines in the sandy soil.

Photo © 2006, Jupiter Images Corporation

What people ate

Animal bones give clues to the animals people kept to provide them with meat. Archaeologists can discover much about the crops people grew from tiny plant remains, such as seeds, as well as remains of insects that lived on the plants.

Text © 2007, Andrew Taylor

Photo © Eugene Wolfe

What is a Tudor theatre?

by Gillian Clements

Background

This explanation text is taken from *Building History: Tudor Theatre* by Gillian Clements. The text can be linked to other English work and to history. It uses questions as headings, going on to explain the answers to those questions.

What's on the CD-ROM

This more basic text provides simple notes about the Globe theatre. The information given can be used as the basis for writing in the second half of the lesson.

Discussing the text

● Highlight the title and explain that the aim of the text is to answer this question. Use the title to make predictions about the content of the text. Note these predictions on the board.

● Read and discuss the opening paragraph, which acts as a general introduction to the text.

● Point out that the subheadings are also questions – an engaging way of organising a text. Make a table for further predictions, with column headings *Question* and *Paragraph prediction*. Note the first two subheadings in the first column and ask the children to discuss in pairs what that part of the text will be about. Take suggestions, then read the text. If the predictions weren't accurate, ask what was missing. You could also set this as an independent activity, provided the children have not read the whole text.

● Highlight the adverbial phrases (see annotations), which explain when, how or why something was done. Discuss how they act as time connectives that introduce or link ideas, because the text is explaining a series of historical events. Point out how some of the adverbial clauses are punctuated by commas. Show that sense and the need to take a breath require a short pause, marked by a comma.

Talk, read and write

● Organise the class into groups, each to focus on a different aspect of Tudor theatres, for example, the buildings, audience, actors, playwrights. Ask each group to use available resources to research information about their topic, making notes on what they find out.

● Now reorganise the groups, so that children

who have researched different topics are working together. Ask them to explain to each other what they have discovered. You might support this activity by underlining the importance of using their notes, and perhaps by providing a 'talking frame'. For example, *I found out four important pieces of information about [the theatre buildings]. The first was…*

● After they have completed the speaking and listening activity, explain that you want each group to make a poster about what they have found out. Discuss how posters use page design, pictures and different fonts and print sizes to make information easily readable and lively. Show some examples if possible to illustrate the various features and techniques. Set some rules for the activity, for example, that everyone in the group has to contribute at least one picture and label or caption, and set a time limit. Provide each group with an interesting collection of paper (different colours and sizes) and equipment (scissors, glue, photographs). Alternatively, this could be a creative ICT activity, using DTP or drawing software.

● When the groups have completed their posters, provide the opportunity for the different groups to view each other's work. Explain the concept of 'envoying', where a representative from each group goes to visit another group and has the poster explained to them. Allow each member of the group to have the opportunity to act as an envoy and explain their own work to 'visitors'.

● As a plenary, work with the children to draft a brief explanatory caption about the posters. Explain that the posters will be displayed and that anyone looking at the display will need an introduction of what it is about. This paragraph should provide an overview of the topic and explanation of the work that was done. Take drafting ideas and construct an introduction, for example, *Class 4 have been finding out about Tudor theatres, the people who worked in them and those who came to watch the plays. We researched…*

Extension

Ask children to find out five pieces of information about the reconstructed Globe theatre. They could do this by visiting the website www.shakespeares-globe.org.

4: 2: W11: to understand that vocabulary changes over time

questions used throughout to structure text; each paragraph answers its subheading question

'an' or 'ean' added to name to make adjective

4: 2: S4: to recognise how commas, connectives and full stops are used to join and separate clauses

adverbial phrases which give information about when something happened; time connectives

powerful vocabulary reflects excitement at the time

4: 2: T24: to improve the cohesion of written explanations

paragraph introduces whole text

commas separate subordinate clause

little-used term nowadays – 'entertainment' that no longer happens

4: 2: W13: to know a range of suffixes that can be added to nouns and verbs to make adjectives

What is a Tudor theatre?

Towards the end of the 1500s, when the Tudor Queen Elizabeth I was on the throne, some extraordinary new theatres were built in London. Everyone flocked to see the exciting new plays!

What other entertainments were there?
There were already many types of entertainment in Tudor times. People could see bear-baiting and bloody executions, church mystery plays and royal processions.

What was the Renaissance?
At this time people were interested in the Classical culture of ancient Greece and Rome and the period became known as the Renaissance (meaning re-birth). During the Renaissance many new scientific and artistic ideas were developed. The new plays performed in Tudor theatres were part of the Renaissance.

Who were the theatres for?
All kinds of people visited London's new theatres from the very poor to the very rich. When a flag was flown over the theatre to announce the latest play, crowds of people crossed over the Thames to enjoy the show. Just one penny bought the cheapest ticket, and nearly everyone could afford that!

Where were the theatres built?
For a long time, people in cities like Coventry, Chester and York had been able to see religious mystery plays. These were put on by local craft unions called guilds and were performed on temporary stages. However, it was businessmen who built the new Tudor theatres. And, as London was the home of business, it became the home of Tudor theatres too.

When were the theatres built?
Most of these theatres were built during the late 1500s and the early 1600s, during the reigns of Queen Elizabeth I and King James I. The theatres built during Elizabeth's reign are often known as Elizabethan theatres and those built in King James's reign are known as Jacobean theatres (after the Latin word for James).

Who put on the plays?
Theatre companies were made up of senior shareholders, actors and boy apprentices. The whole company worked together to put on the plays, meeting at the theatre every day to rehearse new parts.

Who were the actors?
The Lord Chamberlain's Men had some of England's greatest actors. Burbage was their biggest star. Their rivals were the Lord Admiral's Men and their star was Edward Alleyn. He played Doctor Faustus in Marlowe's play about a man who sells his soul to the devil. He was so believable that people thought that there was a real devil on stage.

Who were the boy apprentices?
Women and girls did not perform in public theatres in Tudor times. Female parts were played by boy apprentices who were dressed in skirts, wigs and made up to look the part.

Text extract and illustrations from "Building History: Tudor Theatre" by Gillian Clements © 2004 Gillian Clements (2004 Franklin Watts)

Polka Theatre

 from the Polka Theatre website

Background

Polka is a theatre for children and young people in Wimbledon in London. This text is taken from its website (www.polkatheatre.com), which includes a virtual tour of the theatre, details of current productions and other information. The text here is of mixed genre, giving information about the theatre and also trying to persuade people to visit. It is interspersed with positive quotes from adults and children who have attended the theatre.

What's on the CD-ROM

This text is a rewritten, simplified version of the core text. The persuasive elements have been removed, which makes the piece more straightforwardly an information text.

Discussing the text

● Introduce the text and give some background on the theatre. If possible, explore the website to see what plays are currently being produced.

● Return to the text and explain that it was taken from the 'About the Company' section of the site. Ask the children to speculate what the text might be about. (It is likely to tell us more about Polka and what it does.) Read the first paragraph.

● Clarify difficult vocabulary (for example, *venues, dedicated, exclusively, inspiring*), by encouraging the children to work out meanings from context, using prior knowledge and/or a dictionary. Help them to understand the phrase *Since our doors opened* by asking them to re-read the context and try to explain the phrase in their own words. Paired discussion might be helpful.

● Read the first quote and note how different it is, in terms of presentation and content, from the main paragraph. Elicit that it is in a different font and in speech marks, and that this is what someone has said or written about their experience of Polka, in this case from a newspaper. Point out that quotes like this are dotted throughout the text and are loosely linked to the adjacent paragraph, functioning to highlight and give first-hand examples.

● Summarise the text so far and the information gained. For example, *In the first paragraph we found out about the Polka Theatre, a theatre for children and young people which opened in 1979. It presents exciting plays for children…*

● Go through the rest of the text, using similar techniques; break the text into sections, ask for a prediction about what the text might say next, clarify challenging vocabulary and question difficult ideas. End by asking someone to make a brief summary of what has been read in that section.

Talk, read and write

● Divide the board into quadrants labelled *Theatre, Audience, Plays, Other activities*.

● Focus on one quadrant at a time. First ask the children to locate the paragraphs which give information about this chosen topic and to re-read and discuss the paragraphs. Ask them to tell you what they have found out, for adding to the quadrant. Encourage them to abbreviate the information and to use their own words.

● Once one quadrant is completed, note how the particular paragraphs contain a lot of information about the topic – the text collects information about different aspects of a topic into paragraphs and it may be possible to give a title or heading to each one. Check that this is true by completing the other quadrants.

● Now focus on the final paragraph. Like much of the text this has a persuasive intention. Identify these features: the use of the pronoun *you*, positive or intriguing adjectives such as *magical* and *rare*, and persuasive phrases or claims such as *No two visits are the same*. Give the children the opportunity to discuss the effect of these different language features and explain how they help to persuade someone that the theatre is a good place to visit.

● Highlight the final sentence of the text. This makes a large claim and is rather like an advertising slogan. Help the class to understand the full meaning – in a sense theatre 'begins' at Polka for many children because this is the first place they experience a play on a stage.

Extension

Ask children to identify a text that they would like to see adapted for the stage. They could write a letter to you, in role as Polka's director, to persuade you that this would be a good story to perform.

4: 2: T19: to identify how and why paragraphs are used to organise and sequence information

paragraph topic/focus: audience

quotes from publicity material

punctuates text and maintains persuasive tone

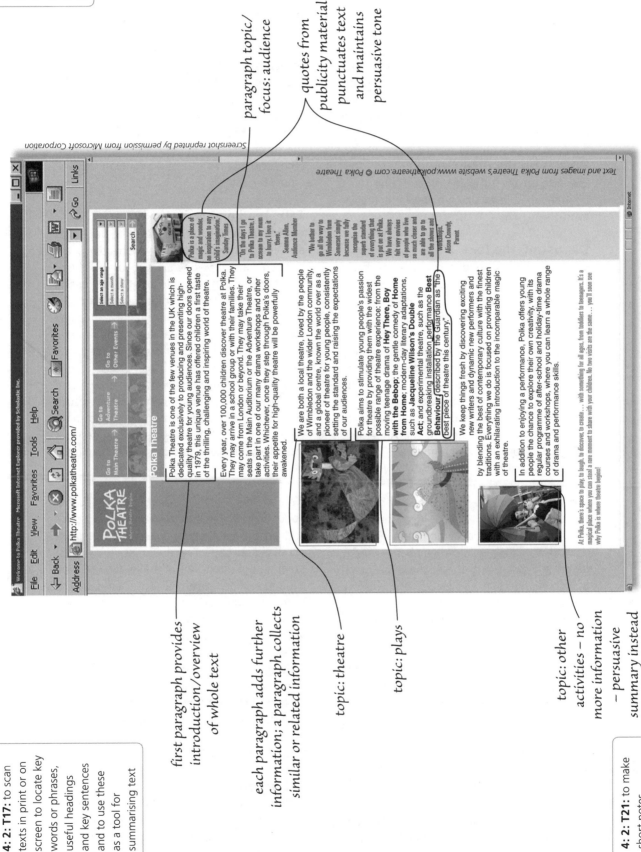

Screenshot reprinted by permission from Microsoft Corporation

Text and images from Polka Theatre's website www.polkatheatre.com © Polka Theatre

first paragraph provides introduction/overview of whole text

each paragraph adds further information; a paragraph collects similar or related information

topic: theatre

topic: plays

topic: other activities – no more information – persuasive summary instead

4: 2: T17: to scan texts in print or on screen to locate key words or phrases, useful headings and key sentences and to use these as a tool for summarising text

4: 2: T21: to make short notes

The Angel of the North
by Andrew Taylor

Background

This text draws on material from Gateshead Borough Council's website. It presents information about a familiar landmark in note form. Through the use of bullet points, information can be presented briefly and simply. The subject clearly links to art and design and geography.

What's on the CD-ROM

The text on the CD-ROM presents the same information in even briefer note and tabular form.

Discussing the text

● Read the text and encourage feedback. Ask if anyone has seen the Angel and if so, what kind of impression did it make?

● Compare the details given with a photograph of the Angel (available at www.gateshead.gov.uk, for example), focusing particularly on the physical features and the materials used. Use the text to add labels to the picture, such as information about the size of the Angel. Labels should help the reader to understand the uniqueness of the Angel and will act as a summary of the notes.

● Clarify challenging vocabulary as you read the text. Most can be understood from context. Demonstrate how re-reading a sentence can help. For example, when discussing the meaning of *prototype* demonstrate how re-reading would allow you to emphasise *model*, *before* and *cast*, giving an idea that a prototype is something that is made first, before something is made in its final form.

● Read the text a second time. Point out that the writing is not continuous and sentences are not linked together. Explain that notes are often listed like this and present just the important information. Making your own notes is useful when trying to remember key facts about something. To demonstrate how the bullet points function, add an extra bullet to one section. For example, *The Angel dwarfs anything which stands close to it* could be added to the second section (beginning *The Angel was designed…*). Emphasise that your addition doesn't follow on from the previous point, nor lead into the next, but adds another discrete detail.

● Point out that there is, however, a loose organisation to the piece – signalled by the gaps between the sets of bullet points. All the points in a section relate to a particular sub-topic about the Angel. The first two bullets, for example, refer to the site. Write this in as a subheading. Ask the class to read the next set of points and suggest a subheading. Repeat for the other sections, listing them on the board. (The headings in the table on the CD-ROM text would be suitable.)

Talk, read and write

● Model how to write even briefer notes about the Angel, using the subheadings the children have developed. Using the first two bullets, write *Site* as a title and *On hill, beside A1 Gateshead; Former colliery bath* as bullet points. Explain how using *Site* as a heading means that you don't need to include *situated* or *set on a site*; and that you decided that *overlooking the Team Valley* wasn't vital information. You used *former* to replace *that used to house*, and have omitted articles such as *a* and *the*. Explain that good notes make clever use of titles, put ideas together, miss out less relevant material and use one word in place of several.

● Now ask the children to try this technique with another section, perhaps the last section, about visitors. Ask the children to work in pairs and encourage them to write a bullet point about visitors to the Angel. Discuss their efforts, pointing out good uses of a title, the focus on key information, and effective use of vocabulary. More able children might make notes of the other sections as an independent activity.

● Show how a table can also help in making notes. Use the table headings from the CD-ROM text to make a table on the board and ask the children to supply information for each section. Point out that the table headings are similar or the same as the subheadings they generated earlier for the core text. Ask groups to complete the table as appropriate.

Extension

Children could take another text from this book, such as 'Mummies' or 'RSPCA', and practise using bullet points and/or a table as a means of summarising the main information.

4: 2: T17: to scan texts in print or on screen to locate key words or phrases, useful headings and key sentences and to use these as a tool for summarising text

4: 2: T21: to make short notes

4: 2: T16: to prepare for factual research by reviewing what is known, what is needed, what is available and where one might search

4: 2: T19: to identify how and why paragraphs are used to organise and sequence information

information about site

information on design and look of Angel

explanation of construction

about people who see Angel

factual information given in note form

gaps suggest grouping of ideas

bullet points give basic information; little development or description

impersonal;

The Angel of the North

Photo used by permission of Gateshead Council, www.gateshead.gov.uk I2I Photography, Colin Cuthbert

The Angel of the North

Height: 20 metres (taller than a five-storey building or four double-decker buses)
Width: 54 metres (almost the same as the wingspan of a jumbo jet)
Weight: 208 tonnes

- Situated beside the A1 road at Gateshead on a hilltop site, overlooking the Team Valley.
- The Angel is set on a site that used to house the baths at the top of a colliery.

- The Angel was designed by the artist Antony Gormley.
- Its form is based on a mould that was taken of his own body.
- A human-size model was made as a prototype before the huge Angel was cast.
- The face has been deliberately left without any features.
- The Angel's wings are not flat but are tilted slightly forward as though wanting to give an embrace.

- The figure is made from weather-resistant steel that includes copper to give a rich red-brown colour.
- The Angel is secured to the ground by concrete piles, 22 metres deep.
- The body is hollow.
- There is an inspection access door in one of the Angel's shoulder blades.
- The Angel was constructed in Hartlepool and then assembled on site. It was designed to last 100 years and withstand winds of over 100 miles an hour.

- More than 90,000 drivers pass the site every day.
- The Angel is also visible from the East Coast rail line which runs from London to Edinburgh.
- About 150,000 visitors a year are expected to see the Angel close up.

Animals of the rainforest
by Suzanne Kirk

Background
This text is taken from a *Literacy Time* poster. It is included as an example of a highly visual text, which uses a tabular form to present information.

What's on the CD-ROM
The CD-ROM includes an extract from the same source. It presents a description of the rainforest area in continuous prose. It might be used to extend understanding of the topic, or as a source text for note-making.

Discussing the text
● Read the text and distinguish the two presentation formats: a table and bulleted sentences. Clarify challenging vocabulary, such as *vegetation, diversity, habitat, nocturnal.*

● Model or revise how to read a table. The headings in the first row identify what information is to be found in the columns below. Explain how the first column of a table also usually helps you make sense of the other information. Demonstrate how to read information, making an explicit link between the columns and the rows. Reiterate that this table needs to be read from left to right. Play a game to reinforce understanding. For example, say: *Name a creature that lives in the rainforest at a 20-metre height*, or, *What name is given to the 30-metre level?* Alternatively, name one of the creatures, such as army ant, and ask the children to use the table to give you information about it.

● Now look at the bullet points below the table. They present further information in short sentences. Each sentence is unconnected to the previous one or the next one. Discuss why the information is presented in this way. (Bullet points just focus on important information; they can form a list of separate pieces of information; they allow information to be presented briefly; key points can be identified easily and quickly.)

Talk, read and write
● Develop another quiz. Ask the children to choose four or five creatures that live in the rainforest. These are the answers to the quiz and should be presented as the top row of a table. The children now have to think up questions which will give one of these creatures as an answer. Demonstrate how to use the text to find information and draft a question: *What creatures live in the canopy and pollinate flowers?* Add the question to the first column of the table. Someone doing the quiz would have to read the question and tick the box for the right answer:

	Harpy eagles	Howler monkeys	Tree frogs	Bats
What creatures live in the canopy and pollinate flowers?				

● Ask the children to set their own quiz and give them time to answer each other's.

● Set up a drama activity based on the text. Explain that the children are a group of expert explorers, and you are a new, very inexperienced visitor to the rainforest. They should use the information in the text to answer your questions, for example, *What is the best time to visit the rainforest if I want to see most creatures? Why are hummingbirds so important?* If responses are not very informed, come out of role, remind them how the text can help, then repeat the activity.

● Develop this by organising groups to prepare advice for the inexperienced traveller. Ask them to underline four or five pieces of important information and to use these points to make a brief presentation to you in role. Explain that they could illustrate the information with made-up stories (*The first time I heard a howler monkey it made my heart stop!*). Follow up their presentation by asking questions in role: *Why is camouflage important?*

● As a plenary, talk about how a table format is a useful way of presenting information succinctly. Make a link to the way they have read and written tables in other activities. Reiterate the importance of the column and row headings, and how they are helpful for identifying and organising key information.

Extension
Provide the table format used for the quiz. Ask children to write a quiz using the same approach, perhaps testing a friend or relative.

read across and down top row and column, like a graph

table is a useful way of collecting lots of information in a small space

lots of scientific vocabulary

these bullets are not connected or sequenced; each bullet point presents discrete information; however they all give general information about rainforest inhabitants (few specific creatures are named)

lots of scientific vocabulary

illustration helps reader to understand information

bullets also 'shorthand'/notes – just main details are given

Animals of the rainforest

Without the special hot and wet conditions which encourage a unique type of vegetation there would not be the huge diversity of animals found in rainforest areas. Some 150 different types of creatures can find a home on one rainforest tree.

Habitat within the forest	Typical animals living there
Super canopy	Harpy eagles
Canopy	Howler monkeys Toucans Snakes Tree frogs Bats Birds
Understorey	Scarlet macaws Paradise tree snakes
Forest floor	Beetles Moths Stick insects Army ants Termites

Height above forest floor

40m
30m
20m
10m
0m

Forest facts
- Scientists are still finding new species of rainforest creatures and identifying them.
- Many rainforest animals are nocturnal.
- Camouflage plays an important part in the survival of many rainforest creatures.
- Insects make up 90% of the animal mass of a rainforest.
- In the rainforest, many plants rely on animals, such as hummingbirds and bats, to pollinate their flowers and spread their ripened seeds.
- 50% of the animal species of the rainforest live in the canopy level.

Text by Suzanne Kirk from "Literacy Time" 3/4: Autumn 2002 © 2002, Suzanne Kirk (2002, Scholastic Ltd); illustration © 2002, Graham Kennedy; parrot photo © Everyday Animals; tree frog photo © Corel

Glossary

by Laura Howell

Background
This glossary of weather terms is from *The Usborne Introduction to Weather and Climate Change*. Glossaries are sometimes included in information books, working as a subject-specific dictionary.

What's on the CD-ROM
This text provides simplified explanations of the weather terms from the core text.

Discussing the text
● Introduce the text and remind the children that a glossary is like a small dictionary that explains technical vocabulary in a book.
● Highlight two head words and read the entries, making your voice distinguish between the head word and the explanation. Show that bold print has been used to pick out the key word and the normal type gives the explanation.
● Read the explanation for *atmosphere*. Draw attention to the numbers and ask what they mean in this context. Elicit that they indicate that there are two meanings and hence two explanations for the term.
● Point out the use of italic in the definition of *barometer*. This indicates that the term *atmospheric pressure* is covered somewhere else in the glossary. Ask the children to find it. Read the two explanations consecutively and explain the links and the way each helps the reader understand the other. Challenge the children to identify other explanations that include cross-references like this (for example, *climate forcing* and *cold front*).
● Ask the children what they have noticed about the way that the text is organised. They should be able to identify that it is in alphabetical order. Explain that glossaries aren't always organised in this way – sometimes words are given in the order that they appear on a page.
● Hand out examples of texts with glossaries. Do they include any of the features highlighted in the core text, for example, the use of bold print and plain font to distinguish the head word from the definition, numbers to make different explanations stand out, italic to enable terms to be cross-checked, and alphabetic order? The different glossaries may use various conventions to do the same thing and this could generate some interesting discussions. You could develop a chart of similarities and differences to collect comparisons.

Talk, read and write
● Choose another curriculum topic and begin to set up a class glossary to explain difficult or technical terms that the children are encountering. If you can do this using word-processing software, follow the same style and layout conventions as in the text. If not, ask the children to help you to develop alternatives, such as underlining or highlighting the key word, using another colour to indicate a cross reference.
● Ask the children to develop their own personal glossary of terms for a particular subject. They should review some recent work on that topic and gather individual specialist vocabulary on large sticky notes. Working in pairs, ask the children to try to explain the term, adding the definition to the note. The explanation could then be checked and an agreed version added to a topic glossary.
● Explain that the conventions used in the glossary, such as using bold print and italic, help to pick out and distinguish certain types of word. These conventions can also be used for note-making and presentation. Basing the activity around a shared experience such as a sports day, work together to agree on an account and then add emphasis to key words. For example, use bold text or a highlighter, numbers to identify different stages in the event and italic or a colour to identify words which will need to be explained in a glossary.
● Taking another text from this book, ask the children to use the note-taking techniques just developed to identify and pick out the main points. You might ask them to find and number five key points in the text, then develop a glossary of terms or simply to highlight what they consider the most important information.

Extension
Ask children to make notes for a glossary about a hobby they enjoy or other topic they are interested in. Ask them to pick out important vocabulary and make a first attempt to explain it. More confident children could present the glossary using the conventions introduced.

Glossary

Here are explanations of some of the more difficult weather and climate terms you may have found.

A

aerosols Tiny particles in the air which scatter sunlight. They can be natural or artificial.

air mass A mass of air with the same temperature and *humidity* throughout.

air pressure See *atmospheric pressure*.

altitude Height above sea level.

anemometer Device used to measure wind speed.

anticyclones or **highs** Areas of high *atmospheric pressure*.

astronomical theory of climate change See *Milankovitch theory*.

atmosphere ① The protective layer of air around Earth that enables plants and animals to live. ② A layer of gases around any planet.

atmospheric pressure or air pressure The force of air pressing down on Earth, measured in millibars (mb).

auroras Patterns of light in the sky, seen around the North Pole (Aurora Borealis) and the South Pole (Aurora Australis).

B

barometer Device used to measure *atmospheric pressure*.

biome An area of Earth with a particular combination of climate, landscapes, plants and animals.

boreal forest or **taiga** A wide area of coniferous forest across Northern America, Europe and Asia.

C

carbon sink Part of the landscape that absorbs and stores carbon dioxide from the air. Forests and oceans are carbon sinks.

CFCs (chlorofluorocarbons) Man-made chemicals that are thought to damage the ozone layer.

circumpolar current An ocean *current* that flows without interruption around Antarctica.

climate forcing Any human-made or otherwise artificial changing of the *climate system*.

climate model A construction of past or future climate conditions, created by feeding various types of data into a computer.

climate system The complex relationships between all the features that create climates on Earth. These include the Sun's heat, living things, water, air and ice.

cloud cover The amount of sky seen to be covered by cloud in any given place.

cold front A boundary at the head of a cold *air mass*.

condensation The process of water vapour turning back into liquid water as it cools down. See also *evaporation*, which is the opposite effect.

Text extract from "The Usborne Introduction to Weather and Climate Change" by Laura Howell © 2003, Usborne Publishing Ltd.

---

headwords shown in bold type

technical vocabulary

numbers within an explantion distinguish between two different meanings of a headword

italics are used to show a term which has its own entry elsewhere in the glossary

explanations shown in normal type

headwords arranged in alphabetical order, like a dictionary. Many glossaries use this convention

---

4: 2: T17: to scan texts in print or on screen to locate key words or phrases, useful headings and to use these as a tool for summarising texts

4: 2: T23: to collect information from a variety of sources and present it in one simple format, e.g. wall chart, labelled diagram

4: 2: W3: to use independent spelling strategies

4: 2: T18: to mark extracts by annotating and by selecting key headings, words or sentences, or alternatively, noting these

4: 2: T21: to make short notes, e.g. by abbreviating ideas, selecting key words, listing or in diagrammatic form

National Coal Mining Museum

from The National Coal Mining Museum for England

Background

This text is taken from a publicity leaflet for the National Coal Mining Museum for England in Wakefield. Like the Polka Theatre text, it has persuasive and informative elements. It is used here to illustrate note-taking techniques. Further information about the museum, including pictures, can be found at www.ncm.org.uk.

What's on the CD-ROM

This simplified version uses bullet points as an example of a note-making technique.

Discussing the text

● Activate children's knowledge of mining as preparation for reading. You could do this by using pictures from the website as a starting point, or draw on relevant experiences children have had. Alternatively invite a visitor to talk to the children, having prepared questions in advance.

● Read the text, clarifying unfamiliar vocabulary. Comment on the imperative verbs used throughout the leaflet, instructing the reader how to enjoy themselves at the museum!

● Discuss the text's layout and organisation. Identify that the bullet points are a kind of 'contents', listing the range of attractions at the museum. The numbers refer to a plan of the site on the original leaflet, giving a brief description of each attraction. To establish understanding, ask questions such as, *What is at number 3?*; *What can you tell me about Inman Shaft?*

● Ask the children why all the text is not written in continuous prose as in the middle paragraphs. The bullet points, use of numbers, headings and brief sentences allows at least some information to be given about many attractions. A museum operator would want to convince the public there is lots to see and try – details can wait until they have convinced someone to visit. The use of note form helps the attractions to stand out.

Talk, read and write

● Re-read the section beginning *Step into the past...* and model how to summarise it, for example, by underlining the important information in each paragraph. This would focus on the factual information and ignore the direct address to the reader. Also demonstrate how to cut back on the text by finding a few words to summarise a sentence or clause: *the people who played a role in our industrial heritage* could become simply *miners*. Write up the summary in note form.

● As an alternative approach for collecting information for a summary, work together to make a spider diagram or mind map. You could include topic headings such as: Compare mining in the past with today; Real life stories of miners; Mining timeline; National Coal Mining Museum for England; Other attractions; Mining buildings; The mining process; The science of mining.

● Explain that the text boxes in a mind map act as headings. Model how some headings should be selected as main topics and that other headings can be treated as subtopics with links to the main headings. Explain that the subtopics provide subheadings for paragraphs and show how additional information or detail can be linked with more lines and text boxes.

● Discuss the differences between a summary presented in note form and as a diagram. Explain that the purpose of the summary is likely to dictate its form. For example, some people find it easier to remember information in a diagram, so use it as a means of learning something for a test.

● Use the text as the basis of some role play. Working in pairs, one child could be a member of the museum staff (an ex-miner) and the other an anxious parent who is not sure about the trip as the mine might not be safe. Ask the pairs to hold the conversation where the 'miner' tries to persuade the 'parent' that the mine is safe and an enjoyable place to visit. Encourage them to use the information in the leaflet to help and prompt them. Give the pairs the opportunity to swap roles. You could also try this as a whole class activity, with different children being hot-seated as the miner.

Extension

Challenge the children to find out more about the museum, by visiting the website. Set a focus for the research, such as: *Find out about three events happening at the museum this year.*

4: 2: T17: to scan texts in print or on screen to locate key words or phrases, useful heading and key sentences and to use these as a tool for summarising text

text after bullet points does not need a full stop

bullet points used as subheads to organise information

photos of attractions add to leaflet's appeal

Text and photos from The National Coal Mining Museum for England leaflet © The National Coal Mining Museum for England

National Coal Mining Museum for England

- **Exhibitions and galleries · Pit ponies**
- **Mining machinery · Train rides**
- **Adventure playground · Nature trail**
- **Under fives' play area · Licensed café**
- **Unique souvenirs · Library**
- **Visit www.ncm.org.uk for information**

Step into the past at the National Coal Mining Museum for England, Overton, and explore the amazing real-life stories if the people who played a role in our industrial heritage.

Follow a time line through twisting tunnels and compare the hardships and risks faced by early miners, with the safety and efficiency of modern mining in England.

Safely back in the daylight again, explore many of the Museum's historic mining buildings, try out cool mining science activities and discover how mining processes worked using our interactive exhibits.

1 **Nature trail**
Enjoy wildlife and scenery over a beautiful half mile stroll. Follow the signs from Caphouse.

2 **Pit Ponies and stables**
See the last ever working ponies now happily enjoying their retirement with us.

3 **1842 Victorian Exhibition**
Uncover the little known stories of the women and children who worked in the cool mining industry.

4 **Coal interface building**
Can you solve some of the safety and communication problems miners had to cope with underground?

5 **Underground tours**
Collect your helmet and lamp, and descend 140 metres underground for an unforgettable 1¼ hour tour.

6 **Visitor centre**
Relax with a variety of refreshments in our licensed café, and discover a range of gifts for everyone in our museum shop.

7 **Settling ponds and reed beds**
Nature gets to work in cleaning water pumped from underground. Get closer to the wildlife with our viewing holes and nature trail.

8 **Workshops**
See science in action with some real heavyweight machinery. Check out our live demonstrations (times vary – ask at Reception).

9 **Inman Shaft**
Hector the Heron gives you an overhead view of the site's water system, plus fascinating interactive displays.

10 **Hope Pit Winding Engine House**
What goes up must come down! Get to grips with pulley wheels – but don't let Frank the virtual Foreman wind you up!

text designed and laid out in an appealing way to attract attention

numbered list details interactive exhibits

brief explanations can give a great deal of information

4: 2: S2: to use the apostrophe accurately to mark possession

4: 2: T18: to mark extracts by annotating and by selecting key headings, words or sentences, or alternatively, noting these

The Early Life of James Cook

by Andrew Taylor

Background

Cook is remembered as a great scientific explorer who 'discovered' large areas of the Earth, including New Zealand, the east coast of Australia and many Pacific islands. This biographical text links to 'A New Resolution' on page 141 and to history and geography.

What's on the CD-ROM

This text uses a timeline to present key dates up to the end of Cook's first major voyage.

Discussing the text

● Ask the children if they know anything about Captain Cook or if they have heard of the *Endeavour*. Some may know of *Endeavour* as the name of a space shuttle, which would allow you to make a connection between astronauts exploring space and nautical men like Cook exploring the seas and discovering lands unknown to Europeans. Briefly explain something of Cook's importance as a sailor and navigator. List the information the children know about Cook.

● Now introduce the text. Ask the children to predict what it is about. Direct them to the title and first subheading if necessary. Then focus on each subheading in turn and ask the children to work in pairs to predict what they will find out in each paragraph. Note ideas and explain that subheadings are useful guides when researching information as they signpost the most appropriate part of the text to read. Challenge pairs to compete in pointing to the right part of the text when you ask a question such as, *What section of the text should I look at if I want to find out about Cook's ship?*

● Recalling the predictions made by the class, read the text a section at a time. Assess the predictions, linking them to the quality or usefulness of the subheading. Clarify any unfamiliar vocabulary or develop a glossary as you read on. For each section, ask the children to discuss two or three points they have learned about Cook. List the major points alongside the original list of information on the board.

● Having read the whole text, prepare the class to make a judgement about the most important points found about James Cook. Return to the full list of information on the board and ask the children, in pairs, to select just three key points about Cook's early life. Ask them to justify their selection using a talk frame, for example, *I think... is one of the most important points in Captain Cook's early life because...*

● See if the children have any unanswered questions about Cook or would like to find out more about him. These thoughts might be used as a starting point for independent research.

Talk, read and write

● Hot-seat a group of five to six children as James Cook. Support them with ideas as the rest of the class prepare questions about his early life which the group being hot-seated can answer, drawing on the information in the text and inventing where necessary. Afterwards, revisit some of the replies and discuss how we could find out if the answers were true or not. This might be an opportunity to introduce other sources to be used for research.

● Explain how a timeline works, by showing the text on the CD-ROM. You might also demonstrate how to draw a timeline using events from your own life. Then ask the class to make their own timeline for the details of Captain Cook's early life, using the core text as their source. You could support this activity for some children by providing a ready-made timeline with a given number of dates or events identified, which they would then complete.

● Play 'Splat' to test the children's growing knowledge of Cook. Write *True* and *False* in large letters on the board and ask two children to stand either side. Make true or false statements about Cook's early life, according to the text, for example, *Cook was born in Whitby.* The players should respond by hitting ('splatting') the correct word on the board as quickly as they can. You could involve the rest of the class as judges or some as expert helpers. Each pair could be asked three questions before allowing other children to have a go.

Extension

Ask children to research the events of Cook's first voyage on the *Endeavour* for presentation on a timeline.

many dates – typical in this kind of text; reader could construct timeline

large amount of precise detail – this voyage highly significant in appreciating Cook's greatness

The Early Life of James Cook

Text © 2007, Andrew Taylor; photos © Fred Brunskill (http://homepage.ntlworld.com/fred.brunskill/)

Early life
James Cook was born in a small cottage in Marton in Cleveland, just outside what is now Middlesbrough, on 27 October 1728.

James first helped his father on a farm, before going to work in a grocer's shop at Staithes. In 1746 he went as an apprentice to John Walker, a ship-owner in Whitby. James spent nine years sailing between the River Tyne and London, shipping coal. In 1755 he volunteered to join the Royal Navy.

Cook in the navy
Within a month of joining the navy, Cook was made a Master's Mate and only two years later he became a Ship's Master himself. His ship, the Pembroke, fought against the French in Canada. Cook also spent time charting the St Lawrence River, which helped General James Wolfe to capture Quebec in 1759. After the Canadian Wars, Cook returned to the seas around Newfoundland to make detailed charts of the area.

A voyage of discovery
Cook's skills at navigation and making charts were noticed and led to him being presented to King George III. The King was interested in scientific discoveries and planned to fund a voyage of discovery to the southern Pacific Ocean. Scientists wanted to measure the distance from the Earth to the Sun by observing the transit of Venus. Cook was chosen to captain the voyage.

Cook's ship
A Whitby collier, the Endeavour, was purchased for the voyage at the cost of £2,800. Although the Endeavour was small – only 106 feet (about 30 metres) long, she was strong enough to allow the hull to rest on shore to receive repairs. There was also enough room to carry 94 people. 12 months' supply of food and stores, and equipment for the scientists, artists and astronomers. While the Endeavour was being refitted, Cook applied to the Admiralty for various instruments to help him navigate accurately, chart his journey and record it in great detail. After months of preparation, the Endeavour sailed for Tahiti on 30 July 1768.

title and subheadings state what text is about

many places from all over world mentioned

subject-specific vocabulary

Physical activity

by Nuala Mullan

Background
This extract is from *Health-Related Fitness* by Nuala Mullan, a book that promotes fitness as a basis for improving the quality of people's lives, linking the text with lessons in PE and PSHE. The text includes bulleted lists and provides a lot of general information about fitness.

What's on the CD-ROM
This text has short sentences and a table to give simpler information, rather than bullet points.

Discussing the text
● Encourage children's engagement with the text by talking about exercise that they undertake, handling this sensitively. Use the bullet points in the text to construct a survey questionnaire, for example:

Activity	Daily	Weekly	Less frequently or never	Length of session
Housework				
Gardening				
DIY activities				

● Establish the distinctions between physical activity, exercise and sport by highlighting the relevant sentences in the text. Ask the children to discuss these sentences and try to explain the differences in their own words.

● Encourage careful consideration of the two main recommendations from the Health Education Authority. Can the children make the distinction between the two? Clarify the difference between the two adjectives *vigorous* and *moderate*. Ask the class to act out the difference by walking (on the spot) *at a moderate pace* and running *vigorously.*

● Go into role as someone who doesn't believe that gentle exercise is really any good for a person. For example, say, *Walking is all very well but it doesn't get you fit.* Ask pairs to use the text to prepare arguments to persuade you that you are wrong.

● Now add to the bulleted lists under general physical activities and exercise. Can the children suggest specific activities someone might do when gardening or dancing? Add a new section under exercise for sport and ask the children to list some of their favourites.

● Demonstrate the use of a two-columned table to display the HEA's recommendations. Give the table a title, such as *Ways of getting fitter and healthier.* Label one column *Vigorous exercise* and the other *Moderate exercise.* Show how to take information from the text and note it in the relevant column. For example, under *Vigorous exercise,* note *20 minutes a time, 3 times a week.* Ask children to discuss this in pairs and then complete their own tables based on the text.

Talk, write and read
● Suggest to the class or a guided writing group that they prepare a very small information card that someone could carry in their pocket or purse to remind them of how to keep fit. In order to do this they need to identify information and summarise the important messages. Set a word limit and give children a credit-card size piece of paper on which to work. Discuss drafts in terms of what is key information, and how the card will be used and what, therefore, is the best layout. (Bullet points are brief and easy to read.)

● Consider how to present the information about the two main HEA recommendations in a more lively way. Children could design a poster (by hand or using ICT), for example. Model how to use engaging headings and questions to draw the reader in, clever use of colour, graphics and illustration to catch the eye, and lively, direct and appealing language.

● Organise pairs and label the children A and B. The As will be someone who doesn't do very much exercise and the Bs will try to persuade them to do more. The Bs should draw on the information in the text to make an argument, and think of good ways of persuading A to change their mind. Discuss how to use the information in the text and how to be persuasive, for example, by emphasising the benefits, presenting a manageable goal, offering support. The pairs could also swap roles.

Extension
Ask children to keep an exercise diary over a period of time. The diary could use a table format, with column headings such as *date, activity, length of time, vigorous/moderate.* Respond sensitively to the returned diaries.

vital to understanding that distinction between these is explored

Physical activity

Physical activity and exercise are recommended as part of a healthy lifestyle, so it is important to understand what these terms mean. Physical activity is the most general term. It includes any activity that involves movement and requires more energy than is needed at rest. Physical activities include:
• housework, gardening and DIY
• moving around – walking and climbing stairs
• exercise, sport, dance and outdoor activities.

Exercise is a type of physical activity. It is often taken in leisure time, and usually for enjoyment or to keep fit. Exercise may be taken in the form of:
• walking – hill-walking and walking the dog
• jogging or running
• dancing – ballet, ballroom, tap, line and folk dancing are all popular forms of exercise
• aerobics – step aerobics and keep-fit classes have become very popular in recent years
• working out in a fitness gym or weights room
• swimming, gymnastics, outdoor activities and all sports.

There are many other types of exercise. Sport is a more controlled form of exercise, with rules, regulations and competitive structures.

How much exercise do you need?
There are two main recommendations that have been made by the Health Education Authority:
• Original recommendation – vigorous exercise at least three times a week for 20 minutes each time.
This is the amount of exercise needed for maximum improvements in aerobic endurance and to reduce the risk of death. However, many people feel that this is too much for them to do. The new recommendation is based on the fact that even moderate levels of physical activity can improve health.
• New recommendation – at least 30 minutes of moderate exercise at least five days a week.

This may seem to involve more exercise than the first recommendation but there are two key differences that make it easier for people to achieve:
• The physical activity is moderate, so walking, cycling and gardening count.
• The 30 minutes can be split into smaller amounts such as two 15-minute sessions. You could take 15 minutes to walk to work every day and walk back again after work every day and you would have reached the recommended level.

Photo © Joseph Zlomek

Photo © Matthew Bowden

Photo © Cheryl Empey

Photo © Robert Van

Text extracts from "Health-Related Fitness" by Nuala Mullan © 1997 Nuala Mullan (1997, Heinemann)

topic sentence opens main subject of text…

…which next sentence defines

bulleted lists of examples

definition of 'exercise'

lots of nouns made from verbs ending in 'ing'

Vikings

from Scholastic Ltd

Background

This text about the Vikings is useful for work on invaders and settlers in history. When teaching about the Vikings it is important that their reputation as ruthless barbarians is challenged, and this text underlines their success as explorers, sailors and traders. It also emphasises the significance of the Viking longboat.

What's on the CD-ROM

The CD-ROM text is a rewritten version of the main text, summarising and reorganising the information given. It focuses on the Vikings' reputation, explorations and the boats they used. Much of the detail has been removed.

Discussing the text

● Before reading, establish what the children know already about the Vikings. Ask them to discuss their knowledge in pairs and write any points down on a large sticky note or on a mini whiteboard. Save their notes and return to them after you have read the text.

● Introduce the text paragraph by paragraph, then allow the children to read the whole text independently. If there are words they need to clarify, such as *legendary, navigators* and *democratic*, prompt them to use context to try to establish meaning and check in a dictionary.

● Encourage the children to ask questions about the first paragraph, such as *Why did the Vikings leave their homes to raid Europe?* Then create a brief summary of the paragraph: *For 300 years, Vikings from Norway, Sweden and Denmark, travelled across the world in search of riches. They were great fighters but also excellent sailors and craftspeople.* Use a similar approach to the other paragraphs, but encourage the children to take the lead on making predictions and summaries.

● Note how the text is rich in adjectives, *expert navigators, excellent sailors* and so on. Remind the class of the function of adjectives and demonstrate how you can use them to present a positive or negative picture. Ask for quick suggestions of positive (*good, happy, beautiful, clever*) and negative (*ugly, mean, violent, rough*) adjectives. Collect the adjectives from the text in a table, asking the class where to put them, for example:

Positive	Negative	Neutral (neither positive or negative)
brave excellent expert	vicious terrifying	shallow light

Discuss where most adjectives are placed and what this tells us about the author's point of view. (The Vikings are generally described using positive adjectives; the writer is presenting a favourable point of view.)

● Set a question before reading the text again. For example: *How do we know so much about Viking longboats?, Why was it important that long boats had a narrow keel?* Ask the children to re-read the text to gather evidence to answer the question(s), discuss with a partner and then present their answers for you to note on the board. Then model how to shape their points into a sentence.

● Return to the ideas about Vikings that were raised earlier. How accurate were they?

Talk, read and write

● Introduce a theme or a few themes, such as Viking voyages, boats or warriors. Demonstrate how to highlight text relevant to that topic. Use a different colour for each topic you focus on. Then collect the information into a table:

Viking voyages	Viking boats	Viking warriors and sailors
The Vikings travelled as far as N. America		

● Ask the class to complete the rest of the table, offering support as necessary to less independent learners.

● Model using the table to write a paragraph about the topic, giving it a title. Emphasise the importance of linking ideas together by highlighting connectives and clauses.

● Give large groups a world map and ask them to work together to label the extent of the Viking voyages of discovery and conquests.

Extension

Give children an illustration of a Viking longboat and ask them to label it, using information in the text.

unlikely adjectival phrase for warship

causal connective links explanation

commas punctuate clauses and indicate where reader should pause

verbs also present Vikings positively; sailing sounds exciting, almost glamorous

Photo © Jon Wisbey

Vikings

Who were they?

THE VIKINGS WERE brave warriors who set out from their homes in Norway, Sweden and Denmark on daring voyages of exploration. These legendary voyages took place over a period of 300 years, from the 8th century onwards. The Vikings went in search of gold and silver, slaves and, perhaps most importantly, new farmland. They sailed to the farthest reaches of Europe in their quest, as well as parts of Asia and North America. The Vikings were notorious for their terrifying surprise attacks on monasteries and towns. But in reality, these ferocious raids played only a small part in their success. The Vikings had a highly civilised, democratic way of life. They were skilled at shipbuilding and many other crafts, as well as being farmers, traders and expert navigators.

Image © Anthony Wootten

At home on the waves

THE VIKINGS WERE EXCELLENT SAILORS. They had to navigate treacherous seas, but their wooden longships were perfectly designed for this purpose. These light, elegant vessels were able to glide past rocks and icebergs and ride out the most vicious storms. The ships were versatile enough to cope with shallow coastal waters and rivers as well as the open sea. The big rectangular sail could be lowered and the ship rowed instead. The Vikings used the sun and the stars to navigate, or simply stayed within sight of land. They also gathered clues from nature to help them find their way – observing fish, seabirds and the pattern of the waves. There are very few longships left – most rotted away. Those that have survived were buried with their rich owners, according to Viking custom.

A specialist ship

PERHAPS THE MOST REMARKABLE of the Viking ships were those used to carry warriors – the warships. These were longer, sleeker and faster than any other ships. They were also highly manoeuvrable, able to quietly dart up the narrowest inlets or even land on beaches under oar-power.

Each ship had up to 50 oars, which the warriors manned in shifts on long voyages. But once it was out on the open ocean, the mast was raised and the rectangular sail unfurled – the ship sailed swiftly away across the waves once more.

Text © 2007, Scholastic Ltd

Photo © Lars Sundstrom

suitably dramatic vocabulary gives more of an insight into subject than some information texts – this evocative style continues throughout text

positive adjectives contribute to argument that counters some of the negativity above

Operation Pied Piper

from the CLUTCH Club website

Background

This text is a report on the main features of the Government's evacuation scheme during the Second World War, known as 'Operation Pied Piper'. The piece comes from the CLUTCH Club website, which features stories documenting aspects of life in Buckinghamshire, Bedfordshire and South Northamptonshire from150 years ago up to the present day. The stories were created and collated by parents in conjunction with local schools.

What's on the CD-ROM

This text presents much of the same information, but in the form of a bulleted list beneath the same headings. It picks out the key points in an immediately accessible way.

Discussing the text

● Prepare for reading by sharing existing knowledge about evacuation during the Second World War. Establish a basic understanding that children were moved from cities to safer parts of the country. Ask why the children think the countryside would have been safer than a city. Elicit that rural areas were less at risk from bombing.

● Read the text and then check understanding. You could do this by making a mind map of the text, using headings such as: Government's evacuation scheme, 'Operation Pied Piper', Finding billets, Census forms.

● Another approach is to play a version of 'Taboo'. Write four or five key words on the board (*evacuation, Government, bombing, billets*). Organise pairs. One of the pair should try to explain the information given in the first three sections to the other, without using the words you have written on the board. Then, the second child should try to explain the last two sections, again without using the taboo words. Discuss whether the task was difficult and how they communicated the information without using the banned words.

● Explain that the text is an information text, with elements of a recount, and point out the characteristic details: orientation, events in chronological order, use of past tense verbs, use of specific names of places and people to bring the incident to life. Encourage children to find other examples.

● Explain that when planning a recount or informative piece a writer needs to answer a set of questions: *When? Who? Where? What?* and *Why?* Write these on the board in a table. Ask the children to find the answer(s) to each question. If it is an effective recount each question can be answered. As an alternative, you could give the text and the question prompts in a table for the children to work on independently.

Talk, read and write

● Use the information gathered in the mind map as the basis for summarising the text. Demonstrate how to use the key information you have gathered to draft one or two sentences that sum up the first paragraph: *The Government's evacuation scheme was planned by a committee advised by a group of experts.* The class could summarise the other paragraphs independently or in a guided group.

● Talk about what else people might want to keep safe in a time of war (for example, precious objects). The children might consider this at different levels. For example, what objects would the nation want to keep safe? What about the local community? What about their family? What would *they* want to protect? Explore notions of objects with a cultural significance, such as valuable paintings or the crown jewels; the shades of meaning in *valuable* or *precious* (something might be important to someone without having monetary value); and why different age groups might consider different objects to be valuable. You could make this a drama activity where the children act out discussions and plans to make objects safe.

● Ask the children to list another set of words in order to play another game of 'Taboo'.

Extension

Ask children to research the website for more about evacuation during the War. Ask them to use a recount planner with prompts *When? Who? Where? What?* and *Why?*

4: 2: T17: to scan texts in print or on screen to locate key words or phrases, useful headings and key sentences and to use these as a tool for summarising text

codename for operation

comma separates subordinate clause that follows, giving extra information

explanation of what will happen (future tense)

explanation of what did happen (past tense)

4: 2: S4: to recognise how commas, connectives and full stops are used to join and separate clauses

From http://duch.open.ac.uk/schools/standrews00/gov_evac.htm

various ways of making past tense

'OPERATION PIED PIPER'

THE GOVERNMENT EVACUATION SCHEME

The Government evacuation scheme had been planned by the 'Anderson Committee', a group led by Sir John Anderson. The Committee met between May and July 1938 and called in experts from railway companies, teachers and the police to advise them.

THE ANDERSON COMMITTEE RECOMMENDATIONS

Factories have to be kept open to produce important materials. People who are not doing essential jobs should be moved away from these factories which will be targets for bombing.

EVACUATION SHOULD NOT BE COMPULSORY

Children not being evacuated with their mothers will be taken in school parties, with their teachers.

Evacuees will be housed in private dwellings. People in the reception areas will have to look after evacuees if they are asked to do so.

The British evacuation was called 'Operation Pied Piper'. It began on Friday 1 September 1939. The Government sent parents a list, telling them what they needed to pack for their children.

Most evacuees travelled to city railway stations to begin their journey to the countryside. Special timetables had to be arranged for the many extra train services. The evacuees did not know where they were travelling to.

FINDING BILLETS

A local 'billeting officer' was appointed to find suitable houses in all areas that were receiving evacuees.

In January and February 1939 the Government conducted an 'accommodation census' to find out how many billets were available. Local people called 'visitors' interviewed householders in reception areas and filled in census forms. Officials used these forms to decide how many evacuees could be billeted in each area.

HOST FAMILIES

After a journey which was often long and tiring, evacuees had to line up and wait for a 'host family' to choose them.

Hosts received money for each evacuee they took in. They were paid by taking a form to the local post office.

Billeting was compulsory. People who refused to take evacuees into their homes without a good reason could be taken to court and fined.

various ways of making past tense

4: 2: T16: to prepare for factual research by reviewing what is known, what is needed, and where one might search

dates and time connectives; events in chronological order

commas separate connective clauses

4: 2: W1: to read and spell words through: blending phonemes; segmenting words; using phonic, grammatical and contextual knowledge

4: 2: T23: to collect information from a variety of sources and present it in one simple format

A new resolution

from *Whitby Today* website

Background

This text is from www.whitbytoday.co.uk and is a copy of a report from the local newspaper the *Whitby Gazette* in December 2005. Like many newspaper reports it combines genre features of information and recount. There is an obvious link to be made with 'The early life of James Cook' on page 137. You may be able to bring this story up to date by revisiting the website or looking for information linked with 'The People's Millions'.

What's on the CD-ROM

The text on the CD-ROM contains most of the same information as the original text, but presented in a tabular form.

Discussing the text

● Remind the children of 'The early life of James Cook' if you have read this. Then give an overview of this text, explaining that it describes a proposal to build a replica of Cook's second ship, the *Resolution*. Explain 'technical' vocabulary such as *ecological, marine, forum* and *eco-centre*.

● Read the text, then remind the children of the what, when, where, who, why questions of a recount. Ask them to skim the text to complete a table of answers. Take each question in turn as a class and highlight the text that answers the question. (The CD-ROM text gives a completed version of the table.)

● Highlight the opening sentence. It provides a summary of the whole article, characteristic of many information texts, including recounts. Discuss why the beginning of this sentence is in capital letters. (In order to make the start of the story stand out from a page of print. It works as a lead line or 'second headline'.) Point out that many of the paragraphs in the text are made up of a single sentence, another characteristic of newspaper articles.

● Highlight the verbs in the passage. Notice that *has been unveiled* is in the past tense and passive voice, characteristic of the recount form. (Identify that the auxiliary verbs *has* and *been* are both in the past tense form and that *unveiled* uses the characteristic *-ed* ending which signals past tense.)

● Note too the frequent use of the conditional *would* and the future tense auxiliary *will* throughout the text. Explain that although this is a report of something that has happened (the submission of a competition entry), the intended outcomes (the building of the ship and marine centre), have not yet been started nor confirmed.

● Look at other features such as the use of causal connectives and specific names and dates. Point out that the connective *as part of* provides a causal link between sentences, and reinforce the speculative, hopeful nature of the piece. Highlight the number of names and titles in the piece. Typically of a local newspaper article, specific names are used throughout to give the text life and to make specific reference to the town.

Talk, read and write

● Using a 'what–when–where…' table as a means of collecting ideas, demonstrate how to plan a recount of a familiar event. Agree on a national, local or school event and ask the children to work in pairs to answer the questions. These will give an outline plan which they can develop using time connectives. In shared writing, draft an orientating introduction which gives an overview of the whole account. They could complete the writing as an independent task.

● To link with history work, you could ask the children to research details of Captain Cook's voyages on the *Resolution*. They could then use the recount planning table to note details as a starting point for writing a prose recount. Children could use maps, timelines and illustrations, perhaps accessed from the internet, to provide information and support their recounts.

Extension

Encourage children to follow up news stories by using web links given in newspapers or by visiting the *Newsround* site at http://news.bbc.co.uk/cbbcnews or going to www.thenewspaper.org.uk. Ask them to note how stories written for the internet (rather than just reproduced from a paper) are similar to and different from printed newspaper reports. Use a large Venn diagram to note the characteristics of web-based reports and newspaper stories and highlight where they overlap.

4: 2: T18: to mark extracts by annotating and by selecting key headings, words or sentences, or noting these

one of few verbs in past tense – indicates this is a recount

caps for first words – common style features of newspaper articles

note – not 'peoples'

frequent use of conditionals reiterates these are proposals – nothing definite yet

another apostrophe of possession

specific organisations involved – typical feature of news reports

Screenshot reprinted by permission from Microsoft Corporation

Photo © Ian Britton/FreeFoto.com

Text extract from "Whitby Today" website 15 December 2005 © 2005, Johnston Press Digital Publishing, www.whitbytoday.co.uk

A New Resolution

AN AMBITIOUS £50 million plan has been unveiled to transform Whitby into an ecological and marine heritage site.

As part of the community project a version of Captain Cook's Resolution ship would be built in the town and then sailed through the Northwest Passage.

The forum aims to win the £50 million of funding necessary from the Big Lottery Fund in a televised competition.

A programme in 2007 entitled 'Living Landmarks: The People's Millions' will showcase various ideas for community projects from towns throughout the country and the nation will then be able to vote on the project they want to see go ahead.

As part of the project, Whitby Beacon Town Forum, which is behind the cash bid, would like to see Whitby and its coast becoming a marine conservation area. A maritime eco-centre would be built on reclaimed land, possibly on the car park near the cargo shed.

The proposed eco-centre would provide exhibitions, information about climate change and the melting of the polar ice caps and also a study centre for universities throughout the area.

It has been suggested that the car park could also be used for actually building the New Resolution with a hole dug in the ground to support the hull.

This would also alleviate future flooding problems by simply providing more space for the water to go.

The proposed eco-centre could be built on stilts or floating pontoons so it would not be at risk of being submerged.

The deadline for submitting the initial application is 6 January and the organisers of Whitby's bid want the people of Whitby to get behind them and simply register their support. No local fundraising will be necessary.

North Yorkshire County Council, Scarborough Council, Yorkshire Forward and Yorkshire Water have already said they back the project in principle.

hint at opinion/point of view; otherwise straight, impersonal report

answers the 'what' question

answers 'when'

answers 'who' and 'where'

more 'what' answers

more on 'when'; what happens next

4: 2: T16: to prepare for factual research by reviewing what is known, what is needed and where one might search

4: 2: S2: to use the apostrophe accurately to mark possession

4: 2: T21: to make short notes

Wallace and Gromit
Grom it from the *Radio Times*

Background
This film review is from the *Radio Times* website. Its subject is the highly successful and acclaimed 2005 feature film from Aardman Animations.

What's on the CD-ROM
This is a simplified version of the core text, retaining genre features such as the synopsis, personal opinions and recommendation.

Discussing the text
● Ask children to tell you what they know about the film and what they think of it if they have seen it. If possible show some clips and discuss it using some of the technical vocabulary in the review, such as *claymation* (the animation technique using photographed clay objects), *voiced*, *feature*.
● Now read the text, and elicit that it is a review, written to advise people whether they should see the film. Note that like many film reviews it mixes a summary of the plot with judgements about it and details about the actors involved.
● Highlight the sentence beginning *The enterprising inventor…* as an example of plot summary or synopsis. It tells the reader something of how the film starts. Ask the children to find other sentences that summarise the plot (for example, *However, business is jeopardised…*).
● Point out the phrases in brackets *voiced, as ever…* and *voiced by…* . Elicit that these tell us the actors playing the parts of Wallace and Victor, in this case, in speech only.
● Highlight the clause: *there are some great references to classic horror movies*. Explain that this is one of the judgements about the film, where the reviewer is giving their own opinion. Encourage the children to identify other examples of judgements and opinions. (For example, the first sentence.) Discuss how adjectives like *delightful* and *great* are used to make positive judgements.
● Revisit the synopsis and explain that a review gives a plot summary so that a reader has an idea of what the film is about, but doesn't tell the whole story. Discuss why reviews, like book blurbs, usually don't say how films end.

Talk, read and write
● Focus on writing a summary. Show a scene from the film (or another suitable film or television programme), lasting just a few minutes. Afterwards, discuss the main events and characters and help the children to distinguish between more and less important information. Challenge the children to describe the scene in the fewest words.
● Explain to the class that you will show the extract again, but this time they should make notes of the main events. They could do this on an individual whiteboard, using a list, or by making a timeline of events. Ask them to compare their events with a partner's, and see if they agree on the most important events. Ask some pairs to explain any differences.
● Using the notes made by one child, demonstrate how to develop a brief scene summary. First, write the information in full and then work together to edit unnecessary detail. Try to link ideas with connectives. Encourage contributions from the class. Aim to produce a three-to-four-sentence summary.
● Re-read the Wallace and Gromit review. Recall how the reviewer gives an opinion about the quality of the film, often through the use of adjectives. Together compose a similar judgement on the extract you have watched, which could then be used to introduce the plot summary. For example, *Wallace and Gromit in The Curse of the Were-Rabbit is a funny and exciting film…* Ask the children to work in pairs to compose their own introductory sentence about the extract.
● Ask the pairs to compare their review with the core text. Prompt them to identify what is missing from their review: information about the actors and director. Go on to explain the purpose of titles and credits sequences and if possible let children research the details using the DVD, for inclusion in the review.

Extension
Ask children to use either a numbered list or a timeline to collect information in note form about another film. Ask them to watch a few minutes of a programme or film at home and make notes of the main plot details. These could be used as the basis for another review and/or scene synopsis in class.

4: 2: T14: notemaking: to edit down a sentence or passage by deleting the less important elements, e.g. repetitions, asides, secondary considerations and discuss the reasons for editorial choices

reviews usually explain the broad outline of the plot but stop short of giving away the ending

judgements made by the reviewer

details about the actors (in this case, providing the voices only as it is an animated film)

4: 2: T22: to fill out brief notes into connected prose

Screenshot reprinted by permission from Microsoft Corporation

4: 2: S1: to revise and extend work on adjectives from Y3 term 2 and link to work on expressive and figurative language in stories and poetry

technical vocabulary

plot summary

adjectives used to make positive judgements

4: 2: T21: to make short notes, e.g. by abbreviating ideas, selecting key words, listing or in diagrammatic form

---

Radio Times | Film review - Microsoft Internet Explorer provided

File Edit View Favorites Tools Help

Back Search Favorites

Address www.bbc.co.uk/films/2005/10/03/wallace_and_gromit_2005_review

Wallace & Gromit in The Curse of the Were-Rabbit (2005)

★★★★

Claymation heroes Wallace and Gromit make their feature-length debut in this delightful comedy adventure. Bursting with wit and imagination, it takes Aardman Animation's Oscar-winning short film format to new levels of technical genius. The enterprising inventor (voiced, as ever, by veteran actor Peter Sallis) and his faithful dog cash in on the approaching Giant Vegetable Competition by offering a humane pest-control service to rid the neighbourhood of rabbits. However, business is jeopardised when a mysterious monster begins destroying local gardens, forcing the pals into a frantic race to catch the veg-ravaging terror. Despite being peppered slightly too heavily with modern innuendo, the tale retains its charm, gaining plenty of comic mileage from its quaint depiction of northern life. Working-class Wallace's rivalry with trigger-happy toff Victor (voiced by Ralph Fiennes) is especially amusing and there are some great references to classic horror movies. But it's facially expressive Gromit who steals the show, causing genuine hilarity without uttering a single word. **SF**

Director **Steve Box**
          Nick Park

Starring **Peter Sallis**
          Ralph
          Fiennes

Tell us what you think
Email us at **rtfilmcomments@bbc.co.uk** to tell us what you think of this film.
Your comments may appear in Radio Times magazine.

Running time   84mins
Country of origin   UK
Genre   Animated Comedy Adventure
Original language   English
Screenplay   Nick Park, Bob Baker, Steve Box,
                      Mark Burton, from characters created
                      by Nick Park, Steve Rushton
Theatrical distributor UIP
UK cinema certificate   U
UK cinema release date   October 2005

Awards information

Award	Category	Name	Nominee/Winner
British Academy Film Awards 2005	The Alexander Korda Award for the Outstanding British Film of the Year		Winner

Extract from The Radio Times website © BBC Magazines Ltd. The Radio Times Word Mark and logo are trademarks of BBC Worldwide Ltd. www.radiotimes.com

A magical day in history!
from the Malcolm Group Events Medieval Festival

Background
This text is taken from a publicity leaflet advertising 'England's Medieval Festival' days at Herstmonceux Castle in East Sussex. As well as describing the attractions of this event in enthusiastic, persuasive language, the text provides practical information about locations and times. It is a good example of the kinds of leaflets and flyers for tourist attractions often displayed at libraries, railway stations, hotels and so on.

What's on the CD-ROM
This is a version of the core text that describes the Medieval Festival in simple, straightforward language, without any persuasive devices or advertising features. Comparing the two texts will highlight the aim of the core text and the way in which it uses language to catch the reader's attention and emphasise the attractions of the event. As a simpler version, it can also provide a helpful introduction to the core text and familiarise children with its factual content.

Discussing the text
● Read the title, strap line and first paragraph together. Ask the children what is being advertised and where they might find this kind of text. Illustrate this, if possible, by showing similar leaflets about other tourist attractions, including local ones that might be familiar.

● Now read the rest of the text, and ask the children to say what they would see and what they could do if they went to 'England's Medieval Festival'. Encourage them to share any personal experiences of this kind of historical re-enactment.

● Move on from the facts of the event to how it is presented in the leaflet. Ask: *What does the leaflet say is special and good about this celebration?* Draw out the idea that the event is presented as big; popular (150,000 visitors); unique (note the use of this word and the phrase *only at*); successful and long-established; 'the real thing' (note the phrases *true flavour* and *authentically costumed*) but also *magical* (note also *time trip* and *fairy-tale*); it's exciting but you can learn about history too. Identify these features as the 'selling points' and introduce this term.

● Now focus specifically on language features, especially word choice. Remind the children of any work done on superlatives and ask them to find three in the text (*largest, most spectacular, finest*). Explain that such words are often used in advertisements to convey that the product or service is better than any others. Collect some examples from other promotional material you have.

● Highlight the word *colourful* in the first paragraph and discuss how this adjective is used to describe the event in a positive and attractive way. Ask children to find other adjectives like this (*magical, thrilling, unique, incredible*).

● Remind the children that they have already talked about what they would see at the festival and ask them now to think about what they would hear and smell. Identify words and phrases that describe this: *crash of broadswords, rallying call, cannon fire, smell of black powder* and *eerie hiss*. Consider the purpose of this kind of writing: the writer is presenting the event in a vivid way and trying to give the reader an idea of what it is like to be there.

● Note the use of other devices to keep readers interested and involved, for example, alliteration (*heraldry and heroism, prestige and prizes*), the use of *you*, and the rhetorical question at the end.

Talk, read and write
● Ask the children to recall what they know about this period of history. Do they think that this festival gives an accurate picture? *What does it emphasise? What does it leave out?*

● Ask: *Does this leaflet make you want to go to the festival? Why/why not?*

● Together, choose a familiar school or local event and use shared writing strategies to plan a short leaflet or flyer for it. Focus on choice of dramatic, positive adjectives and superlatives to describe the event.

Extension
● Ask children to bring in other leaflets advertising tourist attractions, for discussion and display.

● Choose a product, service, place or event and compile a list of words that could be used in writing an advertisement for it.

4: 3: T19: to evaluate advertisements for their impact, appeal and honesty

superlatives emphasise specialness

dramatises event

shows scale and success of event

stresses uniqueness

historical authenticity

alliteration catches attention and makes text lively

focus on fantastical, romantic quality

sights, sounds and smells convey what it was like to be there

dramatic verb choice

use of capitals stresses key points

point of practical information integrated into text

dramatic description

question draws reader in

another superlative

more alliteration

4: 3: S2: to identify the common punctuation marks and respond to them appropriately when reading

A Magical Day in History!

TAKE A TIME TRIP YOU'LL NEVER FORGET

ENGLAND'S MEDIEVAL FESTIVAL
AT HERSTMONCEUX CASTLE, NEAR HAILSHAM

In East Sussex, is England's LARGEST AND MOST SPECTACULAR CELEBRATION of the colourful Middle Ages. Now in its THIRTEENTH THRILLING YEAR, this unique event is held over the three days of the BANK HOLIDAY WEEKEND and has welcomed over 150,000 visitors from around the world.

Only at Herstmonceux can you experience the true flavour, sights and sounds of Medieval England.

OVER 2000 AUTHENTICALLY COSTUMED MEDIEVALISTS help take you back to a time of heraldry and heroism.

The walls of the fairy-tale 15TH CENTURY MOATED CASTLE AND BATTLEFIELD come under siege from the massed forces of opposing armies. You can hear the crash of broadswords on heavy armour; the rallying call of battle cries as the troops are marshalled into position, and you can experience the smell of black powder from SALVO AFTER SALVO OF CANNON FIRE as the castle walls are prepared to be stormed. Witness the incredible sight of the SIEGE ENGINE as it hurls its deadly load towards the castle defenders. SIEGES ARE MOUNTED DAILY AT 11AM AND 3PM.

You can hear the eerie hiss of volley after volley of arrows overhead. And when the fighting is over, you can watch EUROPE'S FINEST BOWMEN gather to compete for prestige and prizes at the Festival's longbow competition. Or try it yourself: ENTER THE HAVE-A-GO ARCHERY, with expert instruction from our archers. Experience displays of FALCONRY in the modern world and learn a thing or two about this ancient craft.

WAS HISTORY EVER SUCH FUN?

Text and photo from a leaflet from The Malcolm Group Events Medieval Festival at Herstmonceux Castle, East Sussex www.englandsmedievalfestival.com; photo © The Malcolm Group Events/The Medieval Image Bank www.englandsmedievalfestival.com

dramatic 'headline' encapsulates idea of event, emphasised by capitals and exclamation mark

4: 3: T18: to investigate how style and vocabulary are used to convince the intended reader

4: 3: T25: to design an advertisement, such as a poster or radio jingle on paper or screen

The great escape!

Background

This is a children's page from the website of Acorn Adventure, a company that runs adventure holidays for individuals, groups and schools in the UK and Europe. The text is aimed at and written specifically for young people, and advertises 'activity camps for children'. There is an accompanying page on the site for parents and carers, providing more practical information, for example, about costs, and focusing on the children's safety.

What's on the CD-ROM

The advertisement on the CD-ROM is for a similar adventure holiday; written in simpler language, but retaining the persuasive devices typical of this kind of text. Headings and lists of bullet points are used to break up the text and make it more accessible. It is suitable for less confident readers but also provides another example of this text type for comparison.

Discussing the text

● Read the first section of the text and ask the children what kind of sentences are used. Identify them as questions, and consider why the author has started like this. *How do they want the reader to answer these questions? What is different about the last question (about frogs legs and snails)?* The intention is to involve readers and present appealing possibilities. The reader is meant to think, *'That sounds good!'* and answer, *'Yes.'* The last question is dropped in as a joke, to make the young reader stop and laugh. Identify this assumption, and see if all of the children respond in the intended way. Maybe some of them are attracted by the idea of these foods!

● Read the rest of the text. Ask the children to describe what is being advertised and who the text is aimed at. How can they tell? Provide some background information about the company.

● Ask the children to describe what this holiday offers, identifying specific activities and facilities. Extend this by asking them to identify the 'pitch', the broader selling points. Confirm that the text emphasises that the holiday offers fun and adventure, and the opportunity to try new things and make new friends. (The word *new* is used four times.) Note also the claims

that the organisers understand what children want and need, for example, in relation to food and changing tents.

● Now look at language and style. What particularly positive words are used? (*Fantastic* and *new* are both repeated.) Explain that the word *new* is frequently used in adverts and discuss the reasons for this.

● Consider the tone of the piece. A good way of doing this is by suggesting a quality that it does *not* have, for example by asking: *Is it serious?* Draw out the idea that the tone is jolly, friendly and informal, as suited to its audience. Focus on vernacular phrases such as *loads of activities* and *laugh yourself silly.*

● At sentence-level, ask the children to find five exclamatory sentences or headings and to discuss the impact they have on the reader. Encourage them to look for other sentences that could end with an exclamation mark rather than a full stop. *How does this alter the effect?*

Talk, read and write

● Ask: *What do the writers think about children – about what they like and don't like?* (For example, that they like being with children of their own age and do not like green vegetables.) *Do you think they are right about this?* Draw out the general idea that writers of persuasive texts, and especially advertisements, need to make assumptions about their readers, about what will appeal to them.

● Develop this discussion by asking: *Who do you think this kind of holiday would appeal to? Who would it not appeal to? Why?*

● Organise the children into groups. Tell them to choose one of the holiday activities mentioned in the text and to compose a paragraph advertising it in more detail. Remind them to consider their audience and pay special attention to tone and word choice.

Extension

Ask children to imagine that they are at an Acorn Adventure summer camp and to write a postcard or letter home about what they are doing and whether they are enjoying themselves. Alternatively, ask children to write a letter to persuade their parents to let them go on this holiday.

4: 3: T19: to evaluate advertisements for their impact, appeal and honesty

direct appeal to young readers

questions get reader thinking; assumes knowledge of reader; that he or she will respond 'yes'

knowledge backed up by experience

exclamation mark adds drama and fun

4: 3: S2: to identify the common punctuation marks and respond to them appropriately when reading

4: 3: T18: to investigate how style and vocabulary are used to convince the intended reader

emotive title given added drama by exclamation mark

use of slang, appropriate to readership

joke question, to amuse; assumes answer this time is 'no'

extravagant positive language

another question to involve reader

4: 3: T25: to design an advertisement, such as a poster or radio jingle on paper or screen

The Great Escape!

How about getting away from your parents for a week or two?

How about going on holiday with just your friends? Or going on holiday to make lots of new friends from all over the country?

How about camping under the stars in France?

How about trying out loads of activities, from sailing to archery, dragon boating to raft building?

How about eating frogs' legs and snails?

Only joking about that last one...

Photo © Brian Ducharme

Photo © Breatte W

Food!

We have a fantastic range of activities for you to try out. All the equipment is provided and our instructors are always on hand to guide you and teach you as much as you want.

We've fed hundreds of thousands of children over the years so we know what you will like. More importantly we know what you won't like. Our food is always tasty and filling and you are guaranteed not to see a brussels sprout all week! If you have any particular likes and dislikes, just let us know.

Camping!

You will share a large tent with two other people – either a friend or two that you bring with you, or newly made friends of the same age. If you want to change tents during the week you can.

Acorn Adventure summer camps are fantastic holidays. Spend a week in France or the UK trying out all kinds of new things, including watersports and other activities such as climbing and caving. Every day there is something new to try, games to play in the centre with our instructors, and evening entertainment to laugh yourself silly.

Why not arrange to go with some of your friends? You can travel together, share a tent, and take part in all the activities together. If you don't want to bring friends you will be sure to meet lots of new ones! Children from all over the UK come to us as strangers and leave as best friends. You will share everything with people of the same age and you can even change tents during the week if you want to change who you share with.

Photo © Betsy Leeuwner

Photo © Tom Denham

Photo © 2006, Jupiter Images Corporation

Text from *The Acorn Adventure website* © Acorn Adventure www.acornadventure.co.uk

Staying fit & active  from Tesco Ltd

Background

This is an extract from a leaflet produced by Tesco, distributed in their supermarkets during the company's 'Healthy Living' campaign. The leaflet promotes exercise. This is the first part, consisting of the introductory paragraphs and sections related to exercise in the context of normal daily life.

What's on the CD-ROM

The differentiated text is a list of ways of taking exercise, briefly described in simple language but with the same enthusiastic, persuasive tone as the core text. It provides an alternative version for less able readers and could be used as an introduction to the core text, as it shares some of the same content and vocabulary.

Discussing the text

● Introduce the extract, explaining where it is taken from.

● Read the introductory paragraphs, up to the subheading *Walk*. Ask why the text starts by saying, *physical exercise can be daunting*? (Check children understand what this means.) *Won't this put people off?* Elicit the idea that this in fact acknowledges readers' worries and assumptions, and is designed to get them 'on side' – a common tactic in persuasive texts.

● Note how the next two sentences are designed to dispel these worries, and ask: *How does the text make the reader feel positive about the thought of exercise? What are the 'selling points'?* Tease out the following key ideas: exercise is easy (in the second paragraph note the words *few*, *little*, *easily* and *easier*), exercise is good for you (in terms of health, appearance and 'feeling good'), exercise is fun.

● Now read the *Walk* section. *How can we tell that this is not a paragraph from an objective report about exercise but a persuasive text?* Guide the children to understand that the text addresses the reader personally, gives advice (not just information), and expresses an opinion (*great form of exercise*). Note also the repeated emphasis on the idea that exercise is easy and simple.

● Read the rest of the text, and ask the children to describe how it is organised: in sections about different kinds of exercise/daily tasks with subheadings.

● Identify how the writer uses language to try to persuade the reader. Focus on the cheerful, friendly, encouraging tone (*Who knows*, *It's fun too!*, *pop round*, *Great for your...*); the inclusion of facts, sometimes supported by statistics; and above all the practical advice for making exercise part of everyday life. Relate these features to the fact that the text is intended to appeal to a very wide audience.

● For a word-level focus, ask the children to find different forms of the word *easy* in the text: *easily*, *easier*, *easiest*. Demonstrate that these words all have the same root, to which different suffixes are added, in this case to make a comparative and superlative. You could extend this exercise by adding prefixes and suffixes to other words from the text, for example, *play* and *gentle*.

● Now highlight the word *But* at the start of the second sentence and explain how this links the ideas in the two sentences by indicating a contrast. Reinforce this by looking at the use of the same connective in the first sentence in *Clean the house*. Compose other sentences hinged round the word *but*.

Talk, read and write

● Ask: *Why do you think people need to be persuaded to exercise? Has the writer chosen a good way of trying to persuade people? Why, or why not? Can you think of other approaches the writer could have used?*

● Work with the children to compile a list of other everyday contexts for exercise. Allocate these to small groups and ask each to write a short paragraph about this kind of exercise, for adding to the leaflet. Prompt them to use persuasive tactics and language. Then share and compare. *Which paragraphs are most effective? Why?*

Extension

Ask children to bring in for display and discussion other leaflets designed to persuade people to do something that is good for them and society, for example, following a healthy diet or recycling. Children could design a poster to promote exercise, focusing (as in this text) on exercise around the house.

4: 3: T25: to design an advertisement, such as a poster or radio jingle on paper or screen

4: 3: W8: to practise extending and compounding words through adding parts; revise and reinforce earlier work on prefixes and suffixes

4: 3: S4: to understand the use of connectives to structure an argument

starts by acknowledging reader's likely worries

imperative sentences give advice

assumes knowledge of reader's attitude

change of direction and less serious tone

healthyliving

Staying fit & active:
A few changes go a long way

Sometimes just the thought of physical exercise can be daunting, let alone doing it. But it doesn't have to mean lifetime membership of the gym and bulging biceps.

A few little changes can easily make activity part of your routine. You'll see and feel the difference it can make – it's your body's way of saying thank you for the effort you've put in. Who knows, you might get a taste for it and be joining us soon on one of the Cancer Research UK runs we sponsor. To make things easier we've got some ways to get moving that you'd hardly notice and don't need special equipment or clothing for. But first, why bother?

Exercise is good for you
Regular exercise can reduce the risk of stroke and heart attack by 50%, reduce the risk of diabetes and improve the way your brain works. It burns off excess fat, tones muscles and actually makes you feel good. It's fun too! Playing in the park and throwing a ball around with the children makes everyone smile and glow.

Exercise is easy
Here are some ways to get active and how they'll do you good.

Walk
It's the easiest and simplest exercise around. Walk to the shops, pop round to see your relatives or use the

photocopier on the next floor (using the stairs, not the lift). There are lots of ways to squeeze this great form of exercise into your day. It tones, shapes up your legs and does your heart and lungs good.

Clean the house
You hate the jobs, but you'll love what it's doing for you. Move quickly from chore to chore to raise your heart rate, tone arm muscles and increase stamina. Vigorous vacuuming, dusting, window cleaning and bath scrubbing all count. Hold in your abdominal muscles while you are vacuuming and slightly bend your legs.

Wash the car
Great for your upper body and reaching over the roof will increase your flexibility. Just look at that shiny paintwork.

Gardening
If you have one, a garden is full of things to do that really burn calories. And it's nice to be outside in the fresh air. Remember to engage your stomach muscles especially when bending or lifting things. A gentle stretch when you've finished is a good idea.

Healthy living logo and text extract from Tesco's "Staying Fit and Active" leaflet © Tesco Ltd; images courtesy of Tesco

4: 3: T18: to investigate how style and vocabulary are used to convince the intended reader

connective indicates contrasting ideas

direct address to reader

familiar, upbeat tone

voices question reader might be asking…

…and goes on to answer it

medical and statistical information makes the case

subheads work as list as well as indicating section content

informal, idiomatic phrase

4: 3: W3: to use independent spelling strategies, including building from other words with similar patterns and meanings

Dear Holly

by Chris Lutrario

Background

In this letter, a child offers advice to a friend and tries to persuade her toward a particular course of action. It has been written in reply to a letter describing feelings, experiences and problems at a new school. The letter provides an example of persuasive writing in a personal, intimate context. This is reflected in the chatty style and warm tone. It combines a clearly reasoned analysis of the situation and practical advice, so is also a kind of instructional text.

What's on the CD-ROM

This is a discarded first draft of the letter. The writer has recognised that the tone is too abrupt and offensive – and therefore likely to be ineffective.

Discussing the text

● Ask the children what kind of text this is, then read the first two paragraphs. Speculate on the background. *What is the relationship between Holly and Bethan? What has just happened?* Note the conventional opening for a personal letter and that the writer starts by referring to the letter received.

● Read the next paragraph and ask what the writer is doing now – explaining what she thinks is the cause of the problem. Focus on tone by asking: *Why doesn't Bethan just say, 'It's your fault. You're too shy.'?* Identify the many different ways in which she softens this judgement: by referring to their friendship, addressing Holly by name, agreeing it's difficult, inserting the word *…well…*, claiming that Holly recognises the truth of what's being said, and the exclamation mark which lightens the whole thing. Note also the use of capital letters for emphasis. The friendship is also reflected in the informal tone – Bethan is writing in very much the way she would talk to Holly.

● Read the next sentence and ask what its purpose is – it signals a shift from diagnosis to remedy. Read the next two paragraphs and ask the children to identify the two key ideas suggested. Again, focus on tone and tactics. Note how Bethan tries to encourage Holly, by saying it's easy, by praise and by anticipating a happy outcome. Re-read the sentence beginning *Go over…* . Note the opening imperative verb, typical of instructions. Ask the

children to point out similar sentences, including ones in which the verb is not at the beginning. Establish that giving advice is a form of instructions.

● Read the rest of the letter and ask: *Why does Bethan end like this? What is she worried might happen?*

● Look back at the second sentence, focusing on the connective *but*. Ask what two ideas are being contrasted. Reinforce this by focusing on the two sentences with *but* in the third paragraph. Similarly, ask children to find and explain the function of *so* in the paragraph beginning *Next,* and *because* in the penultimate paragraph.

● Can the children find different kinds of sentences: statements, orders and a question? Note how the different effects of these sentence types are related to the writer's persuasive tactics (to make a point, to tell the reader what to do, to invite a response or make the reader think).

Talk, read, write

● Ask the children to imagine they are Holly. *How would she feel when she read this letter? Upset? Offended? Pleased? Keen to follow the advice?* Encourage the children to refer to the text to back up their ideas, focusing on the effect of specific sentences and phrases.

● Organise pairs to role play a telephone conversation between Bethan and Holly. Explain that they will first need to decide who makes the phone call and when. For example, Holly could phone Bethan immediately after receiving the letter. When several pairs have presented their conversations, compare different responses. *Do they seem true to the two characters and the situation?*

● Together choose another personal or social problem. Ask the children to write a letter of advice to someone facing this problem. Encourage them to pay special attention to persuasiveness and a careful tone.

Extension

Challenge the children to imagine that Holly followed Bethan's advice and to write the letter in which she tells her what has happened. Alternatively, they could imagine that Holly is offended by the letter, and write her reply.

4: 3: **T23:** to present a point of view in writing, linking points persuasively and selecting style and vocabulary appropriate to the reader

4: 3: **S4:** to use connectives to structure an argument

connectives signal contrast

imperatives show this is a kind of instructional writing

writer encourages and bolsters her friend

connective indicates reason

writer, worried about offence or misunderstanding, makes intentions explicit

conventional salutation

writer refers to letter to which she is replying

analysis of problem; language softens judgement

capitals used for emphasis

two pieces of advice organised in paragraphs, clearly signalled

connective signals consequence

Dear Holly

Thanks for your letter. It's great that you like the new house but I'm really sad to hear that you haven't made any friends at your new school.

You know you said that you sit in the playground on your own and that when someone comes to talk they soon go away again.

You've been my best friend for a long time now, Holly, and, well, it hurts me to say this BUT MAYBE IT'S PARTLY YOUR FAULT. You've always been a bit shy — you know it's true! That was OK when you knew everyone but now you're in a new situation and you need to make more EFFORT.

Here are some things I think you should try.

First, don't just wait for people to come to you. Go over and start a conversation. Maybe say something nice about the person you're talking to. Show that you're interested in them. It's easy!

Next, when someone starts to talk to you for the first time, I bet you just look down at your feet! And don't say anything. No wonder they go away. You need to look up and smile and SAY SOMETHING — something sparky and lively and fun! You're a really interesting person — so I know you can do it. In no time at all you'll have lots of friends, just like you did here at Underwood.

I hope you aren't upset by this letter. I'm only saying this because I'm your friend and I don't like to think of you being sad. I want to help. What are friends for?

So, please, please take my advice — and let me know what happens.

Love
Bethan

4: 3: **T16:** to read, compare and evaluate examples of arguments and discussions

4: 3: **T18:** to investigate how style and vocabulary are used to convince the intended reader

4: 3: **S3:** to understand how the grammar of a sentence alters when the sentence is altered

Vote for me

by Chris Lutrario

Background

This is the text of a speech made by a pupil seeking to be elected by her classmates as a representative on the school council. Although there are some oral features, the style is formal rather than spontaneous, and the piece is carefully organised.

What's on the CD-ROM

This is a skeleton version of the core text, showing its paragraph structure and the key points to be covered. This can be used to show how the ideas have been organised and as an example of a planning technique when children write texts of this kind.

Discussing the text

● If appropriate, link the speech with arrangements for pupil representation in your own school.

● Read the first paragraph. Note how the speaker starts by making her purpose clear. *Why does she include a question?* Explain how this works as a persuasive device by involving the listeners and claiming to know what they are thinking.

● Read the next three paragraphs. Ask what purpose is served by the connectives at the start of each (*First of all, Next, Finally*). Draw out the idea that they signal the sequencing of the three points in the argument very clearly. Can the children identify the main idea in each paragraph: skills, experience, hard work? Note how the speaker goes on to develop and support these ideas in order to convince listeners of her claim to these qualities.

● Focusing on the second paragraph, ask why the speaker ends the second sentence with an exclamation mark. Discuss what the 'story' behind this might be and the effect that the speaker intends.

● Moving on to paragraph four, ask: *Why does the speaker mention other people here?* (She is comparing herself favourably with them.) Explain that this kind of comparison is a common strategy in persuasive texts, especially advertisements. Encourage the children to provide other examples they know.

● Read the next two paragraphs, and ask: *What does the speaker go on to talk about now?* As before, note how the two key ideas (walking bus and school meals) are clearly signalled by connectives, *First* and *Secondly.*

● Read the final paragraph and discuss how the conclusion works. It mirrors and sums up the organisation of the whole speech.

● Shift attention to style and discuss the language used to try to persuade listeners. Focus in particular on the two rhetorical questions and the points at which the speaker assumes agreement (*We all know* and *Surely everyone agrees*). Note that the first three sentences of the last paragraph all have the same structure and rhythm and repetition of *that's*. Explain that these are all common tactics in persuasive texts, oral and written, and discuss their intended effects.

● Ask: *How can you tell that this speech is meant to be spoken out loud?* Note the inclusion of words and phrases more typical of oral texts, for example, *well* (repeated twice), *As you know, OK*. To emphasise the oral qualities, ask some children to read the speech out loud, taking a paragraph in turn. Encourage them to phrase the text in an expressive and persuasive way, thinking especially about where to pause for effect and which words and phrases to stress. Lead the class in commenting on the effectiveness of the reading.

Talk, read and write

● Ask: *Do you think the speaker makes a good case? Would you vote for her?* Prompt those with a negative view to consider how the speech could have been improved, in terms of both content and style.

● Together, choose another idea for school improvement that could have been included in the second part of the speech. Compose a paragraph on this. Focus attention on sequencing ideas and on using persuasive tactics to make the case convincingly.

Extension

Invite the children to imagine that they are candidates in a school council election and to write a short statement putting their case. Challenge able writers to write a longer leaflet, including information about themselves and what they will do if elected (their manifesto).

4: 3: T21: to assemble and sequence points in order to plan the presentation of a point of view

4: 3: S3: to understand how the grammar of a sentence alters when the sentence is altered

4: 3: T18: to investigate how style and vocabulary are used to convince the intended reader

speaker anticipates listeners' thoughts; asks rhetorical questions

makes favourable comparison with 'competitors'

speaker assumes universal agreement

sentences with same structure and notable rhythm

final statement of expected or wished for outcome

Vote for me

I am Wendy and I want to be your class representative on the school council. I expect you're asking yourself: Why should I vote for her? Well, let me give you some reasons.

First of all, I've got the skills you need to be a good rep. As you know, I'm not shy and I'm a good talker! I won't be lost for words at council meetings. But I'm a good listener too. I promise to consult everyone in Year 4 and find out what you think and what you want. Then I'll put forward your ideas clearly and strongly.

Next, I've got the experience you need. I was class rep two years ago at my old school. So I know how school councils work and what a rep needs to do.

Finally, I'm hard-working. Some people just like the idea of being a rep. It makes them feel important. But they don't do much. I will put in the time and the effort that's needed.

OK, so maybe now you believe I can do the job. So you are asking now: What are her ideas for improving the school? Well, I've got lots! I'll mention just two. First, I'd like to develop the 'walking bus' scheme that some parents are starting. We all know that walking to school is good for your health and it reduces the pollution and congestion caused by cars. The 'walking bus' makes it safe — and fun!

Secondly, there's school meals. Surely everyone agrees that they've got better, but they could still be healthier and tastier and offer better choices for vegetarians. My aim will be to get more children more actively involved in a Better Meals campaign.

So that's what I can offer. That's the kind of rep I want to be. That's a taste of what I'd like to do. I hope you'll vote for me on Friday.

Photo © 2006, Jupiter Images Corporation

Text © 2007, Chris Lutrario

suffix 'ive'

introductory paragraph states context and purpose of speech

points are then given in clearly organised paragraphs with temporal connectives

wording typical of spoken language

suffix 'tion'

conclusion reflects and reinforces speech as a whole

4: 3: T23: to present a point of view in writing, linking points persuasively and selecting style and vocabulary appropriate to the reader

4: 3: S4: to use connectives to structure an argument

Welcome to North Devon & Exmoor...
from North Devon Marketing Bureau

Background

The text is the first page of the 2005 guide to North Devon and Exmoor, produced by the local tourist board – an A4 landscape brochure of 96 pages, lavishly illustrated in full colour, and available in tourist information offices around the country. The aim of the introduction in this extract is to impress the reader with the many different attractions offered by the area. Following sections provide more detailed information in similar style on particular aspects, for example, coastline, moor land, attractions for children, catering, history, adventure sports, festivals and events.

What's on the CD-ROM

This is a shorter, simpler text advertising another tourist destination in Devon. As in the core text, enthusiastic language is used to describe the visitor attractions, which are clearly organised in bullet points. This can be use as an alternative text for less confident readers or as an additional example of persuasive writing in this context.

Discussing the text

● Read the title and first paragraph with the children and ask them if they can work out the kind of publication it is taken from, and what its purpose is. Confirm that it is from a tourist brochure and that its aim is to persuade readers to go on holiday in this area. Encourage the children to share any knowledge they have of this part of the country.

● Read the rest of the text, then go back to focus on each paragraph in turn. Ask the children to identify its focus. (Paragraph two, the coastline; paragraph three, inland countryside; paragraph four, various other attractions; paragraph five, conclusion summing up the breadth of the appeal.) Explore the selling points in more detail by asking: *What could you do if you went to this place? What kind of people would enjoy a holiday here?*

● Shift the focus to the style and tone of the text. Highlight the phrase *fabulous coastline* at the start of the second paragraph. Explain that the adjective *fabulous* is used to describe the noun *coastline* in a positive, exciting, even extravagant way. Prompt the children to find other similar adjective–noun pairings by asking: *What is described as golden? Impossible?*

Unchanged? Stunning? Unique? Rolling? Great? Local? Traditional? Exciting? Vibrant? In each case, ask the children to describe what information the adjective adds and what the effect on the reader is intended to be.

● Then focus on *kick off your sandals* in the first paragraph, and ask: *Why doesn't the writer just say, 'take off you sandals'?* Elicit that the verb used is more unusual and precise, and makes readers feel as if they are actually there. Challenge the children to find similar words or phrases that have this imaginative effect: *head off, wide blue yonder, strides, grace us with their presence, rush of the surf, savour.* Discuss that the style is heightened, almost poetic, and that this encourages readers to feel that this is a wonderful, special place.

● At word-level, focus on compound words. Highlight the first one in the text, *everything*, and prompt the children to identify the two words of which it is composed. Then ask them to search for more: *something, coastline, inland, yourself, horseback, seabirds, wildlife, weekend, afternoon* and *sunset*.

Talk, read and write

● Ask the children if they would like a holiday in this area and to give their reasons, referring to the text.

● Encourage them to evaluate the effectiveness of the text. Does it make them want to go on holiday there? If so, what works well? If not, what are the problems?

● Use shared writing strategies to compose a similar beginning for a tourist brochure for the area where the children live. Encourage them to focus on the positive, using powerful adjectives and adventurous vocabulary. Note any compound words used.

Extension

Ask children to choose a product that they like, and to write a list of words and phrases that could be used in an advertisement for it, focusing in particular on adjectives. More able writers could go on to write the advertisement. Alternatively, ask them to imagine that they are on holiday in North Devon and Exmoor, and to write a postcard home, drawing on information in the text.

4: 3: T19: to evaluate advertisements for their impact, appeal and honesty

4: 3: W11: to investigate compound words

4: 3: T18: to investigate how style and vocabulary are used to convince the intended reader

4: 3: T25: to design an advertisement, such as a poster or radio jingle on paper or screen

compound words

paragraph to collate and summarise

poetic, metaphorical style

paragraph focused on inland hills

paragraph focused on other attractions

addresses reader directly, in friendly tone

heightened, poetic style

paragraph focused on coastline

6 powerful positive adjectives in 2 sentences

effective vocabulary makes images come to life in reader's mind

dash indicates linked ideas

compound words

Welcome to North Devon & Exmoor...

Once you've made the first step, the rest is easy. Everything falls into place when you kick off your sandals and feel the golden sands between your toes or pull on your walking boots and head off into the wide blue yonder. Either way, you'll find something to inspire you here.

Our fabulous coastline, with its impossible cliffs, harbours that remain unchanged for centuries and miles of golden sands, is almost entirely made up of Areas of Outstanding Natural Beauty. And a large part of it has been designated a UNESCO World Biosphere Reserve for its stunning and unique environment.

Head inland and you'll find beauty here, too. On Exmoor you can lose yourself in a few strides among the heather and the legends, whilst a journey through the rolling hills always throws up a few surprises, especially if you take your time. See the place on foot, on horseback, on your bike or over a pint – with some great local food and a view to match.

There's plenty to keep you busy on your holiday, from towns with traditional local markets to exciting themed attractions for the kids, as well as a vibrant calendar of Festivals and Events. It isn't hard to see why people come back year after year – like the migrating swallows who grace us with their presence every summer. We even have our own island, home to seals and seabirds and surrounded by the UK's only Statutory Marine Reserve. On some days you'll see more wildlife than you will people. Imagine that! Your own island for a day.

As a holiday destination North Devon and Exmoor can't fail to impress; whether you stay with us for a summer holiday or a long weekend. After the rush of the surf, an afternoon reading, a sunset to savour or just some quality time with your family, you'll soon feel truly at home.

Text from a leaflet 'Guide to North Devon and Exmoor'.
© 2005 North Devon Marketing Bureau www.northdevon.com; background and top right photos © North Devon Marketing Bureau; other photos © Photodisc Inc

What Champs will do for you
by Colin Rose

Background
This text is taken from the introductory double-page spread of *Learning Champs*, first published in 2001. The book explains a programme of techniques designed to improve various aspects of learning, for example, motivation, concentration and memory. These techniques are tailored throughout the book to different learning styles and the approach is practical and encouraging. The aim of the introduction given here is to persuade readers of the value of Champs, to hold out the promise of what it will do for them. In other words, as in much advertising, it makes a 'pitch'.

What's on the CD-ROM
The differentiated text is an advertisement aimed at persuading the reader to learn a foreign language. The text is shorter and simpler than the core text, but follows the same question and answer structure. It can be used with less able readers and to provide an additional example of a persuasive text.

Discussing the text
● Read the six bullet points with which the text begins. Ask what kind of sentences they are, and confirm that they are all questions. Then ask the children to identify the writers' aim and to discuss the effect of using questions. *Who is the likely reader and in what way is he or she supposed to answer?* Draw out the idea that the text is relating to the reader, making a learner's hopes and desires explicit. Tease this out by asking: *What hopes about learning does the writer mention?* Note the use of *you* to address the reader personally.

● Read the next paragraph and ask: *What is the text doing now?* Check that the children understand that the *brilliant book* referred to is the *Learning Champs* book that begins with this introduction. Note that the statement *Well now you can!* is an answer to the questions; the writer claims that the book will enable readers to fulfil their hopes about becoming better learners. Make the general point that persuasive texts, especially marketing material like this, often have this structure: they start by identifying the readers'/audience's hopes and desires (and sometimes fears) and then claim that their product or service is the solution.

● Read the following paragraph (*At school...*) and discuss how the argument again changes course here: the text develops the promise made by the book, emphasising that it is new and different. Note that highlighting these features, too, is a common tactic in advertising.

● Read the first paragraph under the heading *The best techniques for you*, and note how it follows the same pattern as the beginning of the text – posing questions and going on to answer them. Read the rest of this section and discuss the 'promise' being made here: the book will meet your individual needs.

● Focus on the three bullet points. Note the repeated use of the connective *because* to set up a chain of cause and effect, and the key words *easier, quicker* and *fun*, which are chosen to appeal strongly to the reader.

● To extend this sentence-level focus, ask children to identify other connectives and explain how they indicate links in the argument. This is especially marked in the paragraph beginning *At school* and in the final paragraph.

Talk, read and write
● Encourage children to comment on the text by asking: *Does this introduction interest and persuade you? Would you want to read the book? Why? Why not?*

● Use shared writing strategies to write a short marketing 'blurb' for the book, for example, of the kind that would be found in the publisher's catalogue. As part of this, encourage the children to summarise the key ideas in this text, perhaps setting a word-limit, and to use persuasive language and techniques to express them forcefully.

Extension
Ask children to look in magazines, newspapers and catalogues for advertisements that follow the structure of appealing to the reader's hopes, desires, fears, and then claiming that their product is the answer. Challenge the children to write a short advertisement of this kind for a familiar product, such as a drink or a new cleaning product.

4: 3: T19: to evaluate advertisements for their impact, appeal and honesty

variety of connectives make links in argument

repeated use of question-and-answer technique

4: 3: S4: to use connectives to structure an argument

What CHAMPS will do for you

- What if you could learn anything you wanted fast and easily? How would that make you feel?
- What if you could remember difficult things like history dates, maths formulae or science facts more easily?
- What if you could start getting better results at school within the next few days?
- What if you could learn to concentrate and listen better?
- What if you could get yourself going, or motivate yourself to get down to work at any time?
- What if you felt really confident to tackle any school subject, even the ones you don't think you're very good at?

Well, now you can. This brilliant book will teach you all the things you need to become a learning CHAMP – something that will help you for the rest of your life – at home, at school and at work.

At school you get taught lots of different subjects, like maths, English, science and history. But you're not often taught how to learn them. Yet learning is like playing a sport, or playing a musical instrument. It's a skill. And CHAMPS is going to teach you this most important skill of all.

The best techniques for you
Does your face look the same as your friends' faces?
Are your fingerprints the same?
No! And neither is your brain.

Your brain is as individual as your fingerprints or face. Since you learn with your brain, you won't be surprised to know that you have a unique way of learning that suits your unique brain best.

When you use the techniques that match the way your brain learns best, you'll be learning in the way that's most natural to you.

- Because it is natural, it's easier.
- Because it's easier, it's quicker.
- And because it's quicker it's more fun.

That's just what CHAMPS will do for you! It'll teach you the learning techniques that match the way your brain likes to learn best. So if you're already a good learner – you'll get better. And if you find learning a bit of a struggle, your work will get easier and your marks will get better.

Text extract from "Learning Champs" by Colin Rose © 2001, Anova Books (2001, Learning World); photos © 2006, Jupiter Images Corporation

heading clearly states aim

series of bullets all asking reader personal, hypothetical, questions about his/her hopes; prompts a positive response

answers questions above

4: 3: T17: to know how arguments are presented

4: 3: T20: to summarise a sentence or paragraph by identifying the most important elements and rewording them in a limited number of words

4: 3: T25: to design an advertisement, such as a poster or radio jingle on paper or screen

Book Power

by Chris Powling

Background

This extract is the main text of the first chapter of Chris Powling's *The Book About Books*. (Three 'boxes' in this chapter in the book offer interesting facts about books, and are illustrated with humorous cartoons.) The author's aim in this book is to convince readers of the special value and power of books – and, by extension, to persuade them to read. Information and ideas are presented in a light-hearted, appealing way, and the text, in particular this first chapter, includes many persuasive devices.

What's on the CD-ROM

This is a simple statement of the key ideas in the core text, presented as a series of sentences all beginning with the word *Books*. This can be used as an alternative text for less able readers or as a supportive introduction to the core text. It is also useful for purposes of comparison: although this text makes positive statements about books, it does not use persuasive language nor have the friendly, personal tone of the core text.

Discussing the text

● Read the first two paragraphs and ask: *How does the author begin his book? What is he trying to do?* Note the two questions followed by an answer that is emphasised with an exclamation mark. Explain that the author uses this tactic to draw readers in, anticipating their thoughts and answering them. Compare to 'What Champs will do for you' (page 149) if you have worked on that.

● Read the rest of the text and examine its content by asking open-ended questions: *What does the author think about books? What does he say is special about them?* Identify key ideas and encourage the children to express them in their own words. Then distinguish between key statements that are facts and those that are the writer's opinion.

● Now consider how we can tell that this is not a report about books but a persuasive text. Note the choice of positive words, for example, *amazing* and *magical*; the lengthy and enthusiastic listing of things that books can do (*open our eyes, warm our hearts and help us make our dreams come true*); the favourable comparison of books with computers; the invention of new hyphenated words to describe the power of books (*brain-boosting, universe-exploring, time-shifting*); the inclusion of 'amazing facts'.

● Develop this to look at style and tone. Ask: *How does the author try to keep us interested and entertained?* Here, draw attention to the way the author draws in the reader by using *we* and *our*; the use of eye-catching, powerful words such as *hoot, burst, squirm*; the use of short sentences and paragraphs for impact; unfinished sentences (*Meanwhile in other countries…*); the strong expression of a personal view (*For me, that's magical*); the chatty, enthusiastic tone (*You bet they do!*); and the use of humour, notably in the final paragraph with its 'in joke' about the power of books.

● For a relevant sentence-level focus, ask the children to identify the different kinds of sentences included (questions, exclamations, statements and unfinished sentences) and to explain how they identified them – by the corresponding punctuation marks. Discuss how this variety keeps the writing lively and enables the author to guide the reader's response.

Talk, read and write

● Encourage the children to share what they have learned about books from this extract. Ask, for example: *What hadn't you thought of before? What did you think was the most interesting idea? Does the author make you think differently about books and reading?* As they talk, prompt the children to refer to their own experiences as readers.

● Switch focus from content to style, by asking: *What do you like about the way this text has been written? Is there anything that you don't like? How would you improve it?* Encourage the children to refer to details in the text and to consider features of style and tone discussed previously.

Extension

Ask children to write and design a poster to promote books and reading. Alternatively, and posing a greater challenge, ask them to write a similar piece about the special power of a different activity or product, such as playing video games, keeping a pet, playing a sport.

Book Power

A book about books?
Are books really so special that they deserve a book's worth of writing and drawing all to themselves?
You bet they do!
Really? Books have been around for so long, and are so easy to take for granted, we tend to forget how amazing they actually are. A book can fill our heads with someone else's facts and fancies – someone who's far away, or dead, or completely imaginary. Yet, as we turn its pages, those facts and fancies come to life in a way that's utterly personal to us. For what you see, in your mind as you read, will never be identical with what I read, will never be identical with what I see – even if we're staring at the same words.
For me, that's magical.
Books can make us hoot with laughter, burst into tears, or squirm with pain and pleasure. They can teach us about anything and everything – from Acrobatics to Zoology. They're brain-boosting, universe-exploring, time-shifting bundles of endless possibility.
Yet this handy, pocket-sized object doesn't need any power-source, never lets us down by crashing and lasts pretty nearly forever if we look after it properly.
The right book at the right time can open our eyes, warm our hearts and help us make our dreams come true... yet stay entirely private while it does so.
No wonder there's a lot of them about. Last year, we published over 8000 new ones in the United Kingdom alone. Some had a print-run of just a few hundred copies, others flopped off the press by the million. And that was just books for children!
If we're counting those for adults as well, each one with a title trying hard to be different from all the others, then there were more than a hundred thousand new publications altogether.
It was much the same the year before. Not to mention the year before that... and so on.
Meanwhile in other countries...
Yes, maybe we'd better pause a moment. Even a book-lover like me is beginning to feel a little faint. Luckily, another thing you can do with a book is to fan yourself, very gently, till you've built up the strength to move on to the next chapter.

Really?

Text extract from 'The Book About Books' by Chris Powling; text © 2000, Chris Powling; illustration © 2000, Scoular Anderson (2001, A.&C. Black Publishers Ltd)

Annotations:

- 4: 3: S2: to identify the common punctuation marks and respond to them appropriately when reading

- plural personal pronouns suggest writer and reader share views

- striking, powerful vocabulary

- humorous conclusion with in-joke

- two questions to get reader thinking

- answer to the questions

- one word 'sentence' for impact and confirmation

- short paragraphs add to impact in presenting strongly and directly author's point of view

- compares book favourably against its competitor, the computer

- 4: 3: T18: to investigate how style and vocabulary are used to convince the intended reader

- 4: 3: S3: to understand how the grammar of a sentence alters when the sentence is altered

Evacuation

by Vince Cross

Background

This is a straightforward text setting out the pros and cons of the evacuation policy carried out in the UK in the early years of the Second World War. A short introduction describing the policy is followed by bulleted lists of reasons for and against. There is no conclusion and the author's view is not expressed. Making links where possible with work in history would enrich children's study of this text.

What's on the CD-ROM

The text on the CD-ROM is a skeleton plan of the core text, showing the main points in note form, presented in two columns. This text can be used as an introduction to the core text and/ or as a way of highlighting its structure. It is also useful as an exemplar way of planning discussion texts of this kind.

Discussing the text

● Ask the children to share their knowledge about evacuation, drawing where possible on work on this topic in history.

● Then read the introduction. Drawing on the last sentence, ask the children to suggest one reason why people might agree with the policy of evacuation and one reason why they might disagree.

● Read the reasons against and ask the children to state each as briefly as they can in their own words. Then ask which reason they think is the strongest, and why. Guide the following discussion by asking: *Which reasons might be seen as a price worth paying?* (One and two.) *Which one might seem irrelevant or of little importance in the circumstances?* (Four.) *Which were not known at the time?* (Two and three.) Ask pairs or small groups to discuss and sort the reasons into what they see as order of importance. Then share ideas and talk about the results.

● Focus on reasons one and two, and ask how these points are structured. Elicit that the first sentence states the main idea, which is then developed and commented on.

● Can the children identify the point at which the text addresses the reader directly, and explain the effect of this?

● Now read the reasons for. As before, ask the children to summarise the points and discuss their relative importance. Identify those where a main idea is stated and then developed (one, four and five).

● Ask: *What does the author think about evacuation?* Agree that this is never indicated in the text and note that discussion texts are often (but not necessarily) balanced like this.

● Shift attention to structure and presentation by demonstrating that the text is very clearly and neatly organised, and that this is signalled to the reader by the use of subheadings and bullet points.

● For a word-level focus, highlight the word *evacuation* and ask the children to divide it into root and suffix. Note dropping of the final *e* when the suffix is added. Can the children find another example of this in the text? (*education*) Ask them to add the suffix -*tion* to *concentrate*. Invite further suggestions to add to the list.

Talk, read and write

● Organise the class into small groups and give them a few minutes to discuss which case, for or against, is the stronger. Then pool conclusions as a class.

● Highlight one of the reasons that is simply stated and ask children to say how it might be developed or commented on. Use shared writing strategies to add sentences.

● Think about questions that the text raises, for example, *How did Germany's strategy change? How many of the 30,000 people killed were children? How did education, housing and health change after the war?* Organise groups to conduct research and report back. Does the information they have found affect the case for or against evacuation?

Extension

● Ask children to write a conclusion for this text in which they adopt a position, for or against. Encourage them to consider the merits of the two cases and to give reasons for their view.

● The children could write an argument that might have taken place after the war, between two people who have different opinions about evacuation. Less able writers could use speech bubbles and more able writers could present it as a playscript.

both sides of argument presented

nouns ending with 'tion'

Evacuation

From September 1939 onwards, during the first years of the Second World War, the British government evacuated hundreds of thousands of children from the cities to the countryside. They were afraid that if the Germans bombed British towns and cities most of the people who lived there would be killed. Not everyone agrees that evacuating children was the right thing to do.

Photo © EMPICS

Text by Vince Cross © 2007, Vince Cross, previously unpublished.

Reasons for:

The lives of some children were certainly saved. 30,000 people were killed during London's Blitz.

- Evacuation allowed parents to concentrate on keeping Britain going at a very difficult time.
- It showed that the government wanted to look after the British people.
- Many city children had never been to the countryside. This was a new and exciting adventure for them.
- It made different kinds of people aware of each other. Maybe it helped bring about the important social changes that happened after the war in education housing and health.

Reasons against:

- Evacuation made children and parents very unhappy. Families were split up, and didn't see each other for months or even years. Children who were evacuated were sometimes treated very badly by the people they went to stay with. No one knew about this until years later.
- Maybe the children didn't need to be sent away. In fact the German bombing wasn't quite as bad as the government thought it might be.
- Air raid shelters protected people. British air defences proved quite successful. And Hitler stopped the night-by-night bombing of London in 1941 because he decided to fight in a different way.
- It was difficult to keep children in school during evacuation. (Maybe you would think this was a 'plus point'!)

impersonal, factual introduction/ background

sentence signals the issue under discussion

bullets separate and organise points

first sentence states key point

sentences develop key point

author addresses reader directly and lightens tone

Should children follow fashion?
by Adam Hibbert

Background

This extract is from *Read All About It!: Fashion*, a book that presents information and views about fashion and body image through different kinds of journalistic writing. This text takes the form of an exchange of letters between two people with opposing opinions about the issue of children and fashion. The reader has to imagine that the exchange took place over time, with intervals between letters. It is crucial to read the letters in the given order, as the correspondents refer to comments in previous letters.

What's on the CD-ROM

This is a transcript of a discussion between two children with different views about school uniform – a subject referred to in the core text. It is a simpler text, both in content and language, and would be suitable for lower attaining readers. It is also another example of this back-and-forth kind of discussion text.

Discussing the text

● Read the heading and ask the children how they would answer this question. Gather a few contributions on each side of the debate. Show the structure of the text and read the first of Wally's letters.

● Encourage the children to describe in their own words the view Wally puts forward, and to comment briefly on it. Then read Ivor's reply, and ask: *What is his point of view? How does he respond to the ideas in Wally's letter? What do you think Wally might say in reply to Ivor?* Read Wally's next letter and discuss how he develops the argument.

● Follow this pattern as you read the rest of the letters. You could record key ideas in two columns on the board as you go along.

● As the reading proceeds, explain the meanings of more challenging ideas, for example, in Ivor's second letter, *negotiating life's pitfalls* and *influence the way people relate to you*. Help the children to identify the more general issues underlying the two points of view by asking: *What do they think about children?* Wally sees children as needing protection and is concerned about fairness; Ivor thinks children should be treated like adults and be allowed to look after themselves.

● Encourage the children to take a broader view of the text by asking: *What makes this different from the other discussion texts we've been reading?* Help the children to see that the two participants do not just set out their views, but interact and respond to each other's ideas.

● Shift attention to word choice by focusing on the sentence beginning *However* in Wally's first letter. Ask the children why Wally chooses the words *burden* and *trendy* here. Explain that these words both convey value judgements and are intended to have a persuasive effect. Note how different the effect would be if Wally had used *fashionable* instead of *trendy*. Ask the children to find other examples of words being used in this way (*boring old adults*, *frivolous clothing*, *terrible teasing*) and to suggest plainer alternatives. Note how the issue of teasing becomes explicit when Wally changes Ivor's positive *fit in* (Ivor's first letter) to the negative *peer pressure*.

● At word-level, focus on extending words by adding prefixes and suffixes, using *impersonate, sensitivity, appearance, argument* and *isolation* as examples.

● At sentence-level, ask the children to identify the three different kinds of sentences in Ivor's letters and the effect that he creates by using them. (Statement, question, exclamation.)

Talk, read and write

● Encourage the children to forget for the moment about their own view on this issue, and ask them who makes the better case, Wally or Ivor, and why.

● Now give children an opportunity to share their own ideas, ideally by organising a debate on the issue.

● Use shared writing strategies to write Wally's response to Ivor's last letter, then ask the children to write Ivor's response to this individually. In both contexts, prompt them to respond to earlier ideas and to use the language style of the writers to continue their case.

Extension

Ask children to write an exchange of letters between two people with different views on another issue. You could differentiate this by asking the best writers to include a third participant with yet another view.

two contrasting viewpoints set in columns; layout conveys back-and-forth nature of argument

writer states his case, but does not respond to opposing opening argument

point emphasised by punctuation

question challenges opponent to back up earlier statement

title poses question being debated

words chosen for their associations

exaggeration used for effect

writer picks up his correspondent's phrase

root word extended by suffix

assumes agreement; attempt to get others on his side

inverted commas cast doubt on word and idea

Something to talk about

SHOULD CHILDREN FOLLOW FASHION?

No! Wally Wooley	Yes! Ivor Style
Dear Ivor, I suppose I must begin by saying that I'm no enemy of fashion. I know that it brings joy and colour to our humdrum lives, and would be sorely missed if we tried to do without it. However, children do not need the extra burden that being trendy places on them. Fashion is for adults to express themselves with. Nothing is more horrible than expecting a child to impersonate an adult. Yours, Wally	**Dear Wally,** I'm glad we've established that you don't have objections to fashion, as such. Let's concentrate on why you might object to fashion in children's lives. I happen to think that children are fashion's most important fans. Children are immensely sensitive to the way they fit in, and love to experiment, in ways that are beyond boring old adults' abilities. Yours, Ivor
Dear Ivor, It's exactly because of children's sensitivity to peer pressure (fitting in as you phrase it) that fashion is best kept out of the playground. If one has poor parents, or parents who are less keen on frivolous clothing than one's friends' parents, terrible teasing and social isolation can result. Yours, Wally	**Dear Wally,** Children have to learn how to negotiate life's pitfalls for themselves. One of the hardest things to learn is how to influence the way people relate to you. Experimenting with fashion is part of this learning process. By changing how they look, kids learn how unimportant appearances truly are! Yours, Ivor
Dear Ivor, If it were that simple, I would have no problem with your argument. Sadly, some children, for a variety of reasons, are denied an equal chance to 'experiment'. I would rather see children in uniforms. As any teacher will tell you, children will always find a way to express themselves through minor improvements to a dress code. And none of them need feel excluded. Yours, Wally	**Dear Wally,** I remember my brothers insisting that Mum 'take in' their trouser legs in the 80s, when the school trousers were too flared. Uniforms will always be customised, more often than not by put-upon mothers. Why is that any better than other clothes? As for the expense, keep up! Most modern fashions are more influenced by the charity shop than £100 gym shoes. Yours, Ivor

Text extract from *"Read All About It!: Fashion"* by Adam Hibbert © 2000, Adam Hibbert (2000, Franklin Watts)

Zoos — good or bad?

by Jane Bingham

Background

This is an extract from *Animals and Us: Do Animals Have Rights?* which discusses a range of issues related to relationships between humans and animals, such as hunting, and the use of animals as pets, in scientific experiments and for food. In each case, the author presents relevant factual information, draws out different views commonly held on the issues, and allows readers to make up their own minds. Here the issue is keeping animals in zoos.

What's on the CD-ROM

This argument against zoos makes use of ideas referred to in the core text. As well as making its own case against zoos, it counters arguments commonly made in favour of them. Comparing this text with the core text will highlight the difference between a discussion text that examines both sides of an argument without taking sides, and an argument that exhorts a particular view.

Discussing the text

● Read the title. Ask the children what kind of text they think will follow it and why the author chose to write the title in the form of a question.

● Read the first two paragraphs. Note how these provide some background information and make further use of questions. Ask for a show of hands in response to the question at the end of the second paragraph. Allow children on different sides of the argument to share their views briefly.

● Read the three following subheadings and ask the children to predict the focus of each section. Then read the paragraph on *Bad zoos, good zoos* and see if the children can confirm the central issue: the quality of zoos. Help the children to see that the author is providing factual information here, not presenting an opinion. Discuss how this information relates to the main question. *Is it relevant? Does it influence their answer?* Highlight the connectives *however* and *so*, and demonstrate how they indicate links between ideas.

● Read the next paragraph. Ask: *Is the author presenting facts or opinions?* Challenge the children to identify the three opinions summarised here. Note how these statements are signalled by *Some people, Some even* and *others say* and supported by the connectives *because* (twice) and *however.* Encourage the children to talk about which of these opinions, if any, they share.

● Read the next paragraph, and, as before, ask the children whether this is fact or opinion and to summarise the view expressed. There is only one: animals should live natural lives in the wild. Ask: *How does this view relate to the view that zoos are a good thing because they allow people to learn about animals?* Establish that these two views are opposed to each other. Note how this is made explicit in the summary given in the *Think it through* section.

● Read the *Newsflash* and ask the children which view about zoos this information could support. Develop this by identifying how the information relates to facts and opinions presented earlier in the text.

● To finish, ask the children what the author thinks about zoos. Suggest that the text provides no answer to this question and tie this fact in with the purpose of the text: to present a range of views and related facts, but not to take sides. Note also how this impartial, objective approach is evident in the language of the text, which makes no use of persuasive devices such as emotive terms or exaggeration.

● For word-level work, examine words with the same letter string but different pronunciations, focusing on *zoo/room/good, years/learn* and *enough/through*. Extend this by asking pairs to record more words with the two pronunciations of *oo* and *ear* and to find different pronunciations of *ough*.

Talk, read and write

● Work with the class to compile a two-column 'pros and cons' chart about zoos. Start with the points made in the text, but encourage the children to contribute new ones.

● Organise a debate on the question *Zoos – good or bad?* Ask speakers to draw on the text but to offer new arguments and counter-arguments.

Extension

Children could write a conclusion for this text in which they assess the arguments and come down on one side.

Zoos – good or bad?

Are all zoos the same and are they ever a good thing?

People love to see wild animals – and one way they can do this is to visit a zoo. For hundreds of years, people have collected wild animals and kept them in zoos. But is it ever right for animals that were born free to be forced to live in captivity?

Bad zoos, good zoos

In some zoos, animals are kept in small cages without enough room for them to get proper exercise. However, over the last fifty years, many zoos have tried to provide animals with a better living environment. Most modern zoos are in the country rather than in towns, so animals have more room to move around.

see the animals. However, others say that people should watch wildlife documentaries instead.

Born free

People who are against zoos say that animals kept in cages often become ill and depressed. Even if animals seem to be happy in captivity, they are still not living natural lives. They may not be living in a climate that suits them, or they may not be eating ideal food.

A chance to learn?

Some people think that zoos are a good idea because they give people a chance to see wild animals and learn about their behaviour. Some even say that city zoos are a good thing because they allow more people to

NEWSFLASH

Sometimes zoos play a role in preventing a rare species from dying out. In 2003, seven giant panda cubs were born at Wolong wildlife reserve in China. The cubs bring hope for the survival of the giant panda, which has been in danger of dying out. In the next few years, staff at the reserve plan to start releasing the pandas back into the wild.

THINK IT THROUGH

Are zoos a good thing?

Yes
They allow people to learn about animals and help to prevent rare species from dying out.

No
Wild animals should be left alone to get on with their lives. What do YOU think?

Photo © Photodisc Inc

Text extract from "Animals and Us: Do Animals Have Rights?" by Jane Bingham © 2005, Harcourt Education Ltd (2005, Heinemann).

Annotations:
- question initiates discussion
- objective, factual introduction
- signals third view
- connective introduces contrast
- same spelling pattern but different sounds
- 'ough' spelling pattern
- 'ear' spelling pattern
- connective introduces consequence
- recent information relevant to debate
- connective introduces reason
- signals first view
- signals second view

4: 3: T21: to assemble and sequence points in order to plan the presentation of a point of view

4: 3: W6: to spell words with common letter strings but different pronunciations

4: 3: S4: to use connectives to structure an argument

4: 3: T17: to know how arguments are presented

4: 3: T23: to present a point of view in writing, linking points persuasively and selecting style and vocabulary appropriate to the reader

The death of the dinosaurs

 by Fiona Chaplin, Sam Taplin and Jane Bingham

Background

The text was originally a double-page spread from *The Usborne Internet-linked Prehistoric World*. The book is divided into sections on various aspects of the prehistoric world, including the origins of the Earth, first life on Earth, reptiles, mammals and the evolution of human beings. 'The death of the dinosaurs' is taken from the section on reptiles. The extract provided here presents and discusses various theories for the disappearance of these creatures in clear, simple terms, without favouring any particular explanation.

What's on the CD-ROM

This is a spider diagram showing how ideas in the core text are organised and developed. This diagram can be used to introduce the core text and/or to highlight its structure. It also provides an example of a planning or presentation strategy for children to use when writing or otherwise presenting this kind of discussion text themselves.

Discussing the text

● Read the title and the introductory paragraph. Establish what facts are presented here and what is not yet understood. This task will highlight the key issue of what scientists know for certain and what is open to question and still being investigated.

● Focus on the next three subheadings, and ask: *So, what will the text be about?* (Three possible explanations.) *Why are the subheadings given in the form of questions?*

● Read the first theory. Encourage children to explain how a meteorite could have resulted in the extinction of the dinosaurs, helping everyone to understand that it is not the meteorite itself but its several effects. Highlight the role of the connectives *as well* and *also* in indicating these effects.

● Read the next theory and ask the children to tell you which word shows right away that this is a different explanation. (*Another.*) Then ask them to describe in their own words what might have happened, noting again the possible chain of events and the role of the connectives *and* and *also*.

● Read the third theory. Note that its presentation is simpler and more direct than the previous two: because there is no chain of causes to be traced.

● Read the rest of the text, determining the focus of each section and how the author develops the discussion. Discuss how the comments about surviving animals fit in. Highlight again the role of connectives (*as well, but, so, also*) in linking ideas within sentences.

● Draw attention to the clear organisation of the text, showing how the author has used subheadings to engage and provide signals for the reader.

● Refocus attention on the distinction between known facts and possibilities by asking the children to suggest examples of each. Model how the verb forms *must* and *would have* indicate known facts, and *may, might* and *could have* indicate possibilities.

● Ask: *Which explanation does the author think is the right one?* Elicit that the text provides no insight into this; the explanations are presented without comment.

● For a word-level focus, highlight the words *warm/warmth* and *survive/survivor*. Ask the children to pick out the root words and to suggest other words in the same 'families'. Build up families for other words in the text, such as *planation, tidal, poisonous, changeable.*

Talk, read and write

● Organise groups and ask the children to discuss which of the explanations they think is the most likely, and why. Give time beforehand for planning their list of points and ensure that everyone is allowed to give their point of view. Afterwards, see if any of the groups came to a consensus, and find out which is the most popular theory.

● Ask the children to compose a paragraph putting forward a fantastical or absurd reason for the disappearance of dinosaurs, for example, visitors from outer space took them away. Focus attention on how this might start (*Yet another explanation...*) and verb forms such as *may* and *might*.

Extension

Children could take on the role of detective and suggest theories for an incident in a story. They could attempt to explain for instance, who stole an item and how.

4: 3: T17: to know how arguments are presented

4: 3: W7: to collect/classify words with common roots

4: 3: S4: to understand the use of connectives to structure an argument

connective introduces alternative idea

fact

possibility

subheadings in question form consider the main possibilities ('Was it. . .?')

what happened

connective indicates additional idea

what might have happened

introduces event and what is known about it

objective, impersonal presentation

word root added to by suffix

conditional verb form; what might have happened

4: 3: T16: to read, compare and evaluate examples of arguments and discussions

4: 3: T21: to assemble and sequence points in order to plan the presentation of a point of view

4: 3: W8: to practise extending and compounding words through adding parts

---

Photo © Lynne Lancaster

This picture shows what might have happened as the meteorite struck the Earth.

Red-hot lava pouring from a volcano.

The death of the dinosaurs

Around 66 million years ago, at the end of the Cretaceous period, lots of creatures died out completely. All the dinosaurs became extinct, except for some feathered ones that had evolved into birds. Flying reptiles and most sea reptiles also died out. No one is certain why this happened, but scientists have given several different explanations.

Deadly rock?
Near the end of the Cretaceous period, the Earth was struck by an enormous rock, or meteorite, measuring up to 10km (6 miles) across. As it hit the Earth, the meteorite would have smashed into tiny pieces, surrounding the planet in clouds of dust.

The dust clouds would have made the Earth cold and dark for months, killing off any creatures that needed warmth to survive. Without light, many plants must have died as well, leaving the animals with nothing to eat. The meteorite would also have caused massive earthquakes and giant tidal waves.

Lava shower?
Another explanation is that many volcanos all over the world may have erupted around the same time. The erupting volcanos would have poured out vast amounts of hot lava (liquid rock) onto the Earth's surface, and sent clouds of dust and poisonous gases high into the air. These gases could also have caused clouds of harmful acid rain to fall.

Climate change?
By 66 million years ago, the weather all over the world had become cooler and more changeable. Dinosaurs relied on heat from the Sun to keep themselves warm, and they may not have been able to cope with a changing climate.

Several causes
There is probably no single reason why so many animals died out. The meteorite must have killed off many creatures, but animals may also have been affected by a change in the weather.

Text and illustrations from "The Usborne Internet-linked Prehistoric World" by Fiona Chaplin, Sam Taplin and Jane Bingham, illustrations by Inklink Firenze © 2004, Usborne Publishing Ltd.

Owning a car by Chris Lutrario

Background

This is a report of a survey into people's views on car ownership. It presents the range of opinions expressed, organising them into three broad categories: in favour, against, and divided. The report, compiled by children, is entirely objective and impersonal in both content and tone.

What's on the CD-ROM

The main points for and against car ownership are presented here as a double spider diagram. They are stated in a very simple form, with none of the elaboration or explanation provided in the original text. Reading this offers a useful way into the full version. Comparing the two versions highlights the way in which a basic opinion can be developed. In doing so, it provides a useful model of the process children need to go through in planning, developing and presenting their own discussion texts.

Discussing the text

● Read the title and first paragraph. Confirm the meaning of the word *survey* and ask the children to work out what will follow.
● Give the children a few moments to think about how they would answer the question, *Is car ownership a good thing or a bad thing?*, then ask for contributions. Begin to cluster opinions; these are likely to fall into the same broad categories as in the report.
● Read the second one-sentence paragraph and discuss how this helps the reader.
● Read the third paragraph. Discuss its purpose and content. Draw out the idea that it simply presents some reasons against car ownership and does not express the authors' view. Focus on the second and third reasons, and ask how they are different from the first and last. Note how the basic ideas (that cars are dangerous and an inefficient means of transport) are developed and supported by detail, argument and evidence, including statistics. Discuss how this makes them more interesting and convincing. Invite children to respond to this list of reasons in various ways: by adding another reason against car ownership, by agreeing with one of these reasons and developing it further, or by arguing against one of these reasons.

● Read the next paragraph. As before, ask the children to identify the basic reasons and how all except the second are developed. Can they find the reason that is directly opposed to one in the previous paragraph (cars are the quickest way to get about, versus cars are inefficient)? Invite children to offer other arguments in favour of car ownership or to comment on these.
● Read the final paragraph and ask why no actual reasons are presented in it. *What does it do instead?* Note that this paragraph identifies a third, balanced point of view and refers the reader to reasons already stated.
● Consider the structure of the text, noting the clear organisation in paragraphs and the use of bulleted lists. *What would be good headings for each section of the text?*
● At sentence-level, re-read the first paragraph and ask the children to find a question. Note that all the other sentences are statements. Ask the children to find a colon and to explain its function here (it introduces a kind of quotation). Ask them to find two more colons in the text and to explain their function (to introduce lists).

Talk, read, write

● Discuss the general effect of the text. *How does it help you to think about car ownership?* By objectively presenting a wide range of ideas, the text prompts us to reflect on the issue more widely than we might otherwise do. Contrast this with a text designed to persuade the reader to adopt a particular view. Pursue this by choosing one reason and reworking it in a persuasive form.
● Ask the children to choose one reason from the text. If it is one they agree with, ask them to develop it further by providing supporting detail, explanation and evidence. If they disagree with it, ask them to develop an argument against it.

Extension

Children could write a persuasive piece expressing their views about car ownership, drawing on ideas in this text. Encourage more fluent writers to say not just what they think and why, but also to engage with the opposing view and put forward arguments against it.

4: 3: T21: to assemble and sequence points in order to plan the presentation of a point of view

colon introduces quote

colon introduces bulleted list

basic point – cars are dangerous – elaborated on

factual evidence to support point

4: 3: S2: to identify the common punctuation marks and respond to them appropriately when reading

Owning a car

Our group carried out a survey into what people thought about cars. We started the interview by asking "In your opinion, is car ownership a good thing or a bad thing?"

We found that there were three main views on this issue.

Out of the 50 people interviewed, 20 thought car ownership was a bad thing. Reasons for taking this view were:
• Too much of the world's resources are used in the manufacture and running of cars.
• Cars are dangerous. Accidents involving cars cause many injuries and deaths every year. Cars cause pollution, and this is harmful to human health.
• Cars are no longer an efficient means of transport. There are now so many cars that the roads are often congested. Traffic jams cost industry billions of pounds every year.
• Car ownership stops people from taking enough exercise, and this is bad for health.

Sixteen people were in favour of car ownership. Their reasons were: They
• Owning a car means that you can go where you like when you like. They give people freedom.
• Cars are still the quickest way of making most journeys.
• You can take heavy things, such as shopping, buggies and luggage, with you in a car. This is difficult on public transport.
• Cars are fun. People enjoy choosing a car, looking after it and driving it.

The remaining 14 people did not want to answer the question with a simple yes or no. They thought that car ownership had both advantages and disadvantages. They raised the same points as people who were for or against car ownership, but felt that they were evenly balanced.

Text © 2007, Chris Lutrario; notepad © Scholastic

introduction states aim of survey and reproduces question asked

signals the organisation of what follows

outlines reasons against car ownership; presents statistic

summarises survey, indicating mixed views

4: 3: T16: to read, compare and evaluate examples of arguments and discussions

4: 3: T17: to know how arguments are presented

4: 3: T23: to present a point of view in writing, linking points persuasively and selecting style and vocabulary appropriate to the reader

Animal rights and human wrongs
by David Bellamy

Background

The text is an extract from *Tomorrow's Earth: A Squeaky-Green Guide*. In this book, David Bellamy discusses a wide range of issues related to how human beings use animals and the Earth's natural resources. In doing so, he presents the factual background and a variety of different views, always recognising the difficulty of the choices and decisions involved. However, his own position is often made clear in the handling of the argument and especially in the sections titled *What you can do to help*. The original double-page spread from which this extract is taken also has a section on *Animals for food*.

What's on the CD-ROM

This is a persuasive text arguing in favour of the testing of medicines on animals – one of the issues raised in the core text. Comparison of the two will highlight the difference between discursive and persuasive texts, in particular in terms of the different ways in which they use language.

Discussing the text

● Read the title and opening paragraph and ask the children if they can work out what the text is going to be about. Point out how the title signals that the author is concerned with moral issues, not just facts, as the paragraph might suggest.

● Begin reading *New medicines* and *What you can do to help*, asking the children to put their hands up when there is a change from fact to opinion. Confirm this shift of focus at the start of the second paragraph of *New medicines*, read on, and ask the children to summarise the different views. Note how these are signalled at the start of sentences by the phrases *Some people*, *Other people* and *Most people*.

● Ask the children if they can tell what the author thinks about testing medicines on animals. His view is evident in the way he refers to the use of cell cultures as *good news* and in *What you can do to help*, but remind them that he also presents other views.

● Focus on the next subheading, *Animal furs*, and ask the children what they expect to find here. Read the first two paragraphs, pausing to check predictions. As before, prompt the children to identify the different views presented and how these are signalled for the reader. Ask: *What does the author think about people killing animals for their furs? How can you tell?* This becomes clear earlier than in the previous section, through the phrases *gave little thought to* and *thanks to these people*.

● Read the next two paragraphs and identify the new issue introduced here (killing animals for other purposes), the different views about it, and whether the author's view is evident. (No.)

● At sentence-level, focus on different functions of the comma. Ask the children to find examples of its use to separate items in complex lists and to mark grammatical boundaries in sentences.

● For a word-level focus, you could challenge the children to find all the words in the text with the letter string *ow* (*yellow, now, down, own, how*), to identify the different pronunciations, and suggest more words of each kind.

Talk, read and write

● Look again at the section on *New medicines* and ask the children to suggest other possible views on the issue, for example, that testing medicines on animals is acceptable because the lives of human beings are worth more than the lives of animals. Use shared writing strategies to compose a short paragraph presenting this view. Take suggestions on how it could begin: *Another group...* or *Some people go even further. They argue that...*, and include connectives in the sentence constructions.

● Ask the children to put forward and justify their own views on the use of animals. This could be done as a formal whole-class debate or in groups with a chairperson. Allow some informal discussion and planning time first.

Extension

Challenge the children to write a discussion text on *Animals for food*. Alternatively, they could write a persuasive text in which they argue their own view on testing medicines on animals. To increase the challenge, you could ask confident writers to write a response to someone who has an extreme view on one of these issues.

Text extract from "Tomorrow's Earth: A Squeaky-Green Guide" by David Bellamy © 1991, David Bellamy © 1991, Mitchell Beazley); photos monkey © Tash Whiteley, mouse © Daniel Heitz, fur coat © 2006, Jupiter Images Corporation, slippers © Crystal Woroniuk.

4: 3: T23: to present a point of view in writing, linking points persuasively and selecting style and vocabulary appropriate to the reader

4: 3: S2: to identify the common punctuation marks and respond to them appropriately when reading

4: 3: S4: to understand the use of connectives to structure an argument

subheadings identify topics under discussion

wording indicates author's opinion

'ow' letter string

commas mark grammatical boundaries

Animal Rights and Human Wrongs

Scientists working in research laboratories have invented new medicines, antiseptics, vaccines and antibiotics. They help to control many killer diseases, such as malaria, cholera, yellow fever, smallpox and typhoid.

New Medicines

The scientists soon realised that the new cures for the diseases had to be tested to make sure they were safe before they could be given to people. They decided to carry out many of the tests on animals, such as rats and mice, and even cats, dogs, marmosets, monkeys and chimpanzees.

Some people argue that this is all right, as long as the tests are really necessary. And that the work is done by professional, caring people who obey all the rules laid down by the government.

Other people strongly disagree and say that we have no right to treat animals in this way. Most people now agree that using animals to test cosmetics and household goods is wrong.

There is more good news on the way because scientists are now able to do many of the tests on cell cultures in laboratories and not on live animals.

What You Can Do to Help

Always buy cosmetics and household goods which bear the label, "Not tested on animals".

Animal Furs

Until quite recently, many ladies longed to own a fur coat. They gave little thought to how the animals were caught and killed. Farms of mink, chinchilla and Arctic fox boosted the supply of valuable furs.

Some people campaigned that it was wrong to trap such beautiful animals, let alone breed them in tiny cages, just for vanity. Today, thanks to these people, fur coats are no longer as popular. Many new and beautiful synthetic furs look just as good and are as warm.

But what about the problem of leather coats, belts and shoes, and killing animals for food?

Some people say we have the right to kill animals as long as no cruelty is involved. Others say no animal should be killed to provide us with anything at all.

4: 3: T16: to read, compare and evaluate examples of arguments and discussions

commas separate items in lists

comma signals pause

commas separate items in list

'ow' letter string

after factual focus, author's views become evident

4: 3: W6: to spell words with common letter strings but different pronunciations

Telling about bullying
by Rosemary Stones

Background

This text is taken from *Don't pick on me: How to handle bullying*. The book provides a detailed exploration of different kinds of bullying, illustrating the subject with case studies. Its main aim is to arm young people with practical, effective strategies for combatting bullying, and it is written specifically for this audience in a direct, personal style. In this extract, Rosemary Stones presents a range of responses to bullying, but makes her own view very clear.

What's on the CD-ROM

This is a conversation between two people with different ideas on what to do about bullying. The text picks up on several of the ideas in the core text, and brings them to life as they might feature in a real dialogue. It can be used as an introduction to the core text or to show another way of representing a discussion.

Discussing the text

● Read the first sentence and ask: *Whose view is this? What effect does this sentence have?* The author begins by forcefully expressing her own opinion. Encourage children to say whether they agree with this view, giving reasons to support it. Read on to the end of the first paragraph to see how the author develops and supports it.

● Highlight the two-part connective *not only… but*, and check that the children understand the relationship it sets up between the two ideas in the sentence.

● Focus on the four insults in the last sentence and ask why the words are inside speech marks. Explain that these are examples of name-calling that some people use and that the speech marks show that they intended to hurt people's feelings, not to describe what they are really like.

● Read the next paragraph. Focusing on the first two sentences, ask: *Whose views are these? How do we know?* Help the children to see that the author is reporting other people's views, not her own, and that this is signalled by the phrases *Some adults* and *Many of them*, and by the speech marks around *bullying is good for you* and *toughens you up*. Tease out these ideas by asking: *What three reasons do people give for not telling about bullying?*

Show how these are indicated by the repeated use of the connective *or* in the long second sentence.

● Read the final paragraph and consider how the text ends. Elicit that Rosemary Stones' aim is different here. Instead of commenting on how some people respond to bullying, she offers readers support and practical advice. Notice also that she ends as she began – by stating her own opinion in strong terms.

● Finish by making the more general point that some discussion texts work like this: authors present a range of views, comment on and criticise them, and make their own view very clear. You could emphasise this by highlighting sentences expressing the author's view and sentences expressing other views in different colours.

● To extend sentence-level work, ask the children to find and name all the different punctuation marks used in the text, and discuss their functions.

Talk, read and write

● Encourage the children to discuss the merits of the various ideas about bullying given in the text. Remember that this discussion will need to be handled sensitively and with regard to school policy on the issue.

● Alongside this discussion, encourage comment on the text by asking questions such as: *Does the author make you think differently about bullying? Does she express her view clearly and forcefully? Is she fair to people with other views?*

● If the school policy on bullying is presented in a form for children (for example a notice), read this together and discuss it in the light of the text. *Does it give clear and helpful advice? Could it be improved?* If it is not presented for this audience, use shared writing strategies to draft such a notice, drawing on ideas in the text and revising instructional/advice writing styles.

Extension

Ask children to write a story about a bullying incident in which the victim responds in one of the ways mentioned in the text: 'telling' or trying to 'cope on their own'.

4: 3: T21: to assemble and sequence points in order to plan the presentation of a point of view

semicolon between closely related but independent clauses

connective indicates alternative

reminder of the idea given in brackets

text closes with encouragement and advice

4: 3: S4: to understand the use of connectives to structure an argument

Photos: © Jupiter Images Corporation 2006

Text extract from "Don't Pick on Me" by Rosemary Stones © 1993; 2005, Rosemary Stones (2005, Picadilly Press).

Telling About Bullying

The rule that you should never tell about bullying is a rule invented by bullies for their own benefit. Obviously, it makes things very convenient for them! Not only can they bully in peace but a victim of their bullying cannot complain about it without being called a 'grass', a 'telltale', a 'cry-baby' or a 'wimp'.

Some adults are confused about whether telling about bullying is a good thing or a bad thing. Many of them were taught as children that 'bullying is good for you' (it 'toughens you up'); or that it's something you learn to cope with as you get older; or that there's something dishonourable or humiliating in asking for help when you're being bullied – you ought to be able to deal with it yourself. This idea (that bullying is something you should be able to cope with on your own) is very widespread. The people who work on phone helplines report fewer calls from older children even though people in this age group are still bullied – perhaps they are embarrassed to ask for help, feeling that they should be able to cope on their own.

Some people do find ways to cope on their own but some can't. Sometimes the bullying is so severe that no one could deal with it on their own. Remember, even adults are bullied! There is never anything wrong with asking for help. (In fact it takes great courage and strength to do it.)

author begins by giving her own view…

…then teases it out and supports it

connectives join the two ideas

examples of name-calling given in speech marks

speech marks present what other people say, suggests author does not agree

evidence to support point just made

4: 3: T16: to read, compare and evaluate examples of arguments and discussions

4: 3: S2: to identify the common punctuation marks and respond to them appropriately when reading

Slam brake on carnage

from 'Voice of the Mirror' (*Daily Mirror* website)

Background

This editorial is from the *Daily Mirror* website in September 2005. It was written immediately following a major road accident and refers to the photograph and report on this on the front page of the paper. In a thoughtful and concerned tone the editorial expresses the newspaper's response to this event and suggests a number of measures that could be taken to reduce the risk of further accidents. Unconventional sentence structures and dramatic vocabulary hold the reader's attention and emphasise the seriousness of the situation.

What's on the CD-ROM

This is a newspaper editorial urging traffic calming measures where a child has recently been injured on his way to school. It has much in common with the core text, but takes a stronger line in arguing for one particular course of action and is written in simpler language. It can be used as a text for less able readers and is useful for comparing discursive and persuasive approaches in editorials.

Discussing the text

● Explain that this is a newspaper *editorial*, revising the word from Term 1 and earlier this term. Read the headline and ask the children to predict what will follow. *What has happened? What might the editorial say?*

● Ask the children what they notice about the language of the headline: the powerful words, the appropriate image created and the imperative form. Talk about the aim of the headline to attract attention and to shock.

● Read the editorial together. Prompt the children to explore and respond to it by asking questions such as: *What has happened? What kinds of accident are being compared? What does the editorial say is the problem? Where does the text begin saying what could be done about it?* (Paragraph five.) Identify the three suggested measures and reinforce that putting forward suggestions in this way is typical of discussion texts.

● Re-read the text, highlighting features of style. Focusing on the first two paragraphs, ask the children if they can see another way to punctuate the first two sentences. Elicit that these could be joined into one sentence with a comma after *media*. Ask why the writer has used two sentences across two paragraphs. Draw out the idea that this increases the impact. Pursue this by looking at paragraph four, where the three sentences would more usually be linked together as one. Repunctuate in this way (with commas after *gun* and *driver*), and discuss the effect.

● Returning to the start of the editorial, pick out the connective *Yet* (in second paragraph). Check that the children understand the link between ideas that it sets up. Ask them to find other connectives and to identify how they link ideas. These include some less common connectives: *even more so* in paragraph four, *while* in paragraph six, *for* in paragraph seven.

● Remind the children of the dramatic language of the headline and see if they can find other examples, particularly adjective–noun combinations and powerful verbs: *huge coverage, horrific smash, robbed... of their lives, awful consequences, split-second of folly.* Try substituting more neutral words (such as *wide-scale reporting, serious accident, killed,* for the first three examples above), and discuss the effect of such changes. Make the wider point that this dramatic, extravagant style is typical of 'sensational' tabloid journalism.

● For word-level work, focus on extending words with suffixes, using the following words as examples: *coverage, horrific, excessive, motorist, carelessness.* Ask the children to identify the root word and suffix and to explain how the addition changes the word class, such as, from noun *horror* to adjective *horrific*.

Talk, read and write

● Encourage the children to evaluate the effectiveness of the text by asking: *Does this editorial give you new ideas about road safety? Do you think the writer uses language well to hold your attention and make you think? Is it likely to make people change their minds? Why? Why not?*

● Challenge the children to compose headlines and opening paragraphs for editorials on other kinds of accidents.

Extension

Ask children to write a list of safety points for a familiar context, such as a swimming pool.

4: 3: T17: to know how arguments are presented

4: 3: W8: to practise extending and compounding words through adding parts; revise and reinforce earlier work on prefixes and suffixes

describes the problem

connective indicates contrast

temporal connective for things happening at same time

emotive language

4: 3: S4: to use connectives to structure an argument

Mirror.co.uk
THE BEST NEWSPAPER ON THE WEB

Search The web ▾ For

Home | **News** | Sport | TV & Film | More> |

Mirror.co.uk
THE BEST NEWSPAPER ON THE WEB

VOICE OF THE MIRROR

SLAM BRAKE ON CARNAGE

WHEN a plane or train crashes there is huge coverage by the media.

Yet cars remain a greater danger. Each year in Britain around 3,500 people are killed in motor accidents and ten times that number are badly injured.

Today the Mirror reports on a horrific smash which robbed six people – five of them teenagers – of their lives. Yet every day there are accidents which have similarly awful consequences.

A car can be as a dangerous as a gun. Especially in the hands of a young, inexperienced driver. And even more so if the car has been adapted to travel faster.

It might be that young people should be banned from driving vehicles which can move at excessive speeds. The government should be looking at this.

It should also take a twin-track approach to making roads safer by attacking bad driving while educating all motorists on the importance of safety.

For the consequences of a split-second of folly or just carelessness can be seen in the tragic picture on today's front page.

dramatic language and imperative form to grab reader's attention

idea split across paragraphs for impact

refers to news event in powerful, dramatic words

idea split into three sentences for impact

suggestion for action to take

causal connective

4: 3: T16: to read, compare and evaluate examples of arguments and discussions

4: 3: T23: to present a point of view in writing, linking points persuasively and selecting style and vocabulary appropriate to the reader

4: 3: S2: to identify the common punctuation marks and respond to them appropriately when reading

Clean up this mess
from 'Voice of the Mirror' (*Daily Mirror* website)

Background

This is another editorial from the *Daily Mirror* website from June 2005. The preceding few days had seen a succession of extreme weather events in the UK. The cause was being hotly debated and many argued that global warming was to blame. The editorial states that this was *at least partly* the cause. It then goes on to argue that people need to take personal responsibility for the problem and its solution. The editorial includes several concepts that are likely to need discussion with the class.

What's on the CD-ROM

This skeleton plan maps out the ideas raised in the editorial and develops the point about travel. This represents the underlying argument in three steps (problem, cause, solution) and shows how each is elaborated. This plan can be used as an introduction to the core text and/or to highlight the argument. It can also be used to illustrate the 'basic point plus elaboration' structure – an important strategy for planning and writing persuasive texts.

Discussing the text

● Tell the class where the text comes from and outline the background. Read the headline and first two paragraphs and ask the children to explain the point the author is making. As part of this, discuss the meanings of *lifestyle, luxury, great boons* and *heavy price tag*. Note the importance of the connective *But*, prominently placed at the start of a paragraph, in linking the ideas.

● Read the next three paragraphs and ask: *What does the text say is the cause of the extreme weather? What two things does the text say cause global warming?* Check that the children understand the terms *convenience shopping* and *attractive marketing.*

● Ask the children to predict how the text will develop and read the remaining paragraphs. Confirm that the text goes on to try to persuade readers of the seriousness of the problem and of the action they need to take to help solve it. Refer to the causes of global warming identified earlier and ask the children which one is followed through (rubbish, not travel). Note again the connective *But*, used twice at the start of sentences.

● Now shift your focus to the language of the editorial. Ask: *How does the author try to persuade readers that they need to take the problem seriously and do something?* If necessary, provide a clue by highlighting the phrase *destruction of the planet*, and then prompt the children to identify other powerful words and images, such as, *extraordinary extremes of weather, overwhelming mass of packaging, gigantic garbage heap, mess*. Point out too how the comforts of contemporary lifestyles are emphasised by words and phrases like *luxury, great boons of modern living*. Draw out the idea that the author is trying to provoke the reader into action by making him or her feel guilty; the editorial is a kind of 'telling off'.

● For a word-level focus, highlight the words *responsible, attractive, destruction* and *generations* as starting points for work on the suffixes *-ible, -ive* and *-tion*. Ask the children to suggest more words ending with these suffixes and to identify their word class: *-ible* and *-ive* are endings for adjectives; *-tion* and *-ation* for nouns. Then highlight the issue of meaning and use by asking the children to use root and derived words in pairs of sentences. For example, *The wind was strong enough to destroy buildings. There was much destruction.*

Talk, read and write

● Ask the children if they think the editorial will succeed in making people change how they live. Focus their attention on strengths and weaknesses in the argument and the use of evocative language.

● In shared writing, compose additional paragraphs for the editorial about the need for people to travel less. Choose language carefully in order to persuade readers to make changes in their lives.

Extension

Invite the children to write a letter to the newspaper in response to this editorial. Most will probably want to agree and then say what they will do, but you could challenge others to think of arguments against. For example, it's better if recycling is left to big organisations like councils; future generations will just have to look after themselves.

Term 3: Newspaper editorial

4: 3: T18: to investigate how style and vocabulary are used to convince the intended reader

4: 3: S4: to use connectives to structure an argument

4: 3: T17: to know how arguments are presented

4: 3: T23: to present a point of view in writing

4: 3: W9: to recognise and spell the suffixes -ible, -ive and -tion

reference to recent news to show relevance of issue

paragraphs outline causes of climate change; very short paragraphs typical of tabloid newspapers

dramatic contrast

suffix 'ible'

play on words/meanings

suffix 'tion'

prominently placed connective to highlight the argument

powerful words to drive home idea

suffix 'ive'

some concession made, but prominently placed connective highlights rebuttal

strongly worded summing up

Mirror.co.uk THE BEST NEWSPAPER ON THE WEB Search [The web] For

Home | **News** | Sport | TV & Film | More>

VOICE OF THE MIRROR

CLEAN UP THIS MESS

MOST families in this country now enjoy a lifestyle which previous generations would have called luxury.

But the great boons of modern living carry a heavy price tag. They are contributing to the destruction of the planet.

The extraordinary extremes of weather we witness nowadays – like the thunderstorms, floods and heatwaves of the past week – are at least partly due to global warming.

Which is mainly caused by our love of travel by road and air.

And our way of life, dominated by convenience shopping and attractive marketing, produces an overwhelming mass of packaging.

That and the other rubbish we generate, could eventually turn this green and pleasant land into a gigantic garbage heap.

The past few years have seen a significant increase in the amount of rubbish we recycle. But it is still far from enough and some areas lag pathetically far behind.

Councils have a big part to play in making recycling easier. But, ultimately, it is up to us to be responsible for our own mess.

We should not expect to enjoy the pleasures of modern life at the same time as we are destroying the planet for future generations.

Treats with a bit of Wonka magic

Text from "Sussex Express" Friday 5th August 2005 © 2005, Sussex Express; photo posed by model © 2006, Jupiter Images Corporation/John Pilge

Willy Wonka would be right at home in Uckfield's newest sweet shop.

The Sugar Mouse at Bridge Cottage sells the kind of handmade confectionery that would not look out of place at his sweet factory: from humbugs to old-fashioned lemonade sherbet.

The shop, opened only three weeks ago, is owned by 17-year-old Chantel Elliott, who is in her second year of Business Studies at Sussex Downs College.

Chantel's mother, Iris Elliott, said: 'Chantel has been so focused on this venture. She has personally picked every sweet, sweet jar and wrapper. Her father and I have helped out but this shop is testament to her hard work and dedication.'

After dreaming up the idea Chantel spent a considerable amount of time sourcing the best confectioners in the country and eventually discovered 72-year-old sweet maker Dave Keyanne.

Mr Keyanne, who owns Keyanne Confectioners, served as a consultant to the sweet manufacturers on Tim Burton's new film *Charlie and the Chocolate Factory* starring Johnny Depp. He not only makes the vast majority of the products sold in the shop but has also given Chantel invaluable advice and expertise.

Iris said: 'The list of sweets we stock is never-ending, everything from broken rock, original cough candy, bullseyes and carbolic drops to liquorice and sour plums.'

'We get so many different types of people in here. Some of our older customers say they haven't seen some of these sweets since their childhood. Sometimes people ask for specific sweets that we don't stock, so Chantel phones Dave and he either makes them for her or finds out where to get them.'

Not one to sit back and enjoy the sweet rewards of all her hard work, Chantel is looking to expand her empire and is considering the possibility of opening another shop in the foreseeable future.

VOICE OF THE MIRROR

SERVE THE KIDS BETTER

School dinners were never considered gourmet food. But at least previous generations found them edible and nutritious.

Yet years of privatised school lunches have led to a disgraceful state of affairs. It took Jamie Oliver to expose how bad they can be.

Shockingly, the reality in some places is even worse than Jamie found.

Today the *Daily Mirror* publishes photographs taken in one school that reveal just how disgusting the stuff dished up for children can be.

The reason is obvious. The days when all schools had dinner ladies cooking meals on site are long gone.

Instead big companies mass-produce them – often miles from where they are served. They spend as little as possible on the food so they can make profits that run into tens of millions.

So these companies make a fortune while children are given cheap rubbish to eat.

The look of it turns them off and if they do force it down, it does them little good.

Jamie Oliver woke the nation's conscience by reminding us that what people eat is almost as important as what they learn.

The government responded positively to him but it needs to do more than simply say meals should improve.

It must stop companies exploiting children and schools and insist that decent food is always served.

Heading and extract from "Voice of the Mirror" 12 May 2005 © 2005, Mirror Group (www.mirror.co.uk)

HomeNews

Front Page	
Home News	
World News	
Health News	
Earth News	
Science News	
Sport News	
Timeout	
Mailbag	
Competitions	
Conservation	
Subscriptions	
Parents	
Teachers	
Contact Us	

Photo © Vincent Curutchet/DPPI Offshore Challenges Group

Why is Ellen such star?

Ellen MacArthur is a star. She is a yachtswoman who has, against all odds, smashed the solo, round-the-world non-stop speed record at her very first attempt. Only a year ago, Frenchman Francis Joyon had set a blistering pace by taking three whole weeks off the previous fastest time. At 72 days, Joyon's record was expected to stand for at least ten years.

Then along came Ellen.

For 71 days she had no more than 20 minutes' sleep at a time, having to be on constant lookout day and night. Alone she roared on. Up to six times a day she had to haul down and change the sails. It is heavy work. When something broke she had to fix it. Never once could she relax. Never once, until the moment her trimaran B&Q finally crossed the finishing line, could she afford to take her eyes off that ever-ticking clock.

The journey round the world took Ellen all alone through some of the most terrifying seas on earth. She battled difficult winds, mountainous waves and almost collided with a whale. One capsize would have been the end. A trimaran like B&Q, unlike a mono-hull yacht, cannot be righted once it goes over.

Yet, on the very last leg, it was the lack of wind that came close to ruining it for her. A craft with only sails to drive it goes nowhere on a windless sea.

But Ellen is not the first to sail solo around the world. She is not even the first woman to do it. So why have we all been so gripped and amazed as we look on in awe?

It could be that what Ellen does is against all odds.

Ellen MacArthur is a young woman in a man's world. A lone, long-distance sailor must handle and control a large racing yacht single-handed. He must be brave enough to take on the worst that oceans and weather can throw at him. He is big and strong with untidy hair and beard. He is a man, in other words, and a tough one too. He is also not particularly young and will have been at sea since babyhood. Ellen, in contrast is a surprise.

First she is a very young woman, small and neat, and Ellen is from middle England. She was born and brought up in Derbyshire. The sea is far away but, from the age of eight, Ellen was smitten by the sea. Her heroes were famous long-distance sailors, men like Sir Francis Chichester, Sir Robin Knox-Johnson and Sir Chay Blythe. She met them only in books.

The story goes on that, to get her first boat, Ellen had to save up her school dinner money. It took three years. Eight years later Ellen was taking her second boat, a 21-foot (7-metre) yacht all the way round the treacherous British coast.

Yes, Ellen MacArthur is a true star. Now the Queen is to honour her as Dame Ellen MacArthur. She will be the youngest woman ever to have been awarded this highest honour.

That we all adore her could simply be that we are in absolute awe of her utterly amazing courage, her modesty and her quite remarkable skill.

Heading and extract from "The Newspaper" http: thenewspaper.org.uk © 2005, Young Media Holdings Ltd

Search | The web ▼ | For [_____] GO

Home | **News** | Sport | TV & Film | More> |

VOICE OF THE MIRROR

CHARLIE AND THE CHOCOLATE FACTORY
★★

PS2, XBox, PC
£30
Out now

This summer sees the release of *Charlie and the Chocolate Factory*, a madcap remake by madcap director Tim Burton of a madcap movie based on the madcap book by madcap author Roald Dahl.

So a game based on such madcap heritage should be pretty darn fun. Right?

The game attempts to veer slightly from the film's familiar factory-tour plot line, instead finding Charlie Bucket rescuing the other naughty tour goers from the predicaments their greedy exploits place them in.

Charlie has to work together with teams of the iconic Oompa Loompas to free each trapped naughty child, often encountering platforming elements along the way.

Sadly, the missions become repetitive, with objectives often difficult to spot.

Paired with unresponsive controls, you soon wish the game was a simple exploration of Wonka's world, which surely would be entertaining enough?

Graphically the game is inconsistent. The super-stylised character models caricature their Hollywood counterparts marvellously, but the environments they inhabit are less impressive.

The factory, so lush in the movie, appears sparse. The saturated colours often cause confusion too, leading to difficulties in navigating the gaming world.

Charlie and the Chocolate Factory does have a great soundtrack, however. Perky yet slightly creepy tunes complement the quirky settings perfectly.

There are also outstanding voice-overs from all key actors from the film, bar Johnny Depp as Willy Wonka (whose voice double does a remarkable job nonetheless).

So, Oompa loompa dompa dee do, is this game worth recommending to you?

Though children may be enchanted by the prospect of guiding Charlie around the factory, tedious tasks and poor graphics mean this candy caper may lead to an upset tummy.

Catch the movie instead.

Gerald Lynch

Heading and review from www.mirror.co.uk 2nd August 2005 by Gerald Lynch © 2005, Mirror Group

Design and images © 2006, Scholastic Ltd

write here right now!
letters

★ star letter ★

Dear Sir

As an ex-school cook I read your editorial about school dinners with great interest.

Your photos are shocking, but they didn't come as a surprise to me. I know just how bad the food in many schools is nowadays. That's why I left my job. I just couldn't bear to dish out food like that any longer. I wouldn't have given it to my dog. We should all thank Jamie Oliver for exposing this scandal.

And I agree that the big so-called food companies are to blame. They're only interested in one thing: making money.

Certainly bringing back proper school cooks would be a step in the right direction. But we'd be fooling ourselves if we thought it would solve the problem on its own. No, the real issue is money. Good food doesn't come cheap. Like most people, I'd like to see every school serving tasty, nutritious, freshly cooked food. But that will cost. Are parents prepared to pay more? I'm not sure.

And another thing. We need to ditch this nonsense about choice. When I was at school, there was just one meal. We all ate the same thing, and I don't remember any grumbling.

Surely everyone agrees that this is one area where adults know best. We need to give children what's good for them, not what they want.

Yours

Brenda Harley

Text © 2007, Chris Lutrario

TINA BAKER

HER PERSONAL TAKE ON TV

Animal magic

BBC2's forthcoming new series, *Manhunters*, dramatises tales of creatures partial to the Atkins diet chasing their version of fast food – fleeing humans. The drama element is the latest take on natural history, because, it seems, straightforward pictures of wild beasties just aren't exciting enough anymore.

Recently, we had the strange wildlife-meets-CSI hybrid, *Animal Crime Scene* – where investigations of animal 'murder mysteries' were used as a device to jazz up a nature programme. Along with an authoritative voiceover from that nice Mr Attenborough and more experts than you could you shake a stick at, this series also used sophisticated computer-generated images to spice up the visuals.

Before that, there was the wildlife-as-wrestling-fodder genre, using the likes of Steve Leonard to poke, provoke and leap upon unsuspecting species and writhe around on the ground with them a bit. Steve Irwin even made a career out of his enthusiastic crocodile-tormenting tactics.

And, previously, there were the animal docusoaps like *Vets in Practice* and *Animal Hospital*. Human interest was the added element here. When Rolf Harris dabbed his eyes and placed a consoling arm around a bereaved pet owner, the nation sobbed in unison.

All these 'new improved' animal programmes make me quite nostalgic for the days where they'd point a camera at a wildebeest and just see what it did. The most intervention viewers experienced then was Johnny Morris adding daft voices to shots of zoo animals getting on with their everyday business.

But now wildlife shows are like the last series of *Big Brother* – it's all about manipulation. Either the creatures themselves are prodded into a reaction, or we the audience are cajoled into a response thanks to clever editing and emotive storylines.

Perhaps I should start training my cats to juggle – it can only be a matter of time before 'Pet X Factor' is the next big thing.

Extract from 'Animal Magic' by Tina Baker from "TV Times" 1–7 October 2005 © 2005, Tina Baker/TV Times/IPC+ Syndication (2005, IPC Media); photo courtesy of the TFA Group www.tfa-group.com

SCHOOL THINNER

By ROSA PRINCE
Political Correspondent

CHIPS could be rationed in school dinners under Government plans to improve pupils' diets.

Other fried foods such as turkey twizzlers and chicken nuggets may be kicked off the menu altogether if they exceed new fat or salt content limits.

The ideas are being considered by the School Meals review panel, set up in the wake of the *Daily Mirror* campaign to improve pupils' dinners along with TV chef Jamie Oliver.

Panellists are due to report back to Education secretary Ruth Kelly this month and have been ordered to view the proposals favourably.

A Department for Education spokeswoman said: "Part of the panel's brief was to consider rationing or eliminating altogether unhealthy food from school menus.

"They have not reported back yet and we do not know what they will recommend. But certainly it is not unlikely at all that this will happen."

The rationing plan was first suggested by the National Health Forum and Caroline Walker Trust. They demanded salt be banned altogether

Chips rationing plan to cut fat in pupils' food

from school menus and chips rationed to one portion a week.

Fat content would be limited to 10 per cent – so products such as beefburgers, which have up to 19 per cent fat, nuggets, 17, and twizzlers, 21 – would join a food blacklist. Some favourites, such as chips, would be rationed rather than rejected as nutritionists agree children need occasional treats.

But rather than greasy thin fries, dinner ladies will serve relatively low fat chunky

chips with skins for extra nutrition.

Cakes and ice-cream will always be accompanied by fruit and caterers will receive training in healthy food preparation. Oily fish – especially beneficial for growing youngsters – is to be served at least once a week. Out go mushy peas and boiled cabbage. In come lentils, rice, salads and lean cuts of meat.

The Government is also considering banning fizzy pop from schools, with water from fountains or kiosks available all day.

The Department of Education has set aside £90 million over the next three years to improve school kitchens. Many only have facilities to reheat, boil or microwave pre-processed meals, but ministers want all pupils to benefit from fresh ingredients cooked on the premises.

There are now about a million obese children in England.

Ministers were prompted to take action over the poor quality of school meals by Channel 4's *Jamie's School Dinners*.

The *Mirror* also campaigned for an increase in the amount spent on pupils – and we reported last week how it is set to rise from 37p per pupil to between 50p and 60p by 2007.

'School Thinner' by Rosa Prince from "Daily Mirror" Monday 5th September 2005 © 2005, Mirror Group; photo © 2006, Jupiter Images Corporation

Brush and ink paintings

ANY THICK WHITE PAPER

The best kind of brush to use for pictures like these are soft-haired brushes which have a pointed tip. Chinese or Japanese lettering brushes are ideal for these techniques.

Mixing the inks

To do the paintings on these pages, you need to use three shades of one colour of ink. Use ink from a bottle or snip the end off an ink cartridge.

Add a few drops of ink to water in a small container to make a watery ink.

Mix a medium shade by adding more drops of ink to water in another container.

Undiluted ink. Use straight from a bottle or squeeze the ink from a cartridge into a container.

Bamboo

Practise on scrap paper before doing a large picture.

Use a soft brush with a pointed tip.

Use the width of the bristles to paint.

1. Dip your brush in the watery ink, then dab the bristles on a paper towel. Paint a section of a stem.

Don't put more ink on your brush.

2. Paint another two sections above the first one. Leave a small space between each section.

Use the tip of brush to begin with, then increase the pressure.

3. Using the medium ink and the tip of your brush, add branches coming out from the stem.

4. Add twigs onto the branches. Leave a small space between one twig and the next one.

Use undiluted ink.

5. For a leaf, press lightly on the tip of the brush, then press a little harder, then press lightly again.

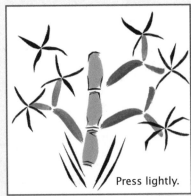

Press lightly.

6. Use the tip of the brush and undiluted ink to paint grass and lines at the joints on the stem.

photos © 2006, Jupiter Images Corporation

illustrations © 2007, Scholastic Ltd:

Extract from "The Usborne Book of Art Ideas" by Fiona Watt © 1999, Usborne Publishing Ltd;

Friction

Down the slippery slope

Equipment

- a small block of wood, about 10cm by 5cm
- a plank of wood, about 20cm wide and 1m long
- large building blocks or bricks

IMPORTANT The blocks must all be the same size

- different materials for covering the plank, for example, carpet, aluminium foil, sandpaper, newspaper, sheet of rubber, shiny paper, cloth
- pencil and paper for recording

SURFACE	NUMBER OF BRICKS
Newspaper	3

Aim

To investigate the slipperiness of different surfaces.

How to carry out the investigation

- Draw up a two-column chart. Give the left-hand column the heading 'Surface'. Give the right-hand column the heading 'Number of bricks'.
- Choose one of the materials and cover the plank with it. Write the name of this material in the 'Surface' column.
- Lean the plank against one of the bricks to make a ramp.
- Place the small wooden block at the top of the ramp, and let go of it. If it moves, write 1 in the 'Number of bricks' column. If it does not move, add another block to the pile to make the ramp steeper. Put the small block at the top again, and let go. If it moves, write the number 2 in the 'Number of bricks' column. If it does not move, keep adding blocks to the pile until it does. Record the number of bricks.
- Repeat for the other surfaces.

IMPORTANT Make sure the test is fair:

Always put the block down at the same point on the plank. Don't push the block. Just let go.

Draw your conclusions

Which surface is the most slippery? The least slippery? You could list the surfaces in order of slipperiness.

What do you notice about the slippery surfaces? What do you think makes them slippery? Do they have anything in common?

Take the investigation further

Did some surfaces take the same number of blocks before the small block moved? How could you find out which of these surfaces was the most slippery?

Text © 2007, Chris Lutrario; illustration © Garry Davies

Pancakes

Makes 8

Ingredients
100g/4oz plain flour
Pinch of salt
1 egg
300ml/½ pint milk
Butter for cooking

Eat with:
SWEET: Maple syrup, freshly squeezed lemon or orange juice, and sugar.
SAVOURY: Grated cheese and cooked ham.

Fancy a bit of early morning juggling? Then try pancakes. These treats tick all the boxes. They're tasty, popular, quick to prepare and make easy eating. Team them with whatever extras take your fancy. If you like, make your mix the night before. Store in the fridge in your measuring jug. Just before you're ready to cook, give the mix a couple of good whisks with a fork. Now it's ready to pour into your pan. Warning: the first pancake of the batch often sticks and needs chucking away. If this happens to you, you're not a failure.

Method

1. Sift the flour and salt into a bowl. Make a deep dent in the flour. Crack the egg and drop it into this hole.

2. Tip a good glug of milk on to the unbeaten egg. With your wooden spoon, start to beat the egg and milk together in a circular movement without mixing in too much of the flour at first.

3. Gradually mix in the rest of the flour and start to beat everything furiously. Hold on to the bowl with one hand as you do this. Tip the bowl to one side slightly if it helps. The aim is to build up some real wrist action to make sure that the batter becomes smooth while it's still very thick.

4. Add the rest of the milk bit by bit, beating until you have a lovely smooth thin batter. If it's not entirely smooth you can always use a balloon whisk to blitz those blobs out.

5. Heat a pancake pan or small frying pan. You want it hot enough to make the butter sizzle when you chuck it in.

6. Use a little knob of butter to coat the pan very lightly. If the butter starts to go brown it's beginning to burn and starts to taste bitter, so whip the pan off the heat if this happens.

7. Pour 2–3 tablespoons of batter into your pan and swirl it round immediately so that it coats the entire surface.

8. Now cook until you think the underside is done. Check by flicking up the edge of the pancake with your spatula. If it's cooked it is lightly browned and it doesn't stick.

9. Tossing time. Or play it safe and use a fish slice or spatula to turn the pancake over.

10. Cook second side till light brown and serve immediately.

Variation
At STEP 6, toss a handful of blueberries into the pan till they're softening and oozing juices, then pour in batter mix. Cook. Don't toss – turn with a spatula.

Extract from "Cooking up a storm" by Sam and Susan Stern © 2005, Sam Stern and Susan Stern; photos © 2005, Trish Gant (2005, Walker Books Ltd)

Lewes town walk

The walk begins at the railway station, and takes about an hour and a half.

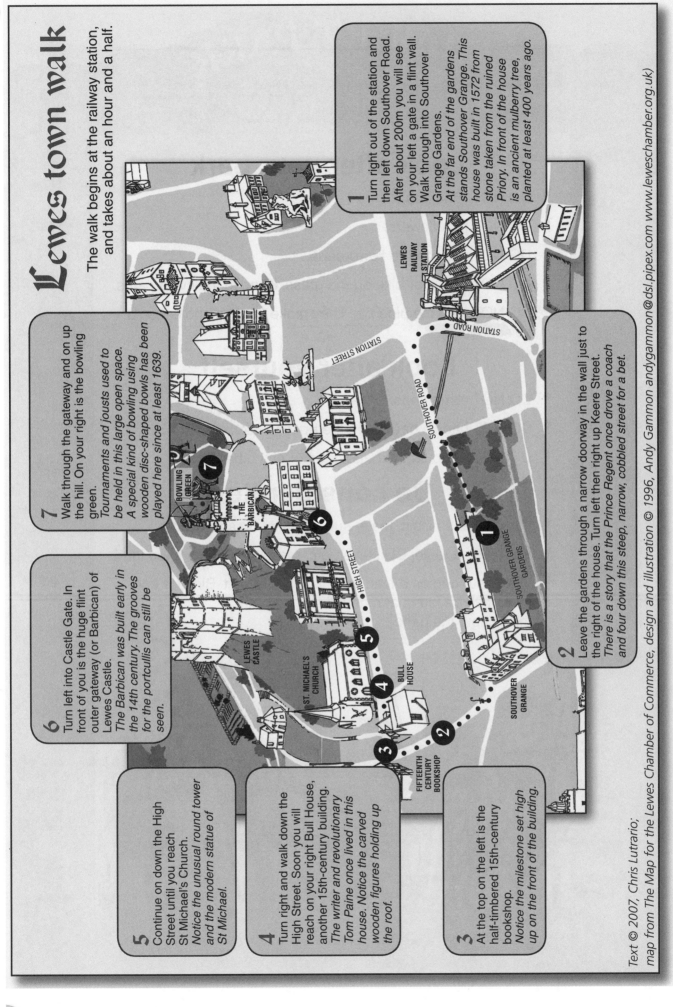

1
Turn right out of the station and then left down Southover Road. After about 200m you will see on your left a gate in a flint wall. Walk through into Southover Grange Gardens.
At the far end of the gardens stands Southover Grange. This house was built in 1572 from stone taken from the ruined Priory. In front of the house is an ancient mulberry tree, planted at least 400 years ago.

2
Leave the gardens through a narrow doorway in the wall just to the right of the house. Turn left then right up Keere Street.
There is a story that the Prince Regent once drove a coach and four down this steep, narrow, cobbled street for a bet.

3
At the top on the left is the half-timbered 15th-century bookshop.
Notice the milestone set high up on the front of the building.

4
Turn right and walk down the High Street. Soon you will reach on your right Bull House, another 15th-century building.
The writer and revolutionary Tom Paine once lived in this house. Notice the carved wooden figures holding up the roof.

5
Continue on down the High Street until you reach St Michael's Church.
Notice the unusual round tower and the modern statue of St Michael.

6
Turn left into Castle Gate. In front of you is the huge flint outer gateway (or Barbican) of Lewes Castle.
The Barbican was built early in the 14th century. The grooves for the portcullis can still be seen.

7
Walk through the gateway and on up the hill. On your right is the bowling green.
Tournaments and jousts used to be held in this large open space. A special kind of bowling using wooden disc-shaped bowls has been played here since at least 1639.

Text © 2007, Chris Lutrario; map from *The Map* for the Lewes Chamber of Commerce, design and illustration © 1996, Andy Gammon andygammon@dsl.pipex.com www.leweschamber.org.uk)

ALBERT PARK

Look after your park

- DO NOT light fires.
- DO NOT pick flowers.
- DO NOT walk on the flowerbeds.
- DO NOT ride your bike on the grass. Keep to the cycle paths.
- DO NOT feed the pigeons. They make a mess and cause a nuisance.

Look after yourself

- DO NOT climb trees.
- DO NOT paddle or swim in the boating lake.
- DO NOT climb on the bandstand or any other buildings.

Be considerate

- If you have a picnic, make sure you tidy up afterwards.
- If you use a radio, CD player, etc, make sure it is not too loud.
- Keep your dog on a lead and clean up after it. Bins for dog mess can be found at many different points throughout the park.

Text © 2007, Chris Lutrario; photos © 2006, Jupiter Images Corporation

Race to 100

for 2 to 4 players

What you need
- number cards 10–100
- a number line
- felt-tip pen
- 2 small counters
- 2 dice

Aim of the game
To move your counter from 1 to 100.

Getting ready
Shuffle the number cards and deal out 12 of them. Write the word UP above each of these numbers on the 100-square. Put these cards to one side. Shuffle the remaining cards and deal out 12 more. Write the word DOWN above each of these numbers.

Playing the game
1 Put your counters on 1. Decide who will start.

2 Roll the dice. Add the numbers shown together. Move your counter on that number of steps. If you land on an UP number, move on 10 steps. If you land on a DOWN number, go back 10 steps.

3 Take turns to roll the dice and move the counters until one of you passes 100. That person is the winner.

NOW make the game harder – and faster! Roll 3 dice each time. Choose two of the numbers to add together. Try to land on an UP number. Make sure you don't land on a DOWN number.

NOW make the game even harder! Roll 3 dice. Choose two of the numbers. Add, subtract, multiply or divide them to get the number that lets you move on the most steps. Try to land on an UP number. For example, if you rolled 6, 2 and 5 you could:
- add 6 and 5 to move on 11 steps
- subtract 5 from 6 to move on 1 step
- multiply 6 by 5 to move on 30 steps
- divide 6 by 2 to move on 3 steps.

You should be able to reach 100 very quickly!

Race to 100

START									
1	2	3	4	5	6	7	8	9	10
20	19	18	17	16	15	14	13	12	11
21	22	23	24	25	26	27	28	29	30
40	39	38	37	36	35	34	33	32	31
41	42	43	44	45	46	47	48	49	50
60	59	58	57	56	55	54	53	52	51
61	62	63	64	65	66	67	68	69	70
80	79	78	77	76	75	74	73	72	71
81	82	83	84	85	86	87	88	89	90
100	99	98	97	96	95	94	93	92	91
FINISH									

Text © 2007, Chris Lutrario; photos © 2006, Jupiter Images Corporation

FENG-SHUI
FOR YOUR BEDROOM

Feng-shui (pronounced foong shway) is an ancient Chinese art. Feng means wind or air and shui means water. According to the Chinese, wind and water carry an invisible life energy called ch'i, and you can bring good ch'i into your life by decorating your house in certain colours or positioning your furniture in certain ways. Why not try these five feng-shui tips to make your bedroom an oasis of calm and tranquility?

1 Think about where you position your bed.

For good ch'i you should be able to see the door from your bed but you shouldn't be facing it. And the head of the bed should always be placed against a wall so that you feel secure when you sleep. Try not to put your bed by or facing a window as this allows the ch'i to flow out of the room too quickly. If you can't avoid this because of the size/shape of your bedroom then hang a wind-chime over the window to disperse the ch'i evenly.

2 De-clutter your room.

One of the basic rules of feng-shui is to get rid of clutter. Clear out everything that you don't use or need. Try to leave the centre of the room clear and unobstructed so that the ch'i can flow through uninterrupted.

3 Don't have any electrical equipment by your bed.

The electro-magnetic fields from TVs, DVD players, stereos etc cause bad ch'i, so always switch off (by the wall socket) anything electric before you go to sleep. Remember to switch off your mobile too, and don't sleep with it by your pillow.

4 Go for soft colours.

Pastel colours or light blues and light greens encourage a sense of calm in your room which will help you rest better. The occasional splash of a vibrant colour such as red, perhaps as a lampshade or cushion is okay. Colours like red or gold are particularly good for energy and stimulation around your desk or study area, but avoid having these colours by your bed.

5 Keep your study area separate from your sleeping area.

Your bed and sleeping area should be a cosy, restful haven so if you have a computer or desk in your bedroom, keep them well away from your bed. Set aside a special study area, with no distractions and don't forget your vibrant colours such as red and gold to promote energy. Blue is also great in a study because it aids concentration.

Things to avoid:

Fans in your bedroom can disrupt the flow of ch'i, as can water such as fountains or aquariums, dried plants and flowers and more than three potted plants.

Daily life

Life in Athens was very different for men and women, the rich and poor, free citizens and slaves. Only wealthy Athenian men could really enjoy the freedom and cultural life that the city could offer. Women were expected to spend almost all their time looking after the home and the children, while slaves had no freedom at all – they were at the command of their masters.

A new birth

Athenians did not have large families. Boys were valued much more than girls. Girls also had the disadvantage of needing a dowry (money paid to the bridegroom's family) when they married. Unwanted babies were left out in the open to die: this was not a crime in Athens. Sometimes a family who could not have children would rescue an unwanted baby.

When a new child was born, its father proclaimed the birth by hanging an olive branch by the front door. About ten days after the birth there was a celebratory meal, and the family gave presents to the new baby. Poor women had to care for their own children, but many mothers had a slave to help nurse the baby.

Childhood games

Until the age of about 7, boys and girls were brought up at home. They played with dolls and balls, and may even have had a toy chariot to ride in. Mothers would tell their children stories and rhymes – they would for example have known Aesop's fables, stories about animals that you can still read today. At the age of about 7, girls began to help around the house – but boys were sent to school.

School

All but the poorest boys in Athens went to school from about 7 years old. They were put in the charge of a slave, known as a paidotribes, who took them to and from school, tested them on their work, and made sure they behaved. School was held in the house of the teacher. Boys learned to read and write, and to do arithmetic. They learned history from Greek writers. And as they got older, they learned to sing and play the lyre or flute.

Text extract from "Ancient Greece" by Peter Connolly © 2001, Oxford University Press (2001, OUP); images © 2006, Jupiter Images Corporation

Photo © Donna Murillo

Photo © Bjorn Lotz

Photo © Michelle Block

A middle-aged river

A stream

An estuary

Rivers

During its journey from source to mouth, a river changes both its look and nature. Rivers begin as narrow, fast-flowing streams in the mountains or hills, but by the time they reach the sea or a lake, they are wide and slow moving. At each stage the river supports different sorts of plants, birds and other wildlife.

What are young rivers like?

Near the source, streams usually move quickly, tumbling over boulders and cascading across moorland or through woods. The water will cut deep channels into the rock. If the water looks white it indicates that the bed or floor of the river is rocky.

What makes a river middle aged?

Gradually, these fast-moving streams will join up with others. The flow of the current begins to slow down and the river begins to get wider. The channels cut by the river get shallower. It is at this stage that this stretch of moving water can be called a river – a river is defined as a stretch of water more than five metres wide.

A middle-aged river often winds or meanders from side to side. Sometimes it will cut several channels in the land and create islands. Rivers at this stage do not often flow over a rock bed so it is rare to see any white water.

What is a river like in old age?

In the final stage of a river's life it moves slowly towards the sea. The course it runs is almost flat and the river banks spread out to form an estuary, or mouth. As the banks get wider they start to form the seashore.

Many rivers are tidal in their estuaries. This means that seawater rushes into the mouth and up the river as the tide comes in.

Text © 2007, Andrew Taylor

Tornadoes

A tornado is a strong, violently destructive wind made up of a spinning funnel of air. Tornadoes are sometimes nicknamed 'twisters', because of the way the air moves in a twisting spiral shape. Air speeds inside a tornado can reach up to 250 miles per hour.

Photo © Lauren Stephens

Tornadoes form beneath thunderclouds. Warm and cool air meet and create strong downdrafts of spinning air. This rapidly spinning air appears as a funnel-shaped cloud, stretching down beneath the storm cloud. As more and more air is sucked in, the funnel gets larger and may touch the ground. If this happens, the winds can cause devastating damage – uprooting trees, ripping buildings apart and lifting cars into the air. As the funnel sucks up the dust and debris in its path, it gets darker. It moves across the ground, following the path of the thundercloud above it.

Photo © Edward Warek

When a tornado forms over the sea, water is sucked into the funnel of air. This is called a waterspout. A tornado that happens over an area of desert sucks up sand and is called a dust devil.

Photo by Ian Dunsford © 2005, Birmingham City Council www.birmingham.gov.uk

Tornadoes can happen almost anywhere in the world, although they are much more common in some places, for example America, than in others. The mid-west states of the USA are known as Tornado Alley because there are so many tornadoes there each year. Tornadoes are much less common in Britain, although they do occur from time to time. On 27 July 2005, for example, a tornado badly damaged houses and cars in a suburb of Birmingham. One passerby described how the tornado in Birmingham picked up a ten-year-old boy, sending him flying through the air. He was lucky to land on his feet!

Text © 2007, Andrew Taylor

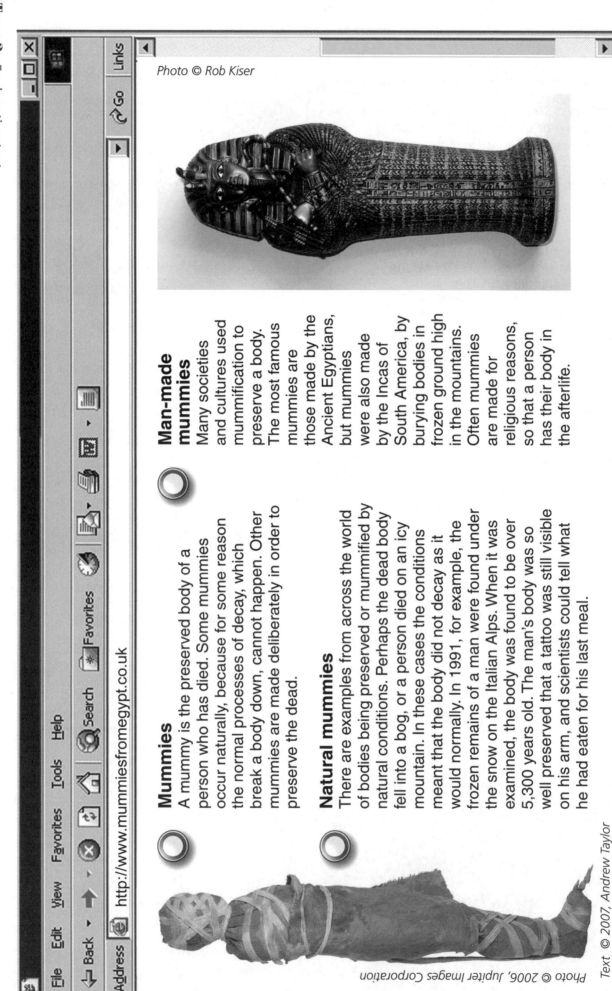

File   Edit   View   Favorites   Tools   Help

Back   Search   Favorites

Address   http://www.mummiesfromegypt.co.uk   Go   Links

Photo © Rob Kiser

Mummies

A mummy is the preserved body of a person who has died. Some mummies occur naturally, because for some reason the normal processes of decay, which break a body down, cannot happen. Other mummies are made deliberately in order to preserve the dead.

Natural mummies

There are examples from across the world of bodies being preserved or mummified by natural conditions. Perhaps the dead body fell into a bog, or a person died on an icy mountain. In these cases the conditions meant that the body did not decay as it would normally. In 1991, for example, the frozen remains of a man were found under the snow on the Italian Alps. When it was examined, the body was found to be over 5,300 years old. The man's body was so well preserved that a tattoo was still visible on his arm, and scientists could tell what he had eaten for his last meal.

Man-made mummies

Many societies and cultures used mummification to preserve a body. The most famous mummies are those made by the Ancient Egyptians, but mummies were also made by the Incas of South America, by burying bodies in frozen ground high in the mountains. Often mummies are made for religious reasons, so that a person has their body in the afterlife.

Photo © 2006, Jupiter Images Corporation

Text © 2007, Andrew Taylor

Internet

RSPCA

WHAT DOES THE RSPCA DO?

The Royal Society for the Prevention of Cruelty to Animals (RSPCA) cares for animals that are in need of help and encourages people to be kind to animals. The Society is a **charity** and does not receive any money from the government. It depends on **donations** from the public to enable it to do its work.

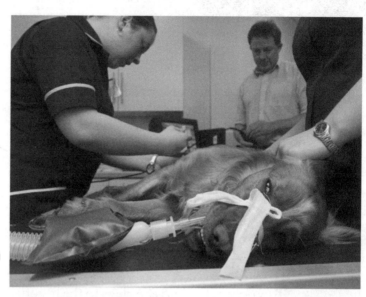

RSPCA Merthyr Tydfil Animal Clinic © Andrew Forsyth/RSPCA

COMMITTED TO CARING

The RSPCA was set up in London in 1824 and is the oldest animal **welfare** organisation in the world. With a team of over 300 inspectors throughout England and Wales, it is also the largest. The Society is so big that it has been split into 10 regions throughout the country, each one with smaller branches run by **volunteers**.

Lots of people know that the RSPCA helps pets, but the Society is concerned about cruelty to all animals – pets, wildlife, farm animals and animals used in **laboratories**.

HOW DOES THE RSPCA HELP?

The RSPCA provides advice and training for animal **welfare** organisations in other countries. It also encourages scientists to find alternatives to animal experiments and asks farmers to improve conditions for their animals.

KINDER FARMING

Freedom Food, the RSPCA's animal welfare food-labelling scheme, is another way the Society is improving animals' lives. Freedom Food farms are inspected to make sure that the animals have proper living conditions and are well cared for. So shoppers buying Freedom Food meat, eggs and dairy products can be sure that the animals had a good life.

The RSPCA works with the police to take people to court who have been cruel to animals. It also persuades the government to improve the law to stop people mistreating animals.

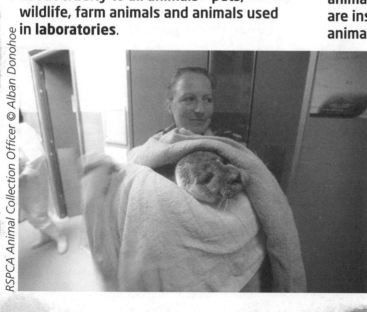

RSPCA Animal Collection Officer © Alban Donohoe

Text extract from "Taking Action: RSPCA" by Frazer Swift © 1997, RSPCA (1997, Heinemann)

Detectives of the past

Archaeologists are like detectives. But instead of solving crimes, they piece together scraps of evidence – metal objects, stone, pottery, leather, building foundations and bones – to understand how people lived long ago.

Metal and stone tools

Archaeologists often find tools made from metals such as bronze and iron, or from rocks such as flint. As well as finding the tools themselves, sometimes they can tell from other objects what kinds of tools were used to shape them. The basic design of many simple tools – including axe-heads and knives – has hardly changed for thousands of years.

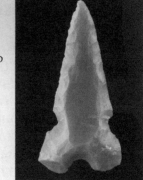

Pottery and crafts

Archaeologists also search for evidence of crafts to build up a picture of life long ago. From even a fragment of pottery, experts can often work out exactly what sort of a cup, plate or dish it was originally part of. Scraps of leather or pieces of woollen cloth provide clues to the history of shoe-making, weaving methods, and the dyes used for colouring yarn and cloth.

Traces of buildings

Among the most important discoveries are traces of the kinds of homes people built long ago. If a building was made of stone, the foundations or even the walls may survive in their original state. But if it was built of wood, there is usually more detective work to be done. The only clues to how it was built may be dark marks in the soil. Sometimes archaeologists find round, dark 'post holes'. These show where the main uprights were sunk into the ground, and so reveal what size and shape the house was.

Photo © Vicky S

Photo © Fons Reijsbergen

Human bones

Human bones provide clues to how long people lived, and sometimes even of the diseases that they suffered or died from. But some acidic soils decay bones, so archaeologists have developed special techniques for identifying where bones once lay even if they are no longer there. On the famous Sutton Hoo dig, archaeologists discovered that the shapes of buried bones showed up as dark lines in the sandy soil.

Photo © Eugene Wolfe

What people ate

Animal bones give clues to the animals people kept to provide them with meat. Archaeologists can discover much about the crops people grew from tiny plant remains, such as seeds, as well as remains of insects that lived on the plants.

Text © 2007, Andrew Taylor

What is a Tudor theatre?

Towards the end of the 1500s, when the Tudor Queen Elizabeth I was on the throne, some extraordinary new theatres were built in London. Everyone flocked to see the exciting new plays!

What other entertainments were there?

There were already many types of entertainment in Tudor times. People could see bear-baiting and bloody executions, church mystery plays and royal processions.

What was the Renaissance?

At this time people were interested in the Classical culture of ancient Greece and Rome and the period became known as the Renaissance (meaning re-birth). During the Renaissance, many new scientific and artistic ideas were developed. The new plays performed in Tudor theatres were part of the Renaissance.

Who were the theatres for?

All kinds of people visited London's new theatres from the very poor to the very rich. When a flag was flown over the theatre to announce the latest play, crowds of people crossed over the Thames to enjoy the show. Just one penny bought the cheapest ticket, and nearly everyone could afford that!

Where were the theatres built?

For a long time, people in cities like Coventry, Chester and York had been able to see religious mystery plays. These were put on by local craft unions called guilds and were performed on temporary stages. However, it was businessmen who built the new Tudor theatres. And, as London was the home of business, it became the home of Tudor theatres too.

When were the theatres built?

Most of these theatres were built during the late 1500s and the early 1600s, during the reigns of Queen Elizabeth I and King James I. The theatres built during Elizabeth's reign are often known as Elizabethan theatres and those built in King James's reign are known as Jacobean theatres (after the Latin word for James).

Who put on the plays?

Theatre companies were made up of senior shareholders, actors and boy apprentices. The whole company worked together to put on the plays, meeting at the theatre every day to rehearse new parts.

Who were the actors?

The Lord Chamberlain's Men had some of England's greatest actors. Burbage was their biggest star. Their rivals were the Lord Admiral's Men and their star was Edward Alleyn. He played Doctor Faustus in Marlowe's play about a man who sells his soul to the devil. He was so believable that people thought that there was a real devil on stage.

Who were the boy apprentices?

Women and girls did not perform in public theatres in Tudor times. Female parts were played by boy apprentices who were dressed in skirts, wigs and made up to look the part.

Text extract and illustrations from "Building History: Tudor Theatre" by Gillian Clements © 2004 Gillian Clements (2004 Franklin Watts)

Welcome to Polka Theatre Microsoft Internet Explorer provided by Scholastic Inc.

File   Edit   View   Favorites   Tools   Help

← Back ▾ → ▾ ⊗ ⟳ ⌂ | Search Favorites | ...

Address 📄 http://www.polkatheatre.com/ ▾ Go | Links

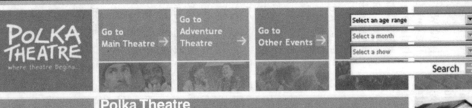

POLKA THEATRE
where theatre begins.

Go to Main Theatre →
Go to Adventure Theatre →
Go to Other Events →

Select an age range ▾
Select a month ▾
Select a show ▾

Search →

Polka Theatre

Polka Theatre is one of the few venues in the UK which is dedicated exclusively to producing and presenting high-quality theatre for young audiences. Since our doors opened in 1979, this unique venue has offered children a first taste of the thrilling, challenging and inspiring world of theatre.

Every year, over 100,000 children discover theatre at Polka. They may arrive in a school group or with their families. They may come from London or beyond. They may take their seats in the Main Auditorium or the Adventure Theatre, or take part in one of our many drama workshops and other activities. Whichever, once they step through Polka's doors, their appetite for high-quality theatre will be powerfully awakened.

"Polka is a place of magic and wonder, an inspiration to any child's imagination."
Sunday Times

"On the days I go to Polka Theatre, I scream to my mum to hurry. I love it there."
Seanna Allen, Audience Member

We are both a local theatre, loved by the people of Wimbledon and the wider London community, and a global centre, known the world over as a pioneer of theatre for young people, consistently setting the standard and raising the expectations of our audiences.

Polka aims to stimulate young people's passion for theatre by providing them with the widest possible range of theatre experience: from the moving teenage drama of **Hey There, Boy with the Bebop**; the gentle comedy of **Home from Home**; modern-day literary adaptations, such as **Jacqueline Wilson's Double Act**; and experimental theatre, such as the groundbreaking installation performance **Best Behaviour**, described by the Guardian as "the best piece of theatre this century."

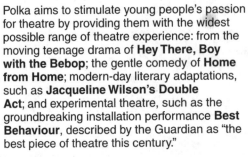

"We bother to go all the way to Wimbledon from Somerset simply because we fully recognise the superb standard of everything that is put on at Polka. We have always felt very envious of people who live so much closer and are able to go to all the shows and workshops."
Alison Crowdy, Parent

We keep things fresh by discovering exciting new writers and dynamic new performers and by blending the best of contemporary culture with the finest traditions. Everything we do is focused on providing children with an exhilarating introduction to the incomparable magic of theatre.

In addition to enjoying a performance, Polka offers young people the chance to explore their own creativity, with its regular programme of after-school and holiday-time drama courses and workshops, where you can learn a whole range of drama and performance skills.

At Polka, there's space to play, to laugh, to discover, to create... with something for all ages, from toddlers to teenagers. It's a magical place where you can steal a rare moment to share with your children. No two visits are the same... you'll soon see why Polka is where theatre begins!

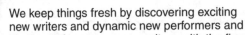

Internet

The Angel of the North

The Angel of the North

Height: 20 metres (taller than a five-storey building or four double-decker buses)
Width: 54 metres (almost the same as the wingspan of a jumbo jet)
Weight: 208 tonnes

- Situated beside the A1 road at Gateshead on a hilltop site, overlooking the Team Valley.
- The Angel is set on a site that used to house the baths at the top of a colliery.

- The Angel was designed by the artist Antony Gormley.
- Its form is based on a mould that was taken of his own body.
- A human-size model was made as a prototype before the huge Angel was cast.
- The face has been deliberately left without any features.
- The Angel's wings are not flat but are tilted slightly forward as though wanting to give an embrace.

- The figure is made from weather-resistant steel that includes copper to give a rich red-brown colour.
- The Angel is secured to the ground by concrete piles, 22 metres deep.
- The body is hollow.
- There is an inspection access door in one of the Angel's shoulder blades.
- The Angel was constructed in Hartlepool and then assembled on site. It was designed to last 100 years and withstand winds of over 100 miles an hour.

- More than 90,000 drivers pass the site every day.
- The Angel is also visible from the East Coast rail line which runs from London to Edinburgh.
- About 150,000 visitors a year are expected to see the Angel close up.

Text © 2007, Andrew Taylor; photo used by permission of Gateshead Council, www.gateshead.gov.uk I2I Photography, Colin Cuthbert

Animals of the rainforest

Without the special hot and wet conditions which encourage a unique type of vegetation, there would not be the huge diversity of animals found in rainforest areas. Some 150 different types of creatures can find a home on one rainforest tree.

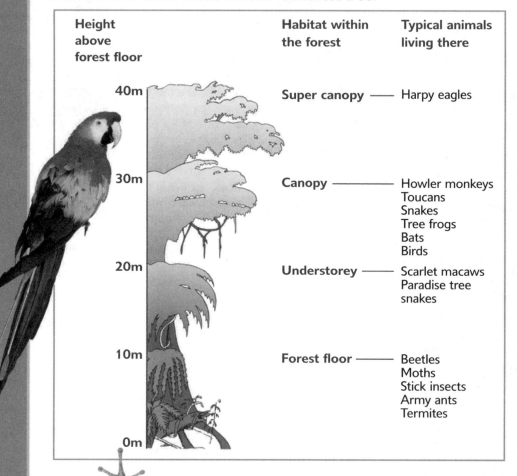

Height above forest floor		Habitat within the forest	Typical animals living there
40m		Super canopy ——	Harpy eagles
30m		Canopy ————	Howler monkeys Toucans Snakes Tree frogs Bats Birds
20m		Understorey ——	Scarlet macaws Paradise tree snakes
10m		Forest floor ——	Beetles Moths Stick insects Army ants Termites
0m			

Forest facts
- Scientists are still finding new species of rainforest creatures and identifying them.
- Many rainforest animals are nocturnal.
- Camouflage plays an important part in the survival of many rainforest creatures.
- Insects make up 90% of the animal mass of a rainforest.
- In the rainforest, many plants rely on animals, such as hummingbirds and bats, to pollinate their flowers and spread their ripened seeds.
- 50% of the animal species of the rainforest live in the canopy level.

Text by Suzanne Kirk from "Literacy Time" 3/4: Autumn 2002
© 2002, Suzanne Kirk (2002, Scholastic Ltd); illustration © 2002, Graham Kennedy; parrot photo © Everyday Animals; tree frog photo © Corel

Glossary

Here are explanations of some of the more difficult weather and climate terms you may have found.

A

aerosols Tiny particles in the air which scatter sunlight. They can be natural or artificial.
air mass A mass of air with the same temperature and *humidity* throughout.
air pressure See *atmospheric pressure.*
altitude Height above sea level.
anemometer Device used to measure wind speed.
anticyclones or **highs** Areas of high *atmospheric pressure.*
astronomical theory of climate change See *Milankovitch theory.*
atmosphere 1. The protective layer of air around Earth that enables plants and animals to live. 2. A layer of gases around any planet.
atmospheric pressure or air pressure The force of air pressing down on Earth, measured in millibars (mb).
auroras Patterns of light in the sky, seen around the North Pole (Aurora Borealis) and the South Pole (Aurora Australis).

B

barometer Device used to measure *atmospheric pressure.*
biome An area of Earth with a particular combination of climate, landscapes, plants and animals.
boreal forest or **taiga** A wide area of coniferous forest across Northern America, Europe and Asia.

C

carbon sink Part of the landscape that absorbs and stores carbon dioxide from the air. Forests and oceans are carbon sinks.
CFCs (chlorofluorocarbons) Man-made chemicals that are thought to damage the ozone layer.
circumpolar current An ocean *current* that flows without interruption around Antarctica.
climate forcing Any human-made or otherwise artificial changing of the *climate system.*
climate model A construction of past or future climate conditions, created by feeding various types of data into a computer.
climate system The complex relationships between all the features that create climates on Earth. These include the Sun's heat, living things, water, air and ice.
cloud cover The amount of sky seen to be covered by cloud in any given place.
cold front A boundary at the head of a cold *air mass.*
condensation The process of water vapour turning back into liquid water as it cools down. See also *evaporation*, which is the opposite effect.

Text extract from "The Usborne Introduction to Weather and Climate Change" by Laura Howell © 2003, Usborne Publishing Ltd.

National Coal Mining Museum for England

- Exhibitions and galleries • Pit ponies
- Mining machinery • Train rides
- Adventure playground • Nature trail
- Under fives' play area • Licensed café
- Unique souvenirs • Library
- Visit www.ncm.org.uk for information

Step into the past at the National Coal Mining Museum for England, Overton, and explore the amazing real-life stories of the people who played a role in our industrial heritage.

Follow a time line through twisting tunnels and compare the hardships and risks faced by early miners, with the safety and efficiency of modern mining in England.

Safely back in the daylight again, explore many of the Museum's historic mining buildings, try out coal mining science activities and discover how mining processes worked using our interactive exhibits.

1 Nature trail
Enjoy wildlife and scenery over a beautiful half mile stroll. Follow the signs from Caphouse.

2 Pit Ponies and stables
See the last ever working ponies now happily enjoying their retirement with us.

3 1842 Victorian Exhibition
Uncover the little known stories of the women and children who worked in the coal mining industry.

4 Coal interface building
Can you solve some of the safety and communication problems miners had to cope with underground?

5 Underground tours
Collect your helmet and lamp, and descend 140 metres underground for an unforgettable 1¼ hour tour.

6 Visitor centre
Relax with a variety of refreshments in

our licensed café, and discover a range of gifts for everyone in our museum shop.

7 Settling ponds and reed beds

Nature gets to work in cleaning water pumped from underground. Get closer to the wildlife with our viewing holes and nature trail.

8 Workshops
See science in action with some real heavyweight machinery. Check out

our live demonstrations (times vary – ask at Reception).

9 Inman Shaft
Hector the Heron gives you an overhead view of the site's water system, plus fascinating interactive displays.

10 Hope Pit Winding Engine House
What goes up must come down! Get to grips with pulley wheels – but don't let Frank the virtual Foreman wind you up!

Text and photos from The National Coal Mining Museum for England leaflet © The National Coal Mining Museum for England

The Early Life of James Cook

Early life

James Cook was born in a small cottage in Marton in Cleveland, just outside what is now Middlesbrough, on 7 October 1728.

James first helped his father on a farm, before going to work in a grocer's shop at Staithes. In 1746 he went as an apprentice to John Walker, a ship-owner in Whitby. James spent nine years sailing between the River Tyne and London, shipping coal. In 1755 he volunteered to join the Royal Navy.

Cook in the navy

Within a month of joining the navy, Cook was made a Master's Mate and only two years later he became a Ship's Master himself. His ship, the Pembroke, fought against the French in Canada. Cook also spent time charting the St Lawrence River, which helped General James Wolfe to capture Quebec in 1759. After the Canadian Wars, Cook returned to the seas around Newfoundland to make detailed charts of the area.

A voyage of discovery

Cook's skills at navigation and making charts were noticed and led to him being presented to King George III. The King was interested in scientific discoveries and planned to fund a voyage of discovery to the southern Pacific Ocean. Scientists wanted to measure the distance from the Earth to the Sun by observing the Transit of Venus. Cook was chosen to captain the voyage.

Cook's ship

A Whitby collier, the Endeavour, was purchased for the voyage at the cost of £2,800. Although the Endeavour was small – only 106 feet (about 30 metres) long, she was strong enough to allow the hull to rest on shore to receive repairs. There was also enough room to carry 94 people, 12 months' supply of food and stores, and equipment for the scientists, artists and astronomers. While the Endeavour was being refitted, Cook applied to the Admiralty for various instruments to help him navigate accurately, chart his journey and record it in great detail. After months of preparation, the Endeavour sailed for Tahiti on 30 July 1768.

Text © 2007, Andrew Taylor; photos © Fred Brunskill (http://homepage.ntlworld.com/fred.brunskil1)

Physical activity

Physical activity and exercise are recommended as part of a healthy lifestyle, so it is important to understand what these terms mean. Physical activity is the most general term. It includes any activity that involves movement and requires more energy than is needed at rest. Physical activities include:

Photo © Joseph Zlomek

- housework, gardening and DIY
- moving around – walking and climbing stairs
- exercise, sport, dance and outdoor activities.

Exercise is a type of physical activity. It is often taken in leisure time, and usually for enjoyment or to keep fit. Exercise may be taken in the form of:

- walking – hill-walking and walking the dog
- jogging or running
- dancing – ballet, ballroom, tap, line and folk dancing are all popular forms of exercise
- aerobics – step aerobics and keep-fit classes have become very popular in recent years
- working out in a fitness gym or weights room
- swimming, gymnastics, outdoor activities and all sports.

There are many other types of exercise. Sport is a more controlled form of exercise, with rules, regulations and competitive structures.

How much exercise do you need?
There are two main recommendations that have been made by the Health Education Authority:

- Original recommendation – vigorous exercise at least three times a week for 20 minutes each time.

This is the amount of exercise needed for maximum improvements in aerobic endurance and to reduce the risk of death. However, many people feel that this is too much for them to do. The new recommendation is based on the fact that even moderate levels of physical activity can improve health.

- New recommendation – at least 30 minutes of moderate exercise at least five days a week.

Photo © Matthew Bowden

Photo © Cheryl Empey

This may seem to involve more exercise than the first recommendation but there are two key differences that make it easier for people to achieve:

- The physical activity is moderate, so walking, cycling and gardening count.
- The 30 minutes can be split into smaller amounts such as two 15-minute sessions. You could take 15 minutes to walk to work every day and walk back again after work every day and you would have reached the recommended level.

Photo © Robert Van

Text extracts from "Health-Related Fitness" by Nuala Mullan © 1997 Nuala Mullan (1997, Heinemann)

Vikings

Who were they?

THE VIKINGS WERE brave warriors who set out from their homes in Norway, Sweden and Denmark on daring voyages of exploration. These legendary voyages took place over a period of 300 years, from the 8th century onwards. The Vikings went in search of gold and silver, slaves and, perhaps most importantly, new farmland. They sailed to the farthest reaches of Europe in their quest, as well as parts of Asia and North America. The Vikings were notorious for their terrifying surprise attacks on monasteries and towns. But in reality, these ferocious raids played only a small part in their success. The Vikings had a highly civilised, democratic way of life. They were skilled at shipbuilding and many other crafts, as well as being farmers, traders and expert navigators.

Image © Anthony Wootten

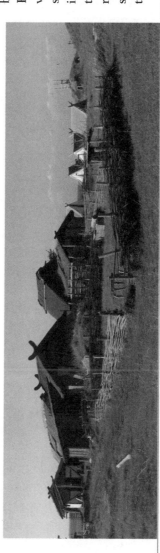

Photo © Lars Sundstrom

At home on the waves

THE VIKINGS WERE EXCELLENT SAILORS. They had to navigate treacherous seas, but their wooden longships were perfectly designed for this purpose. These light, elegant vessels were able to glide past rocks and icebergs and ride out the most vicious storms.

The ships were versatile enough to cope with shallow coastal waters and rivers as well as the open sea. The big rectangular sail could be lowered and the ship rowed instead.

The Vikings used the sun and the stars to navigate, or simply stayed within sight of land. They also gathered clues from nature to help them find their way – observing fish, seabirds and the pattern of the waves. There are very few longships left – most rotted away. Those that have survived were buried with their rich owners, according to Viking custom.

Photo © Jon Wisbey

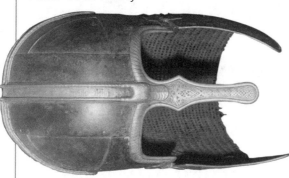

A specialist ship

PERHAPS THE MOST REMARKABLE of the Viking ships were those used to carry warriors – the warships. These were longer, sleeker and faster than any other ships. They were also highly manoeuvrable, able to quietly dart up the narrowest inlets or even land on beaches under oar-power.

Each ship had up to 50 oars, which the warriors manned in shifts on long voyages. But once it was out on the open ocean, the mast was raised, and the rectangular sail unfurled, the ship sailed swiftly away across the waves once more.

'OPERATION PIED PIPER'

THE GOVERNMENT EVACUATION SCHEME

The Government evacuation scheme had been planned by the 'Anderson Committee', a group led by Sir John Anderson. The Committee met between May and July 1938 and called in experts from railway companies, teachers and the police to advise them.

THE ANDERSON COMMITTEE RECOMMENDATIONS

Factories have to be kept open to produce important materials. People who are not doing essential jobs should be moved away from these factories, which will be targets for bombing.

EVACUATION SHOULD NOT BE COMPULSORY

Children not being evacuated with their mothers will be taken in school parties, with their teachers.

Evacuees will be housed in private dwellings. People in the reception areas will have to look after evacuees if they are asked to do so.

The British evacuation was called 'Operation Pied Piper'. It began on Friday 1 September 1939. The Government sent parents a list, telling them what they needed to pack for their children.

Most evacuees travelled to city railway stations to begin their journey to the countryside. Special timetables had to be arranged for the many extra train services. The evacuees did not know where they were travelling to.

FINDING BILLETS

A local 'billeting officer' was appointed to find suitable houses in all areas that were receiving evacuees.

In January and February 1939 the Government conducted an 'accommodation census' to find out how many billets were available. Local people called 'visitors' interviewed householders in reception areas, and filled in census forms. Officials used these forms to decide how many evacuees could be billeted in each area.

HOST FAMILIES

After a journey which was often long and tiring, evacuees had to line up and wait for a 'host family' to choose them.

Hosts received money for each evacuee they took in. They were paid by taking a form to the local post office.

Billeting was compulsory. People who refused to take evacuees into their homes without a good reason could be taken to court and fined.

From http://clutch.open.ac.uk/schools/standrews00/gov_evac.htm

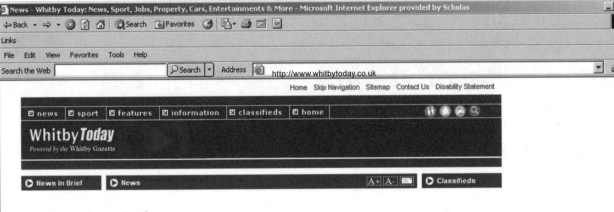

A New Resolution

AN AMBITIOUS £50 million plan has been unveiled to transform Whitby into an ecological and marine heritage site.

As part of the community project a version of Captain Cook's Resolution ship would be built in the town and then sailed through the Northwest Passage.

The forum aims to win the £50 million of funding necessary from the Big Lottery Fund in a televised competition.

A programme in 2007 entitled 'Living Landmarks: The People's Millions' will showcase various ideas for community projects from towns throughout the country and the nation will then be able to vote on the project they want to see go ahead.

As part of the project, Whitby Beacon Town Forum, which is behind the cash bid, would like to see Whitby and its coast becoming a marine conservation area. A maritime eco-centre would be built on reclaimed land, possibly on the car park near the cargo shed.

The proposed eco-centre would provide exhibitions, information about climate change and the melting of the polar ice caps and also a study centre for universities throughout the area.

It has been suggested that the car park could also be used for actually building the New Resolution with a hole dug in the ground to support the hull.

This would also alleviate future flooding problems by simply providing more space for the water to go.

The proposed eco-centre could be built on stilts or floating pontoons so it would not be at risk of being submerged.

The deadline for submitting the initial application is 6 January and the organisers of Whitby's bid want the people of Whitby to get behind them and simply register their support. No local fundraising will be necessary.

North Yorkshire County Council, Scarborough Council, Yorkshire Forward and Yorkshire Water have already said they back the project in principle.

Photo © Ian Britton/FreeFoto.com

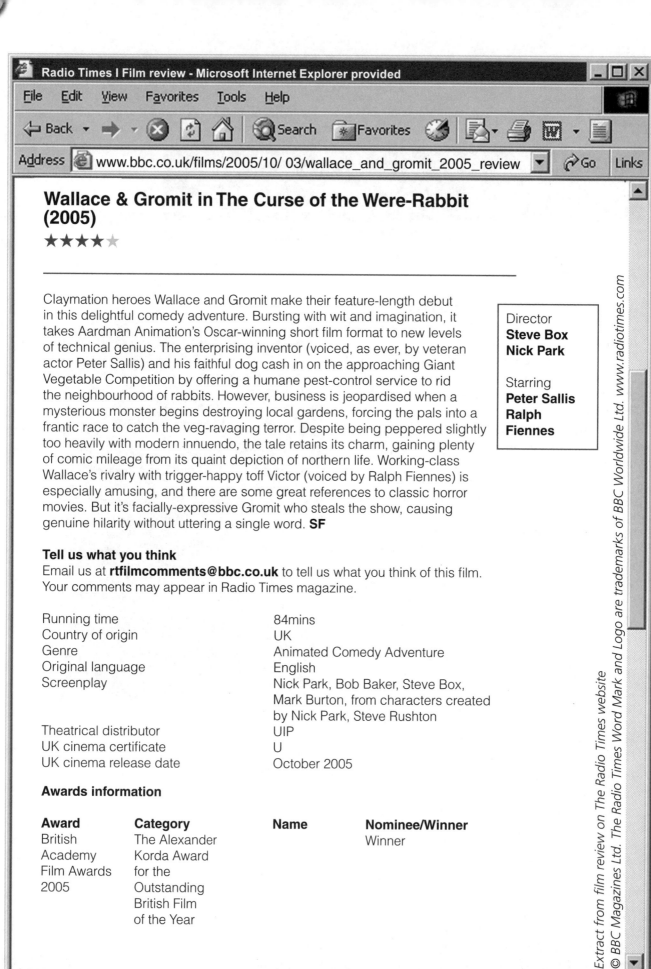

Wallace & Gromit in The Curse of the Were-Rabbit (2005)

★★★★☆

Claymation heroes Wallace and Gromit make their feature-length debut in this delightful comedy adventure. Bursting with wit and imagination, it takes Aardman Animation's Oscar-winning short film format to new levels of technical genius. The enterprising inventor (voiced, as ever, by veteran actor Peter Sallis) and his faithful dog cash in on the approaching Giant Vegetable Competition by offering a humane pest-control service to rid the neighbourhood of rabbits. However, business is jeopardised when a mysterious monster begins destroying local gardens, forcing the pals into a frantic race to catch the veg-ravaging terror. Despite being peppered slightly too heavily with modern innuendo, the tale retains its charm, gaining plenty of comic mileage from its quaint depiction of northern life. Working-class Wallace's rivalry with trigger-happy toff Victor (voiced by Ralph Fiennes) is especially amusing, and there are some great references to classic horror movies. But it's facially-expressive Gromit who steals the show, causing genuine hilarity without uttering a single word. **SF**

Director
Steve Box
Nick Park

Starring
Peter Sallis
Ralph
Fiennes

Tell us what you think
Email us at **rtfilmcomments@bbc.co.uk** to tell us what you think of this film. Your comments may appear in Radio Times magazine.

Running time   84mins
Country of origin   UK
Genre   Animated Comedy Adventure
Original language   English
Screenplay   Nick Park, Bob Baker, Steve Box,
                       Mark Burton, from characters created
                       by Nick Park, Steve Rushton

Theatrical distributor UIP
UK cinema certificate U
UK cinema release date October 2005

Awards information

Award	Category	Name	Nominee/Winner
British Academy Film Awards 2005	The Alexander Korda Award for the Outstanding British Film of the Year		Winner

A Magical Day in History!

TAKE A TIME TRIP YOU'LL NEVER FORGET

ENGLAND'S MEDIEVAL FESTIVAL AT HERSTMONCEUX CASTLE, NEAR HAILSHAM

In East Sussex, is England's **LARGEST AND MOST SPECTACULAR CELEBRATION** of the colourful Middle Ages. Now in its **THIRTEENTH THRILLING YEAR**, this unique event is held over the three days of the **BANK HOLIDAY WEEKEND** and has welcomed over 150,000 visitors from around the world.

Only at Herstmonceux can you experience the true flavour, sights and sounds of Medieval England.

OVER 2000 AUTHENTICALLY COSTUMED MEDIEVALISTS help take you back to a time of heraldry and heroism.

The walls of the fairy-tale **15TH CENTURY MOATED CASTLE AND BATTLEFIELD** come under siege from the massed forces of opposing armies. You can hear the crash of broadswords on heavy armour; the rallying call of battle cries as the troops are marshalled into position; and you can experience the smell of black powder from **SALVO AFTER SALVO OF CANNON FIRE** as the castle walls are prepared to be stormed. Witness the incredible sight of the **SIEGE ENGINE** as it hurls its deadly load towards the castle defenders. **SIEGES ARE MOUNTED DAILY AT 11AM AND 3PM.**

You can hear the eerie hiss of volley after volley of arrows overhead. And when the fighting is over? You can watch **EUROPE'S FINEST BOWMEN** gather to compete for prestige and prizes at the Festival's longbow competition. Or try it yourself: **ENTER THE HAVE-A-GO ARCHERY**, with expert instruction from our archers. Experience displays of **FALCONRY** in the modern world and learn a thing or two about this ancient craft.

WAS HISTORY EVER SUCH FUN?

Text and photo from a leaflet from The Malcolm Group Events Medieval Festival at Herstmonceux Castle, East Sussex www.englandsmedievalfestival.com © The Malcolm Group Events; photo © The Malcolm Group Events/The Medieval Image Bank www.englandsmedievalfestival.com

The Great Escape!

How about getting away from your parents for a week or two?
How about going on holiday with just your friends? Or going on holiday to make lots of new friends from all over the country?
How about camping under the stars in France?
How about trying out loads of activities, from sailing to archery, dragon boating to raft building?
How about eating frogs' legs and snails?

Only joking about that last one…

Photo © Breatte W

Photo © Brian Ducharme

Acorn Adventure summer camps are fantastic holidays. Spend a week in France or the UK trying out all kinds of new things, including watersports and other activities such as climbing and caving. Every day there is something new to try, games to play in the centre with our instructors, and evening entertainment to laugh yourself silly.

Why not arrange to go with some of your friends? You can travel together, share a tent, and take part in all the activities together. If you don't want to bring friends you will be sure to meet lots of new ones! Children from all over the UK come to us as strangers and leave as best friends. You will share everything with people of the same age and you can even change tents during the week if you want to change who you share with.

We have a fantastic range of activities for you to try out. All the equipment is provided and our instructors are always on hand to guide you and teach you as much as you want.

Food!
We've fed hundreds of thousands of children over the years so we know what you will like. More importantly we know what you won't like. Our food is always tasty and filling and you are guaranteed not to see a brussels sprout all week! If you have any particular likes and dislikes, just let us know.

Camping!
You will share a large tent with two other people – either a friend or two that you bring with you, or newly made friends of the same age. If you want to change tents during the week you can.

Text from The Acorn Adventure website © Acorn Adventure www.acornadventure.co.uk

Photo © Betsy Leeuwner

Photo © 2006, Jupiter Images Corporation

Photo © Tom Denham

healthyliving

Staying fit & active:
A few changes go a long way

Sometimes just the thought of physical exercise can be daunting, let alone doing it. But it doesn't have to mean lifetime membership of the gym and bulging biceps.

A few little changes can easily make activity part of your routine. You'll see and feel the difference it can make – it's your body's way of saying thank you for the effort you've put in. Who knows, you might get a taste for it and be joining us soon on one of the Cancer Research UK runs we sponsor. To make things easier we've got some ways to get moving that you'd hardly notice and don't need special equipment or clothing for. But first, why bother?

Exercise is good for you
Regular exercise can reduce the risk of stroke and heart attack by 50%, reduce the risk of diabetes and improve the way your brain works. It burns off excess fat, tones muscles and actually makes you feel good. It's fun too! Playing in the park and throwing a ball around with the children or friends makes everyone smile and glow.

Exercise is easy
Here are some ways to get active and how they'll do you good.

Walk
It's the easiest and simplest exercise around. Walk to the shops, pop round to see your relatives or use the photocopier on the next floor (using the stairs, not the lift). There are lots of ways to squeeze this great form of exercise into your day. It tones, shapes up your legs and does your heart and lungs good.

Clean the house
You hate the jobs, but you'll love what it's doing for you. Move quickly from chore to chore to raise your heart rate, tone arm muscles and increase stamina. Vigorous vacuuming, dusting, window cleaning and bath scrubbing all count. Hold in your abdominal muscles while you are vacuuming and slightly bend your legs.

Wash the car
Great for your upper body and reaching over the roof will increase your flexibility. Just look at that shiny paintwork.

Gardening
If you have one, a garden is full of things to do that really burn calories. And it's nice to be outside in the fresh air. Remember to engage your stomach muscles especially when bending or lifting things. A gentle stretch when you've finished is a good idea.

Healthy Living logo and text extract from Tesco's "Staying Fit and Active" leaflet © Tesco Ltd; images courtesy of Tesco

Walk

Clean the house

Wash the car

Gardening

Dear Holly

Thanks for your letter. It's great that you like the new house but I'm really sad to hear that you haven't made any friends at your new school.

You know you said that you sit in the playground on your own and that when someone comes to talk they soon go away again.

You've been my best friend for a long time now, Holly, and, well, it hurts me to say this BUT MAYBE IT'S PARTLY YOUR FAULT. You've always been a bit shy – you know it's true! That was OK when you knew everyone but now you're in a new situation and you need to make more EFFORT.

Here are some things I think you should try.

First, don't just wait for people to come to you. Go over and start a conversation. Maybe say something nice about the person you're talking to. Show that you're interested in them. It's easy!

Next, when someone starts to talk to you for the first time, I bet you just look down at your feet! And don't say anything. No wonder they go away. You need to look up and smile and SAY SOMETHING – something sparky and lively and fun! You're a really interesting person – so I know you can do it. In no time at all you'll have lots of friends, just like you did here at Underwood.

I hope you aren't upset by this letter. I'm only saying this because I'm your friend and I don't like to think of you being sad. I want to help. What are friends for?

So, please, please take my advice – and let me know what happens.

Love
Bethan

Vote for me

Photo © 2006, Jupiter Images Corporation

I am Wendy and I want to be your class representative on the school council. I expect you're asking yourself: Why should I vote for her? Well, let me give you some reasons.

First of all, I've got the skills you need to be a good rep. As you know, I'm not shy and I'm a good talker! I won't be lost for words at council meetings. But I'm a good listener too. I promise to consult everyone in Year 4 and find out what you think and what you want. Then I'll put forward your ideas clearly and strongly.

Next, I've got the experience you need. I was class rep two years ago at my old school. So I know how school councils work and what a rep needs to do.

Finally, I'm hard-working. Some people just like the idea of being a rep. It makes them feel important. But they don't do much. I will put in the time and the effort that's needed.

OK, so maybe now you believe I can do the job. So you are asking now: What are her ideas for improving the school? Well, I've got lots! I'll mention just two. First, I'd like to develop the 'walking bus' scheme that some parents are starting. We all know that walking to school is good for your health and it reduces the pollution and congestion caused by cars. The 'walking bus' makes it safe – and fun!

Secondly, there's school meals. Surely everyone agrees that they've got better, but they could still be healthier and tastier and offer better choices for vegetarians. My aim will be to get more children more actively involved in a Better Meals campaign.

So that's what I can offer. That's the kind of rep I want to be. That's a taste of what I'd like to do. I hope you'll vote for me on Friday.

Text © 2007, Chris Lutrario

Welcome to North Devon & Exmoor...

Once you've made the first step, the rest is easy. Everything falls into place when you kick off your sandals and feel the golden sands between your toes or pull on your walking boots and head off into the wide blue yonder. Either way, you'll find something to inspire you here.

Our fabulous coastline, with its impossible cliffs, harbours that remain unchanged for centuries and miles of golden sands, is almost entirely made up of Areas of Outstanding Natural Beauty. And a large part of it has been designated a UNESCO World Biosphere Reserve for its stunning and unique environment.

Head inland and you'll find beauty here, too. On Exmoor you can lose yourself in a few strides among the heather and the legends, whilst a journey through the rolling hills always throws up a few surprises, especially if you take your time. See the place on foot, on horseback, on your bike or over a pint – with some great local food and a view to match.

There's plenty to keep you busy on your holiday, from towns with traditional local markets to exciting themed attractions for the kids, as well as a vibrant calendar of Festivals and Events. It isn't hard to see why people come back year after year – like the migrating swallows who grace us with their presence every summer. We even have our own island, home to seals and seabirds and surrounded by the UK's only Statutory Marine Reserve. On some days you'll see more wildlife than you will people. Imagine that! Your own island for a day.

As a holiday destination North Devon and Exmoor can't fail to impress, whether you stay with us for a summer holiday or a long weekend. After the rush of the surf, an afternoon reading, a sunset to savour or just some quality time with your family, you'll soon feel truly at home.

Text from a leaflet 'Guide to North Devon and Exmoor'
© 2005 North Devon Marketing Bureau www.northdevon.com; background and top right photos © North Devon Marketing Bureau; other photos © Photodisc Inc

50 Shared texts Non-fiction ● Year 4

What CHAMPS will do for you

- What if you could learn anything you wanted fast and easily? How would that make you feel?
- What if you could remember difficult things like history dates, maths formulae or science facts more easily?
- What if you could start getting better results at school within the next few days?
- What if you could learn to concentrate and listen better?
- What if you could get yourself going, or motivate yourself to get down to work at any time?
- What if you felt really confident to tackle any school subject, even the ones you don't think you're very good at?

Well, now you can! This brilliant book will teach you all the things you need to become a learning CHAMP - something that will help you for the rest of your life - at home, at school and at work.

At school you get taught lots of different subjects, like maths, English, science and history. But you're not often taught how to learn them. Yet learning is like playing a sport, or playing a musical instrument. It's a skill. And CHAMPS is going to teach you this most important skill of all.

The best techniques for you

Does your face look the same as your friends' faces?
Are your fingerprints the same?
No! And neither is your brain.

Your brain is as individual as your fingerprints or face. Since you learn with your brain, you won't be surprised to know that you have a unique way of learning that suits your unique brain best.

When you use the techniques that match the way your brain learns best, you'll be learning in the way that's most natural to you.

- Because it is natural, it's easier.
- Because it's easier, it's quicker.
- And because it's quicker it's more fun.

That's just what CHAMPS will do for you! It'll teach you the learning techniques that match the way your brain likes to learn best. So if you're already a good learner - you'll get better. And if you find learning a bit of a struggle, your work will get easier and your marks will get better.

Text extract from "Learning Champs" by Colin Rose © 2001, Anova Books (2001, Learning World); photos © 2006, Jupiter Images Corporation

Book Power

A book about books? Are books really so special that they deserve a book's worth of writing and drawing all to themselves?

You bet they do!

Really. Books have been around for so long, and are so easy to take for granted, we tend to forget how amazing they actually are. A book can fill our heads with someone else's facts and fancies – someone who's far away, or dead, or completely imaginary. Yet, as we turn its pages, those facts and fancies come to life in a way that's utterly personal to us. For what you see, in your mind as you read, will never be identical with what I read, will never be identical with what I see – even if we're staring at the same words.

For me, that's magical.

Books can make us hoot with laughter, burst into tears, or squirm with pain and pleasure. They can teach us about anything and everything – from Acrobatics to Zoology. They're brain-boosting, universe-exploring, time-shifting bundles of endless possibility.

Yet this handy, pocket-sized object doesn't need any power-source, never lets us down by crashing and lasts pretty nearly forever if we look after it properly.

The right book at the right time can open our eyes, warm our hearts and help us make our dreams come true… yet stay entirely private while it does so.

No wonder there's a lot of them about. Last year, we published over 8000 new ones in the United Kingdom alone. Some had a print-run of just a few hundred copies, others flopped off the press by the million.

And that was just books for children!

If we're counting those for adults as well, each one with a title trying hard to be different from all the others, then there were more than a hundred thousand new publications altogether.

It was much the same the year before. Not to mention the year before that… and so on.

Meanwhile in other countries…

Yes, maybe we'd better pause a moment. Even a book-lover like me is beginning to feel a little faint. Luckily, another thing you can do with a book is to fan yourself, very gently, till you've built up the strength to move on to the next chapter.

Text extract from "The Book About Books" by Chris Powling; text © 2000, Chris Powling; illustration © 2000, Scoular Anderson (2000, A.&C. Black Publishers Ltd)

Evacuation

From September 1939 onwards, during the first years of the Second World War, the British government evacuated hundreds of thousands of children from the cities to the countryside. They were afraid that if the Germans bombed British towns and cities most of the people who lived there would be killed. Not everyone agrees that evacuating children was the right thing to do.

Photo © EMPICS

Reasons against:

- Evacuation made children and parents very unhappy. Families were split up, and didn't see each other for months or even years.
- Children who were evacuated were sometimes treated very badly by the people they went to stay with. No one knew about this until years later.
- Maybe the children didn't need to be sent away. In fact the German bombing wasn't quite as bad as the government thought it might be.
  Air raid shelters protected people. British air defences proved quite successful. And Hitler stopped the night-by-night bombing of London in 1941 because he decided to fight in a different way.
- It was difficult to keep children in school during evacuation. (Maybe you would think this was a 'plus point'!)

Reasons for:

- The lives of some children were certainly saved. 30,000 people were killed during London's Blitz.
- Evacuation allowed parents to concentrate on keeping Britain going at a very difficult time.
- It showed that the government wanted to look after the British people.
- Many city children had never been to the countryside. This was a new and exciting adventure for them.
- It made different kinds of people aware of each other. Maybe it helped bring about the important social changes that happened after the war in education, housing and health.

Text by Vince Cross © 2007, Vince Cross, previously unpublished.

Something to talk about
SHOULD CHILDREN FOLLOW FASHION?

No! Wally Wooley	Yes! Ivor Style
Dear Ivor, I suppose I must begin by saying that I'm no enemy of fashion. I know that it brings joy and colour to our humdrum lives, and would be sorely missed if we tried to do without it. However, children do not need the extra burden that being trendy places on them. Fashion is for adults to express themselves with. Nothing is more horrible than expecting a child to impersonate an adult. Yours, Wally	**Dear Wally,** I'm glad we've established that you don't have objections to fashion, as such. Let's concentrate on why you might object to fashion in children's lives. I happen to think that children are fashion's most important fans. Children are immensely sensitive to the way they fit in, and love to experiment, in ways that are beyond boring old adults' abilities. Yours, Ivor
Dear Ivor, It's exactly because of children's sensitivity to peer pressure (fitting in, as you phrase it) that fashion is best kept out of the playground. If one has poor parents, or parents who are less keen on frivolous clothing than one's friends' parents, terrible teasing and social isolation can result. Yours, Wally	**Dear Wally,** Children have to learn how to negotiate life's pitfalls for themselves. One of the hardest things to learn is how to influence the way people relate to you. Experimenting with fashion is part of this learning process. By changing how they look, kids learn how unimportant appearances truly are! Yours, Ivor
Dear Ivor, If it were that simple, I would have no problem with your argument. Sadly, some children, for a variety of reasons, are denied an equal chance to 'experiment'. I would rather see children in uniforms. As any teacher will tell you, children will always find a way to express themselves through minor 'improvements' to a dress code. And none of them need feel excluded. Yours, Wally	**Dear Wally,** I remember my brothers insisting that Mum 'take in' their trouser legs in the 80s, when the school trousers were too flared. Uniforms will always be customised, more often than not by put-upon mothers. Why is that any better than other clothes? As for the expense, keep up! Most modern fashions are more influenced by the charity shop than £100 gym shoes. Yours, Ivor

Text extract from "Read All About It!: Fashion" by Adam Hibbert © 2000, Adam Hibbert (2000, Franklin Watts)

Zoos — good or bad?

Are all zoos the same and are they ever a good thing?

People love to see wild animals – and one way they can do this is to visit a zoo. For hundreds of years, people have collected wild animals and kept them in zoos. But is it ever right for animals that were born free to be forced to live in captivity?

Photo © Photodisc Inc

Bad zoos, good zoos

In some zoos, animals are kept in small cages without enough room for them to get proper exercise. However, over the last fifty years, many zoos have tried to provide animals with a better living environment. Most modern zoos are in the country rather than in towns, so animals have more room to move around.

A chance to learn?

Some people think that zoos are a good idea because they give people a chance to see wild animals and learn about their behaviour. Some even say that city zoos are a good thing because they allow more people to see the animals. However, others say that people should watch wildlife documentaries instead.

Born free

People who are against zoos say that animals kept in cages often become ill and depressed. Even if animals seem to be happy in captivity, they are still not living natural lives. They may not be living in a climate that suits them, or they may not be eating ideal food.

THINK IT THROUGH

Are zoos a good thing?

Yes
They allow people to learn about animals and help to prevent rare species from dying out.

No
Wild animals should be left alone to get on with their lives.
What do YOU think?

NEWSFLASH

Sometimes zoos play a role in preventing a rare species from dying out. In 2003, seven giant panda cubs were born at Wolong wildlife reserve in China. The cubs bring hope for the survival of the giant panda, which has been in danger of dying out. In the next few years, staff at the reserve plan to start releasing the pandas back into the wild.

Text extract from "Animals and Us: Do Animals Have Rights?" by Jane Bingham © 2005, Harcourt Education Ltd (2005, Heinemann)

The death of the dinosaurs

Around 66 million years ago, at the end of the Cretaceous period, lots of creatures died out completely. All the dinosaurs became extinct, except for some feathered ones that had evolved into birds. Flying reptiles and most sea reptiles also died out. No one is certain why this happened, but scientists have given several different explanations.

Deadly rock?

Near the end of the Cretaceous period, the Earth was struck by an enormous rock, or meteorite, measuring up to 10km (6 miles) across. As it hit the Earth, the meteorite would have smashed into tiny pieces, surrounding the planet in clouds of dust.

The dust clouds would have made the Earth cold and dark for months, killing off any creatures that needed warmth to survive. Without light, many plants must have died as well, leaving the animals with nothing to eat. The meteorite would also have caused massive earthquakes and giant tidal waves.

Lava shower?

Another explanation is that many volcanoes all over the world may have erupted around the same time. The erupting volcanoes would have poured out vast amounts of hot lava (liquid rock) onto the Earth's surface, and sent clouds of dust and poisonous gases high into the air. These gases could also have caused clouds of harmful acid rain to fall.

Climate change?

By 66 million years ago, the weather all over the world had become cooler and more changeable. Dinosaurs relied on heat from the Sun to keep themselves warm, and they may not have been able to cope with a changing climate.

Several causes

There is probably no single reason why so many animals died out. The meteorite must have killed off many creatures, but animals may also have been affected by a change in the weather.

Photo © Lynne Lancaster

Red-hot lava pouring from a volcano.

This picture shows what might have happened as the meteorite struck the Earth.

Text and illustrations from "The Usborne Internet-linked Prehistoric World" by Fiona Chaplin, Sam Taplin and Jane Bingham; illustrations by Inklink Firenze © 2004, Usborne Publishing Ltd.

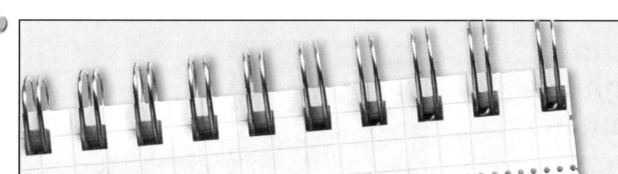

Owning a car

Our group carried out a survey into what people thought about cars. We started the interview by asking: In your opinion, is car ownership a good thing or a bad thing?

We found that there were three main views on this issue.

Out of the 50 people interviewed, 20 thought car ownership was a bad thing. Reasons for taking this view were:
• Too much of the world's resources are used in the manufacture and running of cars.
• Cars are dangerous. Accidents involving cars cause many injuries and deaths every year. Cars cause pollution, and this is harmful to human health.
• Cars are no longer an efficient means of transport. There are now so many cars that the roads are often congested. Traffic jams cost industry billions of pounds every year.
• Car ownership stops people from taking enough exercise, and this is bad for health.

Sixteen people were in favour of car ownership. Their reasons were:
• Owning a car means that you can go where you like when you like. They give people freedom.
• Cars are still the quickest way of making most journeys.
• You can take heavy things, such as shopping, buggies and luggage, with you in a car. This is difficult on public transport.
• Cars are fun. People enjoy choosing a car, looking after it and driving it.

The remaining 14 people did not want to answer the question with a simple yes or no. They thought that car ownership had both advantages and disadvantages. They raised the same points as people who were for or against car ownership, but felt that they were evenly balanced.

Animal Rights and Human Wrongs

Scientists working in research laboratories have invented new medicines, antiseptics, vaccines and antibiotics. They help to control many killer diseases, such as malaria, cholera, yellow fever, smallpox and typhoid.

New Medicines

The scientists soon realised that the new cures for the diseases had to be tested to make sure they were safe before they could be given to people. They decided to carry out many of the tests on animals, such as rats and mice, and even cats, dogs, marmosets, monkeys and chimpanzees.

Some people argue that this is all right, as long as the tests are really necessary. And that the work is done by professional, caring people who obey all the rules laid down by the government.

Other people strongly disagree and say that we have no right to treat animals in this way. Most people now agree that using animals to test cosmetics and household goods is wrong.

There is more good news on the way because scientists are now able to do many of the tests on cell cultures in laboratories and not on live animals.

What You Can Do to Help

Always buy cosmetics and household goods which bear the label, "Not tested on animals".

Animal Furs

Until quite recently, many ladies longed to own a fur coat. They gave little thought to how the animals were caught and killed. Farms of mink, chinchilla and Arctic fox boosted the supply of valuable furs.

Some people campaigned that it was wrong to trap such beautiful animals, let alone breed them in tiny cages, just for vanity. Today, thanks to these people, fur coats are no longer as popular. Many new and beautiful synthetic furs look just as good and are as warm.

But what about the problem of leather coats, belts and shoes, and killing animals for food?

Some people say we have the right to kill animals as long as no cruelty is involved. Others say no animal should be killed to provide us with anything at all.

Text extract from "Tomorrow's Earth: A Squeaky Green Guide" by David Bellamy © 1991, David Bellamy (1991, Mitchell Beazley); photos monkey © Tash Whiteley, mouse

Telling About Bullying

The rule that you should never tell about bullying is a rule invented by bullies for their own benefit. Obviously, it makes things very convenient for them. Not only can they bully in peace but a victim of their bullying cannot complain about it without being called a 'grass', a 'telltale', a 'cry-baby' or a 'wimp'.

Some adults are confused about whether telling about bullying is a good thing or a bad thing. Many of them were taught as children that 'bullying is good for you' (it 'toughens you up'); or that it's something you learn to cope with as you get older; or that there's something dishonourable or humiliating in asking for help when you're being bullied – you ought to be able to deal with it yourself. This idea (that bullying is something you should be able to cope with on your own) is very widespread. The people who work on phone helplines report fewer calls from older children even though people in this age group are still bullied – perhaps they are embarrassed to ask for help, feeling that they should be able to cope on their own.

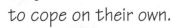

Some people do find ways to cope on their own but some can't. Sometimes the bullying is so severe that no one could deal with it on their own. Remember, even adults are bullied! There is never anything wrong with asking for help. (In fact it takes great courage and strength to do it.)

Photos: © Jupiter Images Corporation 2006

Text extract from "Don't Pick on Me" by Rosemary Stones © 1993; 2005, Rosemary Stones (2005, Piccadilly Press)

Text extract and website border from "Voice of the Mirror" website 9 September 2005 © 2005, Mirror Group www.mirror.co.uk (Voice of the Mirror)

Mirror.co.uk
THE BEST NEWSPAPER ON THE WEB   Search [The web ▾] For [   ] [GO]

| Home | **News** | Sport | TV & Film | More> |

Mirror.co.uk
THE BEST NEWSPAPER ON THE WEB

VOICE OF THE MIRROR

SLAM BRAKE ON CARNAGE

WHEN a plane or train crashes there is huge coverage by the media.

Yet cars remain a greater danger. Each year in Britain around 3,500 people are killed in motor accidents and ten times that number are badly injured.

Today the Mirror reports on a horrific smash which robbed six people – five of them teenagers – of their lives. Yet every day there are accidents which have similarly awful consequences.

A car can be as a dangerous as a gun. Especially in the hands of a young, inexperienced driver. And even more so if the car has been adapted to travel faster.

It might be that young people should be banned from driving vehicles which can move at excessive speeds. The government should be looking at this.

It should also take a twin-track approach to making roads safer by attacking bad driving while educating all motorists on the importance of safety.

For the consequences of a spilt-second of folly or just carelessness can be seen in the tragic picture on today's front page.

50 Shared texts Non-fiction ● Year 4

Mirror.co.uk
THE BEST NEWSPAPER ON THE WEB

Search | The web ▾ | For [   ] GO

| Home | **News** | Sport | TV & Film | More> |

Mirror.co.uk
THE BEST NEWSPAPER ON THE WEB

VOICE OF THE MIRROR

CLEAN UP THIS MESS

MOST families in this country now enjoy a lifestyle which previous generations would have called luxury.

But the great boons of modern living carry a heavy price tag. They are contributing to the destruction of the planet.

The extraordinary extremes of weather we witness nowadays – like the thunderstorms, floods and heatwaves of the past week – are at least partly due to global warming.

Which is mainly caused by our love of travel by road and air.

And our way of life, dominated by convenience shopping and attractive marketing, produces an overwhelming mass of packaging.

That and the other rubbish we generate, could eventually turn this green and pleasant land into a gigantic garbage heap.

The past few years have seen a significant increase in the amount of rubbish we recycle. But it is still far from enough and some areas lag pathetically far behind.

Councils have a big part to play in making recycling easier. But, ultimately, it is up to us to be responsible for our own mess.

We should not expect to enjoy the pleasures of modern life at the same time as we are destroying the planet for future generations.

Acknowledgements

The publisher gratefully acknowledges permission to reproduce the following copyright material:

A&C Black Publishers Ltd for the text 'Book Power' and an illustration from *The Book About Books* by Chris Powling, illustrated by Scoular Anderson. Text © 2000, Chris Powling, Illustration © 2000, Scoular Anderson (2000, A&C Black Publishers Ltd).

Acorn Adventure for extracts from their website www.acornadventure.co.uk © 2006, Acorn Adventure.

Anova Books for an extract 'What Champs will do for you' from *Learning Champs* by Colin Rose © 2001, Anova Books (2001, Learning World). Courtesy of Chrysalis Books Group.

BBC Magazines Ltd for an extract from the film review of *Wallace and Gromit in The Curse of the Were-Rabbit* © 2005, BBC Magazines Ltd (2005, Radio Times website www.radiotimes.com). The Radio Times Word Mark and Logo are trademarks of BBC Worldwide Ltd.

Jonathon Clowes Ltd, London on behalf of David Bellamy (Botanical Enterprises [Publications] Ltd) for an extract from *Tomorrow's Earth: A Squeaky-Green Guide* by David Bellamy © 1991, David Bellamy (1991, Mitchell Beazley).

Vince Cross for the text 'Evacuation' by Vince Cross © 2007, Vince Cross (previously unpublished).

Daily Mirror for 'Slam brake on carnage' from *Voice of the Mirror* 9 September 2005, 'Clean up this mess' from *Voice of the Mirror* 25 June, 2005, 'School Thinner' by Rosa Prince from *Daily Mirror* 5 September 2005, 'Serve the Kids better' from *Voice of the Mirror* website at www.mirror.co.uk 12 May 2005 and the review 'Charlie and the Chocolate Factory' by Gerald Lynch from www.mirror.co.uk 2 August 2005 © 2005, Mirror Group.

Harcourt Education for an extract 'Zoos – good or bad?' from *Animals and Us – Do animals have rights?* by Jane Bingham © 2005, Harcourt Education Ltd (2005, Heinemann Library), an extract from *Health-Related Fitness* by Nuala Mullan © 1997, Nuala Mullan (1997, Heinemann Library).

IPC Media plc for 'Animal Magic' by Tina Baker from *TV Times* 1–7 October 2005 © 2005, Tina Baker/TV Times (2005, IPC Media).

Suzanne Kirk for 'Animals of the Rainforest' and 'Rainforests' by Suzanne Kirk from *Literacy Time 3/4* Autumn Term © 2002, Suzanne Kirk (2002, Scholastic Ltd).

The Malcolm Group Events Ltd for text and photographs from their promotional leaflet for England's Medieval Festival at Herstmonceux Castle © 2005, The Malcolm Group Events Ltd www.EnglandMedievalFestival.com.

National Coal Mining Museum for England Trust Ltd for text and photographs from their promotional leaflet © 2006, National Coal Mining Museum for England Trust Ltd www.ncm.org.uk.

The Newspaper for 'Why is Ellen such a star?' from *The Newspaper* Wednesday 7 September, 2005, www.thenewspaper.org.uk © 2005, Young Media Holdings.

North Devon Marketing Bureau for the extract 'Welcome to North Devon and Exmoor' and images from *Guide to North Devon and Exmoor 2005* © 2005, North Devon Marketing Bureau.

Oxford University Press for the extract from *Ancient Greece* by Peter Connolly, text by Andy Solway © 2001, Oxford University Press (2001, Oxford University Press).

Piccadilly Press for the extract 'Telling about bullying' from *Don't Pick On Me* by Rosemary Stones © 1993, Rosemary Stones (1993, Piccadilly Press – reissued in 2005 by Piccadilly Press).

Polka Theatre for an extract and images from www.polkatheatre.com © 2006, Polka Theatre (2006, Polka Theatre website, designed, developed and hosted by Digital Virtue).

RSPCA for an extract from *Taking Action: RSPCA* by Frazer Swift © 1997, RSPCA (1997, Heinemann).

Scholastic Limited for a marketing page advertising subscriptions in *Nursery Education* magazine, design, text and images © 2006, Scholastic Limited.

Sussex Newspapers Ltd for 'Treats with a bit of Wonka magic' from the *Sussex Express* Friday 5 August, 2005 © 2005, Sussex Express (2005, Sussex Express).

Tesco Limited for an extract and images from Healthy Living leaflet 'Staying fit and active: A few changes go a long way'. Text © 2005, Tesco Limited (2005, Tesco Limited). Images courtesy of Tesco Limited.

Toontastic Publishing for an extract, illustration and characters from the article 'Feng-shui for your bedroom' from *Poppi Extra* © 2005, Toontastic Publishing Ltd and Mr Lucky Bags Ltd (2005, Toontastic Publishing Ltd).

Usborne Publishing for the extract 'The death of the dinosaurs' from *The Usborne Internet-linked Prehistoric World* by Fiona Chaplin, Sam Taplin and Jane Bingham © 2004, Usborne Publishing Limited; illustrations by Inklink Firenze; an extract from *The Usborne Book of Art Ideas* by Fiona Watt © 1999, Usborne Publishing Ltd; an extract from *The Usborne Introduction to Weather and Climate Change* by Laura Howell © 2003, Usborne Publishing Ltd. Usborne Publishing Ltd, 83-85 Saffron Hill, London EC1N 8RT.

Walker Books for the extracts from *Cooking up a storm* by Sam Stern © 2005, Susan and Sam Stern (2005, Walker Books Ltd).

The Watts Publishing Group Ltd for an extract from *Read all about it: Fashion* by Alan Hibbert © 2000, Alan Hibbert (2000, Franklin Watts; an extract and illustrations from *Building History: Tudor Theatre* by Gillian Clements © 2004, Gillian Clements (2004, Franklin Watts). Franklin Wattis is a division of The Watts Publishing Group Ltd, 338 Euston Road, London NW1 8BH.

Whitby Gazette for a text extract from the website www.whitbytoday.co.uk © 2006, Johnston Press Digitial Publishing.